IN THE HOUSE OF THE HANGED

SASHA SOKOLOV

In the House of the Hanged

Essays and Vers Libres

*Translated from the Russian and Annotated by
Alexander Boguslawski*

UNIVERSITY OF TORONTO PRESS
Toronto   Buffalo   London

Published by arrangement with ELKOST Intl. Literary Agency

© University of Toronto Press 2012
Toronto Buffalo London
www.utppublishing.com
Printed in Canada

ISBN 978-1-4426-4330-7 (cloth)

∞

Printed on acid-free, 100% post-consumer recycled paper with vegetable-based inks.

Library and Archives Canada Cataloguing in Publication

Sokolov, Sasha, 1943–
In the house of the hanged : essays and vers libres / Sasha Sokolov ; translated from the Russian and annotated by Alexander Boguslawski.

Includes bibliographical references and index.
ISBN 978-1-4426-4330-7

I. Boguslawski, Alexander Prus   II. Title.

PS8587.O418I513 2012   C891.74'44   C2011-906928-8

---

transcript

This book was published with the support of Mikhail Dmitrievich Prokhorov and the Programme supporting the translation of Russian fiction and intellectual literature abroad – TRANSCRIPT Foundation of Mikhail Prokhorov.

University of Toronto Press gratefully acknowledges the financial support of Rollins College for the publication of this book.

University of Toronto Press acknowledges the financial assistance to its publishing program of the Canada Council for the Arts and the Ontario Arts Council.

Canada Council   Conseil des Arts   ONTARIO ARTS COUNCIL
for the Arts   du Canada   CONSEIL DES ARTS DE L'ONTARIO

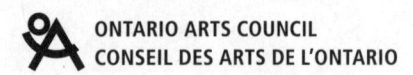

University of Toronto Press acknowledges the financial support of the Government of Canada through the Canada Book Fund for its publishing activities.

Contents

Introduction   vii

On Secret Tablets   3

In the House of the Hanged   8

Having Discovered It – Opened It Wide – Given It Wings   14

Palisandre – C'est Moi?   16

The Key Word of Belles-Lettres   23

A Portrait of an Artist in America: Waiting for the Nobel   30

The Anxious Pupa   37

The Shared Notebook or a Group Portrait of SMOG   44

A Mark of Illumination   52

An Abstract   73

About the Other Encounter   76

Discourse   80

Gazebo   95

Philornist   123

Notes   147

Index of Names and Places   179

Introduction

Sasha Sokolov (Aleksandr Vsevolodovich Sokolov), arguably the most original Russian writer of the past four decades, is known primarily as the author of three extraordinary novels, *A School for Fools*, *Between Dog and Wolf*, and *Palisandriia*. Each of these works is a seminal step in the development of Russian literature: *A School for Fools*, written in the Soviet Union before perestroika and glasnost, is an acknowledged classic of literary non-conformity, innovation, and originality; *Between Dog and Wolf* is a mind-boggling exploration of the possibilities of the Russian language that has been compared to Joyce's *Finnegans Wake*; and *Palisandriia*, a mock epic, is a postmodern parody of literary traditions, politics, sex, and graphomania. English-speaking readers have access to Sokolov's first and third novels; the first in Carl Proffer's translation[1] and the third, with the English title *Astrophobia*, in Michael Henry Heim's spirited rendition.[2] The second novel, in Sokolov's opinion his best and most important, so far has proven impossible to translate into any non-Slavic language.

    The manuscript of his fourth novel perished in a fire in a Greek villa in 1989. Afterwards, Sokolov indicated that he may be moving away from longer literary forms because in his completed works he had sufficiently demonstrated the flexibility and expressiveness of the Russian language, while *Palisandriia* was written 'to end the novel as a genre.'[3] Responding to a question about the small number of his published novels, Sokolov pointed out that Griboedov was immortalized by his single work, *Gore ot uma* (Woe from Wit) and Ershov became famous for his single fairy tale in verse, *Konek gorbunok* (Little Hunchback Pony). Moreover, he noted that the exigencies of the Russian book market (publication of his works in runs of three thousand copies, as opposed to a hundred fifty thousand at the end of the Soviet period) as well as the small number of readers of 'his type of literature' contribute to his silence.[4] Because he insisted that he was no longer searching for fame or prosperity but was writing 'for the drawer,' some scholars feared that the author of A School for Fools would remain silent, like J.D. Salinger.[5] However, Sokolov never proclaimed that he would not write or publish again. In fact, in addition to his three novels, from 1981 to 2006 he wrote a number of shorter literary texts, which often have been described as essays, even though they do not fit the traditional essay form. Almost all of these texts were presented orally before their subsequent publication; one was specially written for a prestigious literary journal in Russia. In recent years, the author published in the Tel Aviv–based Russian literary journal *Zerkalo* (Mirror) remarkable new texts, which clearly exemplify his notion of *proeziia* (prose elevated to the level of poetry).

Today, Sokolov's achievements are indisputable. He is acknowledged in the West and in Russia as a ground-breaking innovator, a literary maverick, an unsurpassed master of the Russian language, and an ingenious stylist, whose enormous importance for Russian and world literature is unquestionable. He is the recipient of three prestigious literary awards: the 1981 Andrei Bely Prize for best prose; the 1989 Oktiabr' Prize for the journal's best publication of the preceding year; and the 1996 Pushkin Prize, for, among other accolades, purity of style, advancement of the Nabokovian tradition of literary mastery, and his contribution to the development of literature through the exploration of language.[6]

Sokolov was born in Ottawa, Canada, in 1943, into the family of a Soviet diplomat. His father, Vsevolod Sokolov, and his mother, Lydia Chernykh, were posted in Ottawa as members of the Soviet legation and, as it became known later, both were involved in an attempt to steal plans for the atom bomb (the Guzenko Affair). As a result of their implication in that plot, in 1947, the Sokolovs were forced to leave Canada and return to Russia. After years of disillusionment and alienation from the Soviet system, exacerbated by learning his family history (the death of his paternal grandfather during the purges) and by constant problems in school, in 1963 Sokolov enrolled in the Military Institute for Foreign Languages. This decision and his experiences of regimented life made him even more aware of the Soviet system's pitfalls and more desirous of leaving the country; he attempted to cross the Soviet border with Iran, but was caught. Sokolov simulated mental illness by pretending to be an unexploded bomb and was finally discharged from military service. In 1966, he entered the Department of Journalism at the Moscow State University and graduated in 1971. Employed by the prestigious paper *Literaturnaia Rossiia* (Literary Russia), Sokolov thought that the hectic intellectual life of Moscow was preventing him from creating a substantial longer work; he quit his job and became a game warden at a hunting reserve on the Volga, not far from Tver'. There, he completed his first novel, *A School for Fools*, in 1973. The same year, he returned to Moscow, divorced his first wife, Taisiia Suvorova, and met Johanna Steindl, an Austrian teacher of German and his future wife, through whom he shipped the manuscript of his novel to the West. In an attempt to obtain permission to leave the country, Sokolov began a hunger strike in Moscow, while Johanna did the same in Vienna. The international publicity brought the case to the attention of the Austrian Chancellor Kreisky, who intervened on Sokolov's behalf with Leonid Brezhnev. Unexpectedly, Sokolov was given an exit visa, and on 8 October 1975, he landed in Vienna. There, he met Carl Proffer, the director of the publishing house Ardis, who had earlier received the manuscript of *A School for Fools*. Proffer immediately realized that he was dealing with a unique masterpiece written by an extremely talented and mature author. The publisher obtained a job for Sokolov in Ann Arbor, Michigan, which allowed Sokolov to arrive in 1976 in the United States, a few months after the publication (in Russian) of his novel. Trying to procure the most distinguished reviewer for it, Proffer asked Vladimir Nabokov to read and comment on the book. Nabokov's evaluation of *A School for Fools* – 'an enchanting, tragic, and touching book ... by far the best thing you published in the way of modern Soviet prose' – in many ways assured the recognition of Sokolov in the West. A year later, Proffer's English translation of the *School*, with Nabokov's endorsement on the cover, received favourable reviews in numerous papers and journals. After the publication, Sokolov, who was given Canadian citizenship in 1977, divorced Johanna Steindl and began a nomadic life, moving frequently between Canada and the United States, living in Vermont, Quebec, and California. Later, he expanded his travels, spending considerable time in Israel, Slovenia, Italy, Greece, and Russia. The most remarkable year was 1989, when Sokolov was given an entry visa and returned triumphantly to Russia. After almost a year of constant meetings, contract negotiations, radio, television, and newspaper interviews, travels, and public readings, Sokolov, exhausted, returned to Vermont, recognized as perhaps the most important and influential living Russian author.

Three years earlier, in Vermont, Sokolov had met Marlene Royle, a world-class rower, who worked as a coach at the Craftsbury Sculling Center and whom he later married. In the winters, Sokolov, himself a champion cross-country skier, taught the sport to winter vacationers. After Marlene became the director of the Florida Rowing Center in 2005, the Sokolovs moved to Wellington, Florida. At the end of 2009, the couple returned to Canada and settled near Vancouver.

Besides the literary prizes and translations of his novels into eighteen languages, the importance and international reputation of Sasha Sokolov is best confirmed by two separate issues of *Canadian American Slavic Studies* (*CASS*) entirely devoted to him. The first, edited by Don Barton Johnson, appeared in 1990 and included Sokolov's biography, bibliography, and eleven scholarly studies of his fiction. The second, commemorating the thirty-year anniversary of the publication of *A School for Fools*, edited by Ludmilla Litus, came out in 2006 and included eight studies of Sokolov's works, a new biographical essay, an updated bibliography, a section of photographs and illustrations, and three interviews. Incidentally, this publication contained the first two scholarly studies of Sokolov's essays, by Don Barton Johnson and Lisa Ryoko Wakamiya.[7]

These studies clearly draw attention to the significance of the essays and validate the idea of making the essays available to readers of English. The present collection contains fourteen texts written by Sokolov between 1981 and 2010 and published in various papers and journals in Russia and in the West. Not surprisingly, this time span presents a challenge to the readers who are not familiar with Russia's modern history and with the tremendous political changes that have taken place in that country.

In the middle of the 1980s, Mikhail Gorbachev's policies of openness and restructuring relaxed censorship and permitted critical voices to be heard. Ultimately, they led to the demolition of the Berlin Wall, the independence of many Soviet-bloc countries, and the dissolution of the Soviet Union in 1991. Subsequently, these new policies allowed Sasha Sokolov to emerge from the underground and become a celebrity in his native country. Many early texts discuss the problems of the Soviet system which, at least partially, vanished after the downfall of the 'evil empire.'

However, even today, most of the ideas expressed in the texts are important and valid, since they concern universal truths about literature, language, the role of the artist, talent, and mastery. Only one of the included texts has been translated into English before; consequently, the new translations will add considerably to our understanding of Sasha Sokolov as an author and literary craftsman, a unique voice in Russian and world literature. The essays demonstrate the development of Sokolov's shorter forms and reveal more fully his originality and literary gifts. According to Don Barton Johnson, the texts are 'small, highly concentrated works of art' written in a 'style no less ornate than the fiction.'[8] In this collection, they are presented chronologically, as follows: 'On Secret Tablets' (1981); 'In the House of the Hanged' (1983); 'Having Discovered It – Opened It Wide – Given It Wings' (1984); *'Palisandre – C'est Moi?'* (1985); 'A Portrait of an Artist in America: Waiting for the Nobel' (1985); 'The Key Word of Belles-Lettres' (1985); 'The Anxious Pupa' (1986); 'The Shared Notebook or a Group Portrait of SMOG' (1989); 'A Mark of Illumination' (1990); 'An Abstract' (1996); 'About the Other Encounter' (2006); 'Discourse' (2007); 'Gazebo' (2009); and 'Philornist' (2010).

'On Secret Tablets,' the first of Sokolov's essays in this volume, was originally a speech delivered at the conference 'Russian Literature in Emigration: The Third Wave,' at the University of Southern California, Los Angeles (14–15 May 1981). The essay begins with fundamental questions whether beauty selects its own apprentices and whether it can exist if the world is addicted to ugliness. What was in the beginning – the art or the artist? How and out of what should one create works of art? Who is called and who is chosen? Posing all these questions leads to lamentation about the lowering of artistic standards, the dominance of mediocrity in Western literature, and the situation of an exiled artist, for whom literature is sacred. In the West, the word *writer* had lost its primary meaning and is applied to graphomaniacs or authors of letters, manuals, treatises, and pulp fiction. Sokolov describes his encounters with émigrés and with Canadian border officials for whom the profession of writer indicates insanity or is a sufficient reason to suspect the individual of being a spy. Giving as an example his novel *Between Dog and Wolf*, in which he fictionalized the lives and deaths of several acquaintances from the hunting preserve where he once worked (and where he wrote his first novel), Sokolov asserts that life often follows fiction and the question of the primacy of art or artist is irrelevant because everything has been prerecorded on secret tablets. Ultimately, fate will decide what will remain – the word or silence.[9]

'In the House of the Hanged' was first a speech given at the conference 'Reevaluation of Human Rights' at Emory University, Atlanta, in the spring of 1983. It was written during Sokolov's work on *Palisandriia* and initially followed the experimental format of the early drafts of his third novel – no capital letters, no periods, and no paragraphs. After its first publication, however, the text was 'normalized' and in all subsequent editions appeared in more standard form, with capital letters and proper punctuation marks, just without paragraphing. The essay explores the fundamental human right – freedom. More politically engaged than the rest, the essay, like 'On Secret Tablets,' is structured around a number of questions the narrator asks himself, and partially explains Sokolov's reasons for emigration from the Soviet Union – curiosity about the world, inability to live in a lawless society, and disapproval of the passive suffering and constant humiliation of Soviet citizens by their government. Since people's actions determine their fate, they should not be afraid to follow the example of the phoenix – escape from their cages by burning themselves up and beginning a new life, reborn and free.[10]

After Carl Proffer's untimely death in 1984, during a memorial evening organized at the New York Public Library, Sokolov read a eulogy, originally entitled 'The Alpha of Ardis: In Memory of Carl Proffer,' but renamed in subsequent publications 'Having Discovered It – Opened It Wide – Given It Wings.' The title, a quotation from the ending of the essay, employs three perfective verbal adverbs – *otkryv, raspakhnuv, okryliv*. In English translation these three words lose much of their euphonic power, density, and spark, not only because they have to be preceded by the word 'having,' but also because their meanings are difficult to render exactly. As in 'On Secret Tablets,' the author discusses predestination and fate, attributing to it the transformation of Proffer, who with his wife, Ellendea, founded the publishing house Ardis and not only 'launched' Sokolov's career, but gave wings to many other Russian artists.[11]

The three texts written in 1985, '*Palisandre – C'est Moi?*,' 'A Portrait of an Artist in America,' and 'The Key Word of Belles-Lettres' are literary statements about Sokolov's art.

In '*Palisandre – C'est Moi?*,' a speech given at a conference 'Russian Writers in Exile: Josif Brodskii and Sasha Sokolov,' at the University of Southern California, Los Angeles, 13 April 1985, he addresses several topics important to his writing: his dislike for plot, his admiration for slow writing (which cannot be learned and is 'God given'), his aversion to fast scribbling, and his wish (as well as his right) not to be identified with the heroes of his novels. In a text filled with humorous anecdotes but quite serious in intent, the author explains why he should not be identified with the hero of his novel, Palisandr. At the end, realizing that the readers will find his arguments insufficiently convincing, he finishes with a poem from his novel in which Palisandr ponders his own identity.[12]

'A Portrait of an Artist in America: Waiting for the Nobel' was a Regents' Lecture given at the University of Southern California, Santa Barbara, on 14 November 1985. Originally entitled 'Portret russkogo khudozhnika v Amerike: V ozhidanii Nobelia' (A Portrait of a Russian Artist in America: Waiting for the Nobel), the essay talks about the torments of literary creation in general and about the difficulties of those writers who, having chosen freedom from the oppression and restriction of Socialist Realism, found themselves in countries where Capitalist Primitivism, characterized by isolationism, departure from tradition, and the lowering of artistic criteria and artistic levels, reigns supreme. Many of them had to choose a new language; doing this they decided in advance to write below their abilities. Sokolov, a master of the Russian language, acknowledges that he could never abandon his native idiom and sacrifice the quality of his work. Therefore, he ends the text, literally overflowing with the names of Western and Russian cultural icons, examples of his nostalgic reverence, with a hilarious story describing what would happen if he decided to change his profession. He would become a painter, but because of his absolute lack of talent for drawing, he would remove the paintings and even the frames, putting only nails in the walls, not to be accused of excessive minimalism.[13]

The third text from this 'literary' series, 'The Key Word of Belles-Lettres,' called by Johnson 'Sokolov's literary manifesto,'[14] was another Regents' Lecture presented at the University of California, Santa Barbara, a week later, on 21 November 1985. The essay addresses several of Sokolov's essential concerns. All writers need good readers; not just admirers, but intelligent and sensitive critics. Authors do not create ex nihilo: they follow the existing literary tradition (the foundation of art); they also need freedom (the art's wings and light). Each work requires an effective opening that reveals God's mysterious spark. The first phrase is the verbal key to the fortress of form. This verbal key is shaped like the word *how: How* is the passage to truth. After quoting examples of great opening lines by Hemingway, Belyi, Voznesenskii, Melville, and Maiakovskii, Sokolov suggests that art should be beautiful and prose should be superior and refined, like poetry. He also praises Impressionism, his favourite art movement, for being a protest against all norms and rules. The essay ends with the writer's terrifying dream about literature, which has not followed the developments of all other arts, but hit the Hollywood pavement. Everybody became a writer. And yet, the writer hopes, the Word will remain God.[15]

'The Anxious Pupa' was a keynote address at the 'Fourth Annual South-East Conference on Foreign Languages and Literatures' at Rollins College in Winter Park, Florida, in February 1986. The audience, expecting a traditional keynote speech of no great interest or significance, was literally stunned by the depth, artistic quality, and the beauty of the text. Not surprisingly, the essay was published in *Kontinent,* and this prestigious publication affirmed the recognition of Sokolov as an important Russian author living in exile. 'The Anxious Pupa' is the only essay translated into English prior to this collection. Johnson called it 'a meditation on the prison-house of language.'[16] The work continues and expands the theme of Sokolov's mastery of Russian and his unwillingness to abandon it for another language; here, however, the author presents it in a highly poetic, emotional, and dense form. In the beginning, the protagonist (named simply *you*) regrets being born in Russia rather than in Buenos Aires, Uppsala, Jerusalem, Rome, or Athens. He feels entrapped by the dialect given to him a priori, and falls into a depression, which culminates in a nightmarish conversation with his native language, disguised as an Inquisitor. The language advises the protagonist to work hard. Slowly, the protagonist awakens, rebels, is released from a military hospital, grows, accepts his language and, ultimately, begins to soar. The text segues from a personal essay into a generalized story about any artist who, through hard and tormenting work, experiments, and sacrifices, discovers and embraces the possibilities of his native language.[17]

Three years later, during his visit in Russia, Sokolov created one of his most difficult texts, 'The Shared Notebook or a Group Portrait of SMOG,' dedicated to the art group SMOG (Samoe molodoe obshchestvo geniev – The Youngest Society of Geniuses), to which he belonged in the 1960s. Originally presented at a gathering dedicated to dissident writers, held at the Krasnyi Tekstil'shchik (Red Textile Worker) in Moscow, on 26 June 1989, this is an impressionistic and hermetic text, which recreates the atmosphere of those years, using as a leading metaphor the streetcar ride from Nikolai Stepanovich Gumilev's poem 'The Streetcar that Got Lost' and cleverly interweaving into the tale loose portraits of the members of SMOG. Three of them, Vladimir Aleinikov, Leonid Gubanov, and Nikolai Nedbailo can be identified by the quotations from their poems, the titles of their works, and anagrams or stylistic devices; others are presented as generalized outlines and fragments intended as a group portrait. Johnson calls the essay 'a stylistic tour de force.'[18] Although without notes it is difficult to identify the protagonists of the text, its poetic quality and beauty, its richness of language, and its stylistic complexity are obvious to any reader.[19]

This extraordinary work was followed a year later by the longest of Sokolov's essays in this volume, 'A Mark of Illumination,' written to commemorate the hundredth anniversary of the birth of Boris Pasternak. According to Johnson, the text is 'an unsettling examination of the anxiety of influence.'[20] Saturated with quotations from Pasternak's autobiography and his poems, as well as references to popular songs and the works of famous poets, the text describes the 'awakening' of the authorial persona, his rediscovery of Pasternak's poetry, becoming a poet, and his attempt to break away from those who silenced and forgot about the greatest lyric poet of the century. The attempt to be like the idol, to merge with him, even to become him, leads to disappointment, but, in the end, the protagonist (again referred to in the text simply as *you*) discovers that a poet does not need to be exactly like the master. It is enough to be an inspired admirer, a witness of the other's art, and to realize that what you have in common are eternity and speech. The essay, written in breathtakingly complex and varied syntax, with sentences alternating from one word to many subordinate clauses, has one more dominant stylistic feature – it replaces question, exclamation, and quotation marks with their proper names or periphrases.[21]

These last two texts, published in Russian literary journals, added greatly to Sokolov's popularity in Russia and, perhaps, secured for him the 1996 Pushkin Prize. During the award ceremony on 26 May 1996, the author read his acceptance speech, entitled 'An Abstract,' dedicated to those who believed in his talent and to friends of Russian literature. It is a single three-page long sentence, starting with the question why Sokolov has not written for the theatre and developing into a dialogue of several voices about various events related to Sokolov's life. It is an autobiographical recollection of his grandparents, his friends, the places close to his heart, and of his departure from the fatherland caused by his love of freedom and his desire to be an eternal traveller – a hero of space, not time. At the conclusion of the text, the authorial persona, overcome by nostalgia and longing, contemplates going back to his native land, but hesitates and ... no longer hears the voices, the play of imagination remains unfinished. Only now the readers realize that the play is the author's life, therefore, only its abbreviated variant can be presented. The poetic quality of the text, its astonishing structure and style make it one of Sokolov's most significant works. Moreover, the essay is a clear indication of the dramatic changes that would occur in Sokolov's subsequent writings.[22]

Sokolov aficionados had to wait ten years for the next text. It is a tribute to the Russian writer Aleksandr Gol'dshtein, read in Tel-Aviv at the Gol'dshtein memorial evening on 26 October 2006, by the editor of *Zerkalo*, Irina Vrubel'-Golubkina. Sokolov's 'About the Other Encounter' is a response to a text written by Gol'dshtein about Sokolov; it describes two brief meetings between the writers and their conversations about literature. The author praises Gol'dshtein for his mastery, and for practising the same kind of writing – *proeziia*. The writers also talk about less important things and decide to write a biting epigram against the boring and uninspiring town, Afula. After Gol'dshtein's death, Sokolov finishes the epigram, but, unexpectedly, the epigram becomes a eulogy. At the end of the text Sokolov includes an ironic statement indicating that he will present the poem to maestro Iosif (Iosif Brodskii), the friend of the Roman poet Catullus (a character in the eulogy). Mentioning Brodskii in a humorous way is the author's subtle stab at the dominant personality of Brodskii, whose tremendous influence as a Nobel Prize laureate and supposed connoisseur of Russian literature destroyed or put insurmountable obstacles in the career paths of many Russian artists. The eulogy to Afula, playful and linguistically inventive, consisting of seven rhymed stanzas written without capitalization and without punctuation marks of any kind, closes this short, but important text.[23]

A year later, Sokolov surprised his readers again, publishing in *Zerkalo* the extraordinary 'Discourse,' the first part of a triptych of vers libres. The idea, hatched in 'An Abstract,' of a conversation, dialogue, a theatrical discourse of many voices, is further developed here, but the conversing voices, rather than discussing facts from Sokolov's life, are talking about eternal truths and ideas, primarily about art, creativity, literature, and writing. Thus, the text becomes a testimony to Sokolov's powers of invention and a revelation of the elements used in his fiction and discussed in his earlier essays. In fifty numbered stanzas of an uneven number of lines written in blank verse, with the initial capital letter and a period after the last word but no further capitalization or punctuation besides commas and colons, Sokolov shows us the process of the creation of an artistic text, a text that exemplifies his term *proeziia*.

Plot is replaced by a circular construction joining the first and the last stanza, and by repetitions of themes and imagery. The discussion of style, presented in a form appropriate to poetry, confirms Sokolov's earlier statements about his style and technique (slowness of writing, importance of listing, repetitions). The *proema* is saturated with foreign expressions, which point out the significance of languages (Spanish, Greek, Latin) and foreign cultural heritage, adding beauty, complexity, and finesse to the text.[24]

Two years later, the author created the second part of the triptych, 'Gazebo,' in eighty-eight stanzas (representing the number of piano keys) of uneven-numbered lines, in blank verse, with only the initial capital letter and with punctuation consisting exclusively of commas, colons, and the final period. Writing the triptych, the author considered 'Gazebo' to be a centrepiece, linking, joining, and cementing all the pieces together. The poem's main topics are theatre, music, writing, refinement (finesse), and the spirit of wandering. Unlike the 'Discourse,' this multilayered text consists of amusing short plots linked, as in the two previous texts, by the device of conversation among several narrative voices. Sokolov's fascination with and fondness for foreign cultures is again reinforced by fragments of Italian, Spanish, French, German, Polish, and Latin woven into the verbal material and contributing to the sumptuousness of the whole, perhaps the best example of *proeziia* created by the author to date. The seriousness and importance of the text, which demonstrates vividly the narrative's birth out of sound similarities and trigger words, is apparent when the reader realizes that 'Gazebo' is about as long as the dramatic Pasternak tribute. The fanciful, madcap combinations of words, neologisms, and foreign expressions placed within syntax often reminiscent of the Bible, leads the astonished reader from a story about the wandering Italian composer Antonio Scandello, through stories of several fascinating invented characters, to the final conversation between eternal wanderers. It is a playful recycling and mocking of some popular plots in fiction presented in a highly concentrated form in which, literally, every word counts. Symbolically, a careful reader can interpret the two prevalent images – the arboretum and the gazebo, as the world and the abode of literature. Asserting that everything in literature has been done before and that the present does not create anything lasting forever, Sokolov defies his own assertions by constructing this amazing text.[25]

To finish the triptych[26] of vers libres, in 2010, Sokolov wrote the newest text, 'Philornist,' using the same devices as in the two earlier poems, but dividing it into ninety-nine stanzas of uneven number of lines, from three to fourteen. The poem, which can be understood as a reflection on death, aging, and writing, again considers the idea of a play, but develops the idea into a nostalgic requiem about the disappearing culture and, ultimately, disappearing world of beauty. The story, consisting of short vignettes of unparalleled power, is framed by the image of a heron communicating soundlessly and advising the protagonist to repent; metaphorically, it can be understood as a journey and fate of an artist amid desolation and ugliness of the modern world.

In the text, Sokolov continues to challenge Russian readers, introducing a large number of foreign words and expressions, ranging from Sanskrit terms related to Hindu beliefs to English, Italian, Spanish, Latin, German, Slovenian, and Japanese. He adds to this international mixture his own neologisms and unorthodox uses of Russian expressions. The result is a text that shimmers and sparkles, masterfully changing in tone and 'flavour' from Russian to Japanese, Chinese, and Italian. Sokolov's nostalgia for international cultural heritage reaches its apogee, even though it was already well developed in the earlier texts, particularly in the 'Gazebo.' And it is not surprising to discover in all three poems common themes and imagery, ranging from theatre, music, birds, language, and refinement, to artistry and the life journey of the writer.[27]

Preparing Sokolov's texts for their first English publication, I followed one guiding principle – verity – to Sokolov's language, to his style, and to the graphic appearance of the texts. In other words, if the author does something unusual or extraordinary in the original, the translation should attempt to render this as faithfully as possible (of course, if it can be done at all). Special attention must be paid to the choice of words, to puns and word plays, to rhymes, neologisms, and sound similarities. Stylistically, the common literary devices used by the author, like anaphoras (beginning of sentences with the same word), anagrams (words formed by changing the place of letters), ananyms (words spelled backwards), aposiopesis (incomplete or broken-off sentences), and paronomasia (placing similar-sounding words next to each other or close to each other), are rendered as close to the original as possible because, even though they may contradict what English teachers have told their students, they are essential to the preservation of the unique rhythm of the texts. As for the graphic appearance of the works, all of them follow Sokolov's ideal – nothing on the page should distract the reader from the 'mellifluous flow' of the narrative; therefore, there are no paragraphs and no footnotes.[28] In Sokolov's latest texts, even capital letters are eliminated; because the poems are in essence single sentences in which every word is an autonomous, meaningful part of the whole, capitalization would be distracting and misleading. Needless to say, creating this kind of translation is a painstaking and challenging task. Since many things cannot be translated literally, achieving verity is often a task that tests the translator's inventiveness and imagination. And in such cases the author's guidance, help, and suggestions are invaluable. Therefore, I must express my gratitude to Sasha Sokolov for his friendship and his assistance during the preparation of these renderings. In many instances, the author's ingenuity and his feel for the language enriched the final versions and allowed me to provide intertextual and cultural references revealing the text's depth, richness, and extraordinary complexity. I will never forget the hours we spent together, surrounded by food, drink, and piles of dictionaries, searching for the perfect word and often finding pearls that not only made us both laugh hysterically, but now and then found their way into the Russian originals. And I will never forget Sasha's inspired readings (recitations) of his texts, which confirm my conviction that these masterpieces, now appearing finally in print, are equally beautiful when presented orally. In addition, there are no words in English that could express how much I owe to my wife, Kay Davidson-Bond, who, despite her illness, was the best first, second, and third reader of my renderings and whose knowledge of English allowed me to find a happy balance between what is possible and what is impossible in translation. I extend similar thanks to my friend, Professor Paul Licata, who read all the texts and whose editorial talents were invaluable in the long process of preparing the manuscript for publication. I also wish to express my gratitude to the University of Toronto Press, particularly to Richard Ratzlaff, for believing in this project and guiding it to its completion. Finally, preparing notes and annotations to the texts, I depended on dictionaries, encyclopedias, and on-line sources too numerous to mention individually, but gratefully acknowledged. Taking full responsibility for any errors that may have remained unnoticed, I sincerely hope that the essays and vers libres will astonish, touch, and enchant the readers as much as the author's novels do, vividly revealing the astounding erudition, wit, curiosity, and ever-developing talent of Sasha Sokolov, the wide-eyed globetrotter and citizen of the world.

A Note on Rendering Russian Names

Rendering Russian names in English is particularly difficult because in common usage many names are spelled in their English equivalents (for example, Alexander instead of Aleksandr). To avoid confusion and to achieve uniformity in translation, I am transliterating all Russian names, using the Library of Congress's system, but I provide the possible other spellings of the names in the Index of Names and Places.

NOTES

1 Sasha Sokolov, *A School for Fools*, translated by Carl Proffer (Ann Arbor: Ardis, 1977).
2 Sasha Sokolov, *Astrophobia*, translated by Michael H. Heim (New York: Grove Press, 1989).
3 See D. Barton Johnson, 'Sasha Sokolov: A Literary Biography,' *Canadian American Slavic Studies* (hereafter *CASS*) 21/3–4 (1987), 217.
4 Based on personal conversations with the author as well as on some of his interviews. See Ivan Podshivalov, 'A Conversation with Sasha Sokolov: Moscow 1989,' *CASS* 40/2–4 (2006), 364; Naum Vaiman, 'A Conversation with Sasha Sokolov (Over the Barrier: A Special Broadcast in Honor of Sasha Sokolov's 60th Birthday),' *CASS* 40/2–4 (2006), 374–5.
5 See Georgii Mkheidze, 'Snezhnyi chelovek' (The Snow Man), compiled and edited by Ludmilla Litus, *CASS* 40/2–4 (2006), 380.
6 See Ludmilla Litus, 'Sasha Sokolov's Journey from "Samizdat" to Russia's Favorite "Classic" 1976–2006,' *CASS* 40/2–4 (2006), 412–13.
7 D. Barton Johnson, 'Sasha Sokolov's Major Essays,' *CASS* 40/2–4 (2006), 233–49; Lisa Ryoko Wakamiya, 'Transformation, Forgetting and Fate: Self-Representation in the Essays of Sasha Sokolov,' *CASS* 40/2–4 (2006), 317–29.
8 Johnson, 'Sokolov's Major Essays,' 233.
9 The importance of this essay is confirmed by its subsequent publications. In periodicals: *Sintaksis* (Paris), no. 10 (1982), 156–61; *Dvadtsat' dva* (Tel Aviv), no. 24 (1982), 177–82; *Al'manakh panorama* (Los Angeles), no. 59 (1982), 11; and *Sobesednik* (Moscow), no. 30 (1989), 10–11. In conference proceedings: *The Third Wave: Russian Literature in Emigration*, edited by Olga Matich and Michael Henry Heim (Ann Arbor: Ardis, 1984), 203–7, as 'Sokolov o sebe' (Sokolov about Himself). In the following books: *V ozhidanii Nobelia ili obshchaia tetrad'* (St Petersburg: no publisher, 1993); 'Esse. Vystupleniia,' in *Palisandriia* (St Petersburg: Symposium, 1999); *Trevozhnaia kukolka* (St

Petersburg: Azbuka-klassika, 2007); and *Shkola dlia durakov, Mezhdu sobakoi i volkom, Palisandriia, Esse* (St Petersburg: Azbuka-klassika, 2009).

10 Published in *Literaturnyi Kur'er* (New York and Glenn Ellyn, IL), no. 10 (1983), 4–6, and in the subsequent Russian-language editions of Sokolov's essays (see comments to 'On Secret Tablets').
11 Published in *Vremia i my* (New York-Paris-Jerusalem), no. 79 (1984), 243–4; renamed in subsequent publications.
12 Published in *Al'manakh panorama*, no. 267 (23–30 May 1986), 24–5.
13 Published in *Al'manakh panorama*, no. 254 (21–8 February 1986), 31–2; reprinted in subsequent Russian publications as '*Portret khudozhnika v Amerike: V ozhidanii Nobelia*' (A Portrait of an Artist in America: Waiting for the Nobel).
14 Johnson, 'Sokolov's Major Essays,' 237.
15 Published in *Al'manakh panorama*, no. 267 (20–7 December 1985), 30–1; reprinted in *Znanie-sila* (Moscow), no. 1 (1994), 83.
16 Johnson, 'Sokolov's Major Essays,' 240.
17 Published in *Kontinent* (Paris), no. 49 (1986), 84–91; reprinted in *Literaturnaia gazeta* (Moscow), no. 18 (1990), 8; and in subsequent Russian collections. A free translation into English by Benjamin Sher, with the title 'Persona non grata,' appeared in the *Journal of Literary Translation* (New York), 22 (Fall 1989), 226–32, and was later revised by the translator for his publication on the Web. Another translation, by Olga Pobedinskaia and Andrew Reynolds, entitled 'The Anxious Chrysalis' appeared in *The Penguin Book of New Russian Writing: Russia's Fleurs du Mal*, edited by Viktor Erofeev and Andrew Reynolds (London and New York: Penguin, 1995), 199–207. Two translations into German and one into Polish exist.
18 Johnson, 'Sokolov's Major Essays,' 244.
19 Published in *Iunost'* (Moscow), no. 12 (1989), 66–8.
20 Johnson, 'Sokolov's Major Essays,' 249.
21 Published in *Oktiabr'* (Moscow), no. 2 (1991), 178–86.
22 Published in *Nezavisimaia gazeta* (Moscow), no. 99 (31 May1996), 7.
23 Published in *Zerkalo* (Tel Aviv), no. 27 (2006), 169–71. The text is available at http://magazines.russ.ru/zerkalo/2006/27/ss13.html.
24 Published in *Zerkalo*, no.29 (2007), 3–16. Available at http://magazines.russ.ru/zerkalo/2007/29/ss2.html.
25 Published in *Zerkalo*, no. 33 (2009), 3–27. Available at http://magazines.russ.ru/zerkalo/2009/33/so1.html.
26 The three vers libres were published in a separate edition: Sasha Sokolov, *Triptikh* (Moscow: Ob"edinennoe Gumanitarnoe Izdatel'stvo, 2011).

27 Published in *Zerkalo*, no. 35 (2010), 3–24. Available at http://magazines.russ.ru/zerkalo/2010/35/2so.html.
28 To make this collection more user-friendly, the texts are supplemented with notes that provide comments and explanations of particular words, phrases, ideas, and quotations. Moreover, besides the notes, the collection features an Index of Names and Places that will help readers see the scope of Sokolov's cultural 'travels' and learn a few details about the persons, places, and things immortalized in his writing.

IN THE HOUSE OF THE HANGED

On Secret Tablets

Does beauty itself look for apprentices among the neglected and mischievous in spirit and, enchanting them with the non-extinguishable light of its uselessness, promote them to masters? Do they owe many of their skills to the maudlin mentors from vocational slaughterhouses of the soul? Or does everything begin and go on according to the will of wonderful dissimilarity – detachedly and despite? In other words: where did we stop? What did we figure out during our vacation lasting thousands of years? What was and will be in the beginning: the artist or the art? And – does our beauty exist if we don't think about it, if we've turned away and become insensitive? Or if we've become addicted to the ugly? Let's assume – addicted to the ugliness of prosperity, of non-existence, to this abysmal shame, to the ugliness of the gossip about the truth. By the way, where, at what ball, is she dragging her precious train trimmed with the noble skunk? And what should we do without this genteel lady, since so many questions used to hang around during our gatherings? After all, we are set not only on comparing them to the old-fashioned umbrellas and canes hanging on our hooks, but also on straightening out their curves, correcting their interrogative hunch-backed form – supposedly servile and obsequious, but in reality pushy and usurpatorial. The questions captivate us. What was Aleksandr Sergeevich doing in the country in the winter and how fair or, more precisely, how fresh were the roses of Ivan Sergeevich? How – and most importantly – out of what should one create poems and all things refined and wonderful? And if out of nothing, what should we do in such a case? Shouldn't we create a biography of Nebuchadnezzar, concoct some memoirs, become fathers of the nation, or join the ranks of saints? Who is who? Who is called and who is chosen? Or point-blank: do you respect me? Outside, there is a fiesta of questions requiring an immediate answer. And in the booths of politics, ideology, and vainglory – a full collection of queries. There, the specialists in beating around the bushes make orations and the prophets pronounce prophesies. Precisely there, Mediocrity herself, all in white, appears to the public, inundated and moved by the verbal slush. Well, and what about those who are mischievous in spirit? In culture, which has experienced many times the crushing of the spirit by the lacquered packaging overstuffed with mind-boggling rubbish, they are the voice crying amid the indifference: give a kopeck to the holy fool. And what, in fact, can be done, but not by Aleksandr Sergeevich and not only in winter at his estate, but by me, Aleksandr Vsevolodovich, the entire year and in a completely different land, where strawberries, lilacs, and bird cherries don't smell, the trees have forgotten their names, where about the habits of tree frogs I can talk only with the dedicated Sokolov scholar Don Barton Johnson, and where, in graveyards, instead of wise undertakers with their humane ropes, pipe-layers and bulldozers work? What can do all these, for whom a semiconductor is no more than a conductor serving half of the train cars? Of course – teach, follow in the footsteps of Prometheus and ignite the torches of wisdom, since the number of universities is legion. How is it possible not to know the writings of Damocles, the labours of Sisyphus, the philosophical views of Procrustes? – shouted the professor, astonished to tears by the ignorance of his student. Gimme a break – the student retorted – you keep your company, we keep ours. That's true, what gave this exalted examiner the right to assume that his discipline is worth anything; why did he bother the representative of our youth? Apparently mister professor is not from here – perhaps he is an émigré from some Russia, where, we hear, the Writers' Union plays almost the role of an opposition party. And why do they bother with these scribblers? When someone cuts off all their dogs' heads, to use the Chinese saying, they'll know their place. I'm not sure about Paris, London, and Copenhagen. Perhaps the process of healing the United Nations from literary depression is not uniform and in a number of decrepit capitals, like some Brasilia or Siberia, people still do not realize that it is time to close the shop of belles-lettres. But here, in the New World, when you say 'writer,' you must immediately explain that you allow yourself the use of the word in the sense retired long ago and vague. Because in the understanding of the non-reading masses a writer is a person who knows how to quickly draft a letter, an application, a manual on running, a treatise on diet or some *Gorky Park*.

For that reason the word 'graphomaniac' in the local dialect has a narrowly clinical meaning. And why would you want to turn into an aesthete and an elitist? This is not some kind of Petersburg salon from the time of the wonderful poet-nudist Konstantin Kuz'minskii, even if he himself moved to Texas. Leave your Mnemosyne alone, dear sir, don't bother her and don't tire her out. When I, healed by my latest experiences, describe to my colleagues what it means in the land of my language to be a writer or just to have a reputation of being one, even I feel that I am telling tall tales. And when, during my travels from Canada to America, the customs officials ask me about my occupation and I answer that I am a writer, they immediately begin to search me. Then some plain-clothes egghead arrives and we begin an edifying discussion about the location of my heart. You say that you were born in Canada? And you say that you write and speak Russian? And where is your heart, you say? My heart is a bat, which during the day hangs above the abyss of my intestinal cavity and at night flies out to suck the heroic blood of future conscripts with the purpose of weakening your military forces, sir. This is how I should answer evasively, but I am afraid to be seen as excessively romantic. After all, my literary reputation is already sufficiently damaged. Do you know why I am scrutinizing you with my lorgnon? – a princess from the first wave asked me, when we were sitting with her at one of her Napoleonic tables, doing lunch. Pray, tell – I replied, making myself inconspicuous. I read your *A School for Fools* twice – the princess continued – and, would you believe, at first I concluded that you were a freethinker, a mason, but now I have figured it out: you are simply insane. Her Majesty's Canadian Mounted Counterintelligence also keeps scrutinizing me. However, it came to a different conclusion. The game is over – I and my friend were told in a proper bureau in Montreal. We have proved without a doubt that both of you – Sasha and Alexander – are spies. Evidence? There's more than enough. First of all, we are both writing something all the time, and, secondly, we have the same last name. However, one of us, being a monarchist, writes our name with two letters 'f' at the end, and the other, being himself, with one 'v.' When I am finally arrested, I will cheer myself up by the following recollection. Once a German scout was detained in Italy because he methodically made drawings of old towers. And even though he tried to convince the investigating authorities that he was simply a well-known poet, Goethe as a matter of fact, his name did not tell anybody anything. Needless to say, Johann Wolfgangovich also acted according to the slogan 'Literature beyond

Politics.' And, after all, uncle Petia, the drunk, the barely literate seer who lived not far from Tver', where I worked as a game warden and wrote my first book, kept warning me, kept warning: San'ka – he used to say – don't be goin' to America. At the time when the old man was giving me this advice, I did not even think about leaving. And I was genuinely surprised: God be with you, Petra Nikolaich, what gave you the idea, what America? I see it, I see it – he kept reading my fate – you'll leave. His words were even more puzzling because he and I never talked about politics. In our village, we did not get newspapers, we did not listen to the radio, and we lived only by thinking about the conditions of the river, the weather, and the hunt. And in the unsophisticated beauty of the table talk, the prediction of uncle Petia suddenly seemed to lose sense and meaning. Strange, mysterious, and tragic events occurred in that indigent place, where, besides me, Chaikovskii, Prishvin, and Rilke with his Russian translator Drozhzhin used to find peace and freedom, but where a man's soul is not worth much more than a pair of boots. There the Volga, otherwise known as the Lethe, flows until it runs into the Turkish sea of oblivion. Enjoying tea made with its water and learning what is going on around its banks, you become forever privy to the unexplainable and unfamiliar – in the river itself and in the fates of those doomed to be with her. Not long ago I received a letter from a poacher friend. Now look, begins this unvarnished village prose, didn't Petra Nikolaich tell you not to go where you shouldn't? You didn't listen and you don't know about our life here. After Vit'ka Lomakov drowned, many things happened while you were absent. Do you remember Iliukha the dimwit? Iliukha went across the Volga on Constitution Day to have a drink, but the ice was still weak – so later only his skis were found. Kostia Mordaev, the handicapped ferryman, knew his end in advance. And so he fell asleep in the boat. The water, where he plopped in, was no more than half a metre deep. But for Mordaev even that was enough. And now about Val'ka, the lame Vit'ka's wife, and the Lady-Bugger. One November day, when the river's edges were already iced up, they went to the other side to the store. After a few drinks inside, they went rowing back. And when they were getting out, the ice broke and they fell in. They were standing in the water, screaming. People in the houses around heard the women and tried to wake up their husbands, but the husbands were out cold themselves. They woke up in the morning and found their wives lying in the entrance-hall, frozen stiff. The fellows started drinking worse than before. Then, Bor'ka, the hunter, somehow fell asleep with a lit cigarette. And his hut burned down. Nothing remained of Bor'ka either. And many more such events took place here and in the neighbouring villages – concludes this martyrology, shortened by me because, to describe them all, one would need to write a book. And I wrote it. With a photograph of the village clairvoyant Petr Krasolymov on the cover, the book, *Between Dog and Wolf,* was published by Ardis several months before I received this sad report. Nevertheless, some incarnation of all these events can be discovered in it. And as far as the misfortunes of the man who became the prototype of the sailor Al'batrosov are concerned, they befell him almost in complete agreement with the book. Because things described in fiction come true; fate suggests to the neglected in spirit solutions that it has already found. And it does not make any difference whether the master creates life myths or they create him: the text has been recorded in the same place, on secret tablets. And nothing else but fate will answer all the questions and decide what will remain – silence or the word. And, if necessary, it'll rip out our sinful tongues.

In the House of the Hanged

Trying to assess my understanding of human rights, I could not find anyone more specific than myself to serve as an example of a human, so I asked this human a number of leading questions. Which circumstance of your biography, I asked him, do you consider the most unfortunate? Not counting my birth as such, he answered, I consider the most upsetting the fact of my initial belonging to a lawless society. Of course, it could have been much worse. I could have been born a citizen of China, Cambodia, Vietnam, or Greater Albania, a black resident of the Republic of South Africa, or simply a guinea pig. But such musings bring little comfort because it is impossible to forget that it also could have been much better. And, naturally, the answer to the question about my happiest circumstance would place it on the 8th of October 1975 at 6 p.m., when the plane in which I left Moscow landed in Vienna. I was walking through the underground tunnel towards the passport control and feverishly, but with absolute clarity, felt – nevermore. And the feeling of freedom I experienced then and later walking around the paradisiacal garden of Europe was complete and supreme. Freedom was almost material: it was the music of a mechanical top that incessantly rang in my heart. With time that feeling subsided, but even now, so many years later, I still congratulate myself on my departure from my hoodwinked motherland. Why did they let me go, I wonder, me in particular out of so many who wished, suffered, and hated? Why me, asked Stalin's famous companion-in-arms and the enemy of the state, Lavrentii Beria – the hero of my novel *Palisandriia*. It was the same question, but asked in a different situation: the minister was being dragged out to be shot. He meant: why not Khrushchev, not Voroshilov, not Kaganovich or Molotov, not the entire remaining Central Committee, but him, Lavrentii Pavlovich? He could not perceive the logic of the cruel gesture of fate and to him his leading question seemed justified. But we, his descendants, especially the physiognomists, know better. It was enough to examine closely the features of the murdered executioner's face and the prognosis was clear: this one would end badly. Right. And our future is revealed by the close scrutiny not only of our faces, but of our actions as well. After all, we repeat ourselves, and the circumstances in which we find ourselves as a result of these actions frequently happen to be similar. Once I knew a certain pathological reader. He was born and grew up in Moscow and never went any farther than to visit the grave of Boris Pasternak, approximately twenty kilometres from the capital, just because that acquaintance of mine preferred reading books to travelling around the world. And there was another man, who never argued, never broke up with and never stopped seeing anyone, regardless of the price he had to pay for it. In front of you stands a man diametrically different from those two. Throughout his entire life he has kept breaking up with something, has not appreciated any acquaintances, and has constantly kept departing to somewhere else – far away and for a long time. An idealist, an egocentric, and a romantic, he has valued truth more than friendship and considered his departure from the common and frequently repulsive milieu as a means of growth, as a way of defending his ego. He looked back at that, what he left, like a snake looks at its abandoned old skin: without pity, with a feeling of becoming lighter; and in his ability to act like that he saw a pledge of individual freedom. He considered it his fundamental and the most important human right. He started considering it on the 1st of September, 1950, when, taken for the first time to one of the many stifling Moscow schools, he ran away without regaining consciousness. He was captured only in the evening. The sad hours spent in classes, being always regarded as the worst, the laziest, and the most rebellious student, will not pass for naught. They will constitute food for thoughts about Chekhov's ordinary grey days as well as about the narrow-mindedness and lawlessness of the teachers and their students; they will also provide the material for his first novel, which he will write after running away from a prestigious literary paper and becoming a game warden on the Volga. The manuscript will secretly leave Russia two years before its author because it will be unthinkable to try to publish it there. By a twist of fate it will find its way to America, to the publishing house Ardis, where it will be published in English and Russian. It will be a book about student so-and-so, a subtle and strange boy afflicted by a split personality, who cannot make peace with the surrounding reality. An anarchist by nature, he protests against everything and at the very end comes to the conclusion that in the world there is nothing-nothing-nothing except the wind. The author sympathizes with his hero. Their opinions about human rights in general and the Russians' lack of rights in particular agree with the opinion of the third, more famous dissident. The book quotes the testimony of the latter which dates back to the antedeluvian seventeenth century. It shows that even time is not able to improve the situation of our people or change their points of view on it. Satan begged for and received from God the radiant Russia, says the archpriest Avvakum, to redden it with martyrs' blood. You devised it well, devil, and to suffer for the sake of Christ, our light, pleases us too. End of quote. The patient suffering of the Russian people is the talk of the town. And enough has been written about it. I just want to add several words, even though they are not my own. I made one of the epigraphs for *A School for Fools* out of eleven Russian verbs constituting a well-known exception to the rules still unknown to me. To chase, to hold, and to rotate, to hear, to see, and to offend, to run, to breathe, likewise to hate, and to endure, and to depend. In the ten years that have passed since the writing of *A School*, my opinion about the situation in Russia has become even darker. Apparently, I have been affected by age and the experience of living in countries with humane regimes. In addition, and this happened unintentionally, I assumed the role of an almost detached observer. And many things became clearer. Today, looking at the lives of our people before and after me, I cannot avoid making the statement that the entire history of Russia is the history of Russian leaders trampling on the rights of their citizens and the citizens of neighbouring countries. I do not force my opinions on anyone. But I will be dissuaded by neither the communists nor the monarchists. And yet, hope for better times still flickers. It flickers as long as, at least in our novels, we can meet people like Pavel Norvegov, the geography teacher from the school for fools, who died long ago but still continues to appear. Here is a fearless man with unlimited inner freedom. Because what should I fear facing eternity, we shout with him, if today the wind tousles my hair, freshens my face, blows into the collar of my shirt, flows through my pockets, and rips off the buttons of my jacket, while tomorrow it breaks unwanted old buildings, uproots oaks, stirs and swells reservoirs, and carries the seeds from my orchard all over the world – what should I fear, I, geographer Pavel Norvegov, honest suntanned man from the fifth suburban zone, a modest but well-qualified pedagogue, whose thin but still regal hand from morning until evening keeps turning the empty planet made of deceptive papier-mâché! Give me time – and I'll prove to you which one of us is right; one day I'll whirl your squeaking lazy ellipsoid so hard your rivers will start to flow backwards, you'll forget your false books and newspapers, you'll get nauseous hearing your own voices, last names and titles, you'll unlearn how to read and write, and you'll want to babble like aspen leaves in August. An angry draft will blow down the names of your streets, lanes, and sickening signs, and you'll want the truth. O, you lousy cockroach tribe! – Pavel Norvegov and I reproach our readers – O, brainless Panurge's herd, covered with fly and bedbug excrement! You'll want the great truth. And then I'll come. I'll come and bring with me those you killed and humiliated, and I'll say: Here is your truth and vengeance against you. And from horror and anguish the servile manure flowing in your veins in place of blood will turn to ice. End of quote. And so, long live freedom. Freedom, about which *Bartlett's Dictionary of Quotations* says as much as it does about God and love. Nevertheless, after repeating the words of some luminary who said that freedom is his God, I would like to add something from me personally. So, when Protagoras tells me that man is the measure of all things, I continue his thought. And freedom, I tell him, is the measure of every man. That is – his understanding of freedom, his attitude towards it. The attitude of the majority of my compatriots towards freedom, their inability to understand it, consistently made me furious. Especially in my youth. From time to time, in the heat of a chance discussion on the street or in a restaurant – ultimately, a discussion about rights and freedoms – I would use the heavy argument of my fists, but even there fate was favourably disposed towards me: I was never arrested for brawling. I was arrested for something totally different – for a series of unauthorized absences from the stinking barracks where I was taking classes. Even in that case I was lucky. I was sitting in the same prison and in the same wing where the perplexed Lavrentii Pavlovich awaited his execution. Except that he was sitting there eleven years earlier than I and two floors above – in the deluxe room. I cannot guarantee what was happening on that floor, but on ours human rights were not discussed, even though there were extremely few of them. For example, a cell of about nine men was given one *Pravda* per day and two minutes for the morning and evening ablutions. And, in general, I cannot recall that human rights were ever discussed in any company – even among students. That is, discussed not in passing, but thoroughly and seriously, with particulars. In parentheses: perhaps I was socializing within the wrong circles; it happens. If forbidden literature was ever discussed, nobody inquired by whom and why it was forbidden. That was self-evident. We told anti-Soviet jokes, sang underground songs, shouted in jest and under our breath seditious slogans, and related to each other the news about so and so going to trial and so and so already tried. But none of that was ever supported by a theoretical base. Nobody claimed that thanks to this or that article of the Constitution we, Soviet citizens, had the right to freely listen to the broadcasts of foreign radio stations and to travel abroad, yet we were not allowed to do so. On the one hand, everyone, from adolescence on, knew that no good would come from such statements: forbidden means forbidden. On the other hand, you don't mention the rope in the house of the hanged. It's not ethical to babble in vain. Everything is clear without words. Everyone understands everything. And this universal understanding – understanding of the hopelessness of your own situation – liberated me internally and I became incomparably freer. And I realized that I was no longer able to live or to write as I did before. After the high military medical commission officially acknowledged that I was an unexploded bomb, I received a white ticket and merged with the brilliant crowd of the free artists of the capital. Moreover, these were the sixties – the most democratic period in the history of the regime after the New Economic Policy. In the evenings, in the city squares, the young geniuses read poems to each other. I was one of them: part poet and part vagabond. The authorities were almost indifferent towards us. Nevertheless, precisely in those happy months I understood that sooner or later I would escape from my country. If for no other reason, at least out of healthy curiosity. It is boring, gentlemen, to languish throughout your entire incarnation in your cherished but solitary fatherland. Either on a boat across the Black Sea, on skis across the Spitzbergen, or on foot across Lapland or the Pamir – our citizens have many ways to assert their right not to be citizens. I kept making plans and proposed to my friends that they depart together with me. And only one – from roughly thirty initiated – became interested in my proposal. Accordingly, today he resides in California and the rest live and, apparently, will live to the end of their days at their former addresses. At that time I was a desperate, uncompromising maximalist. I believed the situation that had developed in our country demanded one single solution: mass emigration. The masses did not justify my hopes. And glory be to Allah, I say now, not everyone is obliged to run away, break cleanly with something, and act on a whim – after all, someone needs to populate the country. But even now, having become twice older than that freedom-loving poet of the sixties, I secretly – secretly, so I don't ruin my reputation as a respectable man with an attaché case – fail to understand: why the heck millions of my compatriots – nice, wonderful, spiritual, wise, and honest people – tolerate the conditions of their existence. Is it not humiliating to live in a country where the thing we so freely re-evaluate here is trampled? And isn't it a shame to populate it? I had a friend in Moscow – a young diplomat. He worked for a long time in New York as a secretary of the Soviet legation. One day, when he came back to Russia for his latest vacation, I asked him directly: Listen my friend, I said, your wife has left you anyway, you have no children, you are free as a bird; tell me why do you keep returning here all the time, what have you lost here? And even though by that time we had drunk quite enough, he simply did not understand my question. More precisely, he understood, but it so astonished him that, when someone came in just then, the question remained open. Trying to close it, I occasionally employ the most banal parallel. There are various birds, I tell myself. And right away memory suggests a line from a poem by Jacques Prévert: To paint a bird, you need to draw a cage first. Of course, of course, I answer, there is a cage too. And there are different birds in it. The secretary bird, for instance, wonderfully tolerates its imprisonment; it just gets a little fat. But a nightingale in the same cage keeps silent and dies. And the phoenix? O, the phoenix is true to itself even in captivity. As a sign of protest it burns itself, and when its ash is swept out from the cage, it is reborn and flies away. It has a sharpened – you might say fiery – sense of its own dignity. *Jedem das seine* or let the dead bury their dead, their own rights and freedoms. I did. I quickly threw into my suitcase a few unnecessary things and, without saying goodbye to anyone, executed the latest departure from my repulsive milieu. Since the masses did not justify my hopes, I solved the question of emigration in an individual way. It was my most difficult departure. I think that it succeeded because I was ready to sacrifice for it almost everything. And, essentially, I did sacrifice almost everything. Still, life in the West appears to be perfectly suitable. I find here exactly what I hoped to find. Here people have precisely those rights and freedoms that are most dear to me. Freedom of assembly and demonstration. The right to leave the country in which you live and the right to return to it. The right to freely express your ideas in any form and the right not to express anything. As a writer, I am particularly impressed by the absence of censorship in newspapers, journals, and publishing houses. A footnote: several Russian-language publications are the exceptions. Paradoxically, some of them appear with American support and in America. Apparently, even emigration can't cure servile cowardice, dishonesty, and stagnation. So, enough about that.

Having Discovered It – Opened It Wide – Given It Wings

The ways of inspiration, writing, and publication are inscrutable. The feeling that we choose them ourselves is just an illusion. Let's consider me, for example. To gather my thoughts and compose my first novel, I acted instinctively. In those years, as a newspaper columnist from the capital, author of whatever, I suddenly realized that it was time to undergo a transformation. I left the editorial office, travelled north, to the backwoods, and settled in the house of a game warden. Killed by poachers, the host was almost always absent and his profession as well as the objects in his household unintentionally became mine. An ascetic's cot for one, a chair, and a table. On the latter – a pen, some paper, and a kerosene lamp. And while during the day existence is lit by the steel-coloured glow from above, in the evening – you need to illuminate the existing picture yourself: strike a match, light the wick, and the face of the young artist in the portrait created by the window frame instantly becomes divinely yellow. And the killed game, the fish from the river, and the potatoes turn into locusts and wild honey. Unlike his living quarters, that introspective anchorite was not humble. On the contrary, he was daring. Realizing clearly that it would be impossible to publish the book in his fatherland, he did not become despondent or doubtful. Because all this was happening in Russia, where literature, which involves the restless and poor in spirit, is a thing of honour and valour, not to mention heroism. And it is also sacred. And it is also a cornerstone of culture. And while there in times of economic problems the word replaces currency, in years of sluggishly progressing repressions it replaces lead bullets. The doubts, I may add, came later, when on a chance occasion I sent the manuscript abroad. I sent it blindly, not knowing to which publishing house it would find its way or whether it would find its way to any at all. There was no answer for several months and I thought that I was waiting completely in vain: either the manuscript had not arrived or I lacked talent to such a degree that it did not even make sense to answer me. Both alternatives seemed fatal. In other words, how I, a man of little faith, could have known that Providence had taken care of everything long before, that somewhere in Niagara thirty-five years earlier a man was born who at a certain moment in his life also experienced the necessity of transformation – was transformed and dedicated himself entirely to the same business as I had: to Russian literature. This man will be the first to read, fall in love with, translate, and publish my first book. To this man I will be indebted for practically everything that is related to my actual literary situation. Today it seems natural to look back. To look back and realize once more that in those daring days of early attempts I was not as much an unacknowledged genius as a typical representative of my unacknowledged generation. A generation of the transformed, who, in the cabins of game wardens, the huts of trackers or janitors, and nooks of lift-operators, made up the Russian literature of the seventies and the eighties. And acting like that, without visible reasons to do so, this generation nurtured great hopes, which are the only thing that gives life to art in the epoch of despair. For many, including me, these hopes materialized: Proffer appeared, Ardis was opened. It was opened in America, and in Russia immediately a lot of wings grew, a lot of feathers became stronger. Ardis was established at the perfect moment for exactly this kind of publishing house. Again, it was the work of the instinct mentioned before; fate once more took care of things. It may be called a shared fate. Ardis began and continues as a phenomenon unique not only in Russian but in world publishing. After all, the main evaluating principle of its editorial board – artistry – is also the only one. All Russian literature – regardless of the place where its creators live: in the motherland or scattered around the globe – is at this moment – as it was yesterday – practically in exile. Its status is marginal. But it will survive because it is necessary. Because having discovered it – opened it wide – and given it wings, Carl Proffer became not only a prophet of literature's future recovery, but also helped in its present. He helped concretely and visibly. After his departure, Carl remains in books he published and translated, in the fates of many writers and readers here and in the land of my language, in the fates of Russian literature and Slavic Studies. One day, when Russia at large wakes up from its lethargic oblivion and begins to speak in a human voice, it will honour and recognize him. The enlightened America does it already today.

Palisandre – C'est Moi?

Dedicated to OM, AB, DJ, AZ, AT

Nabokov, the creator of refined prose scores, did not understand the purpose of music. Sartre floated down the stream of existence and lost its meaning. Their unworthy contemporary, I lost only the taste for the plot. A loves B, B–C, C–D. What tedium. If every simile is claudicant, every plot is an invalid of an even higher order, a member of the privileged guild of wandering cripples, whom a charitable widow lures home at sunset to wash the legs of the legless. A samovar is being prepared – dusk is coming – and howling to the moon is heard. And before the torch has time to burn down, we already cannot distinguish the cunning blindman's bluff from the burning passionate caress. It's the genre worthy of Fedotov's brush. Post mortem. The plot is forced on the painter by the writer S, in whose illegible memory an occurrence in a bakery is coming to life. Lo: in no way defiant and not acting up at all, someone comes to the bakery and asks: Do you have any raisins? Since the Russian truth – regardless of its bitterness – stands above the saccharine chicanery of Japanese etiquette, he receives a straight answer: No, we don't. However, the results of his inquiry do not placate the visitor. And do you have any raisin rolls? – he says with a barely noticeable bow. And receives in reply: Yes, we do. And then he says calmly and simply: In that case be so kind and extract a pound of raisins for me. And from that moment he finds himself in the annals of urban folklore. What makes the image of the given buyer so dear to us? What qualities attract us in this hero? Inquisitiveness? Resourcefulness? Implacability? Undoubtedly. But first of all – daring. It is enchanting. And contagious. Therefore, when I hear criticism of my disregard for plot, I want to take the loaf of literature, extract from it all the raisins of plot and throw them all as alms to the surrounding voracious masses. And the daily bread of the primordial, autonomous word I want to give to the humble in spirit, to the persecuted, and to the other chosen ones. Are you talking about the separation of the refined from the state – politics – means of information – means of production and production of means? – a person with ears will become agitated. You are talking. I am shouting. Because what besides a shout can allow us to clear the surrounding fog? But life continues and no day passes without a plot. Look, look, D loves E! You are joking. I swear. And E? E adores F. And over there, to the left, in the musty corner, F–G. And in the meantime, every winter, Z, a professor from the University of Southern California, visits the writer S in Vermont, where Z comes to ski. Sitting all day long on the glass-enclosed veranda of the villa overlooking the ice-glazed peaks, the friends drink *glintwein* and gracefully trill their r's talking about Russian literature. And while around dinner they both still quite definitely believe that there is only one, closer to supper they clearly distinguish two. And if they want anything for breakfast, it is just the police tea. But if the poet divides all literature into that written with permission and that without, the journalist Iurii Mal'tsev into free and not free, the chronicler Vladimir Kozlovskii into censored and uncensored, the translator Barbara Heldt into masculine and feminine, the fifth husband of my grandmother, the Pushkin scholar Dmitrii Darskii into related to Pushkin and not, if the Franco-English writer and pianist Valerii Afanas'ev advises itemizing within it – besides the village prose – the special proses of the workers' outskirts, Cossack *stanitsas, kishlaks* of the urban type, et cetera, the author S and the professor Z from the University of Southern California – my God, how comfortable, how cozy they are there, in front of the fireplace, in those curvaceous rocking chairs and cocoons of Shetland goat-wool blankets – through the magical crystal of their sparkling goblets they are able to distinguish between literature slapped together quickly and that created slowly. The latter evokes in the interlocutors a feeling of inexplicable amity. The friends consider themselves apologists of slow writing and their opinions about its nature are the same. In short, the beautiful simply must be majestic. At least relatively. And even though the majestic does not have to be beautiful, it willy-nilly is. Exceptions like huge piles of garbage or giant squids are not only rare, but questionable. Whatever the case may be, the majestic appears to be so much more enchanting than the hectic as Ravel's *Boléro* is more sublime than Khachaturian's 'Sabre Dance.' Besides, in the same way that the Day of Creation does not have anything in common with a calendar day, so artistic slowness – for instance, that of Leonardo – is not the slowness of an idiot or a somnambulist. It is the unhurried pace of another kind. The text, put together in the tempo of *largo*, is dense and thick. It resembles the heavy water of the river Lethe. Ah, Lethe, Lethe, wrote a painfully familiar acquaintance of mine, how captivating is your mellifluous slowness, how lovely. The text, similar to the water of the Lethe radiates an invisible, but quite tangible energy. The theoreticians of slow writing labelled this energy with a term as archaic and as mentally hermetic as the game of chess, and borrowed from its vocabulary – quality. However, besides this bare abstraction, the unhurried stylist also acquires something essential. Blessed are the deliberate, says my painfully familiar acquaintance, because they are able to notice the flow of Eternity. The slow ones are gourmands, Epicureans of art, since only they appreciate the true delight and the benefit of the artistic process with its ennobling torments. Not by accident Dostoevskii, up to his neck in passions, dreamed about creating without hustle and bustle, like Turgenev: he wanted to cleanse himself. Fedor Mikhailovich thought that as soon as his life settled down, his creditors stopped following him, and his epilepsy and conscience did not torment him anymore, he would start writing for pleasure – with feeling and with reason. He was wrong. The ability to write slowly does not depend on life's circumstances. It is given by God. And for one who has not been given this gift, it is as impossible to learn how to write without haste as it is to learn to fly without first growing wings. The author S was given the gift. He had demonstrated the genius of slowness already in his mother's womb. As if predicting all of the turmoils, anticipating all of the discomforts of earthly existence, and suspecting any kind of haste to be the work of the evil one, he was born at ten months. On his arrival, the baby appeared both huge and majestic. The Canadian capital's birth-size records were broken. And, completely encumbered by plots, life began to flow before his astonished eyes: G–H–J–K–L–M–N. Several years after his appearance, S was forced to abandon the land of his birth, but thirty-three years later returned to its boundaries. That autumn, in the glorious city of Detroit, in the consulate shaded by the maple leaf, he was supposed to give his oath of allegiance to Her Majesty Elizabeth. On the day of the ceremony, in the morning, the consul O called the author S. We've never met, he said excitedly, but I'm extremely well informed about you. As a matter of fact, my father attended your *maman* during her delivery. Your case was the greatest success of his entire practice. By the way, have you had a chance to visit the Ottawa Museum of Pathological Embryology? Don't miss it; my father was its founder and first trustee. It is a wonderful exposition. Specialists consider it the best in all of Ontario. Various kinds of fetuses are collected there. Dad put his entire soul into this thing. But I would never forget with what genuine sadness he used to say that he would have exchanged without hesitation all the embryos in the world for only one – yours. Oh, no, no, don't even think it! As a gynecologist and humanist he was absolutely genuinely glad that everything went well. However, he was also an irrepressible scholar, a passionate collector, and a fanatical conductor of experiments. In other words, nobody can take a dream away from a person, don't you agree? S did not answer. O continued: All those years we, the Os, regularly thought about you. You became our family legend, our relic, and we never failed to celebrate your birthday. Apropos, do you realize you were fortunate that your birth coincided with two dates – of the revolution and of Tolstoi's death? And how do you like this consonance – Ottawa, Ostapovo? It's mystical. In short, I can hardly wait to see you; come as quickly as you can, my friend, said the consul O. S set out. But in an attempt to preserve spiritual balance, we will substitute for the description of the slightly gloomy suburbs of Detroit a small elegiac digression. To acknowledge my future nostalgia for our Vermont conversations on the glass-enclosed veranda overlooking the ice-glazed peaks, I, the author S, dedicate the above discussion, of literature resembling the waters of the Lethe, to my interlocutor, professor Z. And now I have reached my destination. As I, preceded by the announcer, was entering the prescribed office, the face of the gentleman – who was slowly getting up from his deep, comfy, and soporific diplomatic chaise-lounge to welcome me – was perceptibly changing. This face was falling. Carelessly attached panty hose and curtains fall like that. Leavened dough falls like that. Anamnesis: the son of doctor O expected to see a hero of family myths, a being approximately the size of Väinämöinen or Hiawatha, while the man who entered the office was no larger than S. Diagnosis: the consul O was stricken by an intense disappointment, accompanied by an involuntary dropping of the face. Exactly the same kind of disappointment is experienced by a reader who meets the author of some heroic work, but the author – upon verification – turns out to be not a hero at all. And the author of a sentimental work turns out to be a total cynic, a hooligan. And the creator of an excellent detective story – is unequivocally boring. And Chekhov, who sang the glory of the little man, was, on the contrary, huge: seven feet tall. And Galich, who wrote a number of songs in the labour-camp genre, was never in prison. And when this became known, people began to think that Aleshkovskii also never did time, and they got it wrong again. Therefore, this integral part of us, which we call the reader, stubbornly refuses to take into account the difference between heroes and authors and to distinguish between artistic invention and the description of facts. When my first novel was brought to Moscow, one of the closest relatives of the author S began to assure her acquaintances that I had invented the whole thing and that in reality everything was completely different because we really had never even considered selling the dacha and I had never gone to the suburbs to take music lessons, and, most importantly – could she have cheated even once on her husband with some pedagogue? I can imagine what troubles she will have in connection with *Palisandriia*. You're wrong, you're wrong, she would tell her neighbours, he was never interested in old women, he went out exclusively with young girls – Q, R, T, U, V. Of course, of course, they would believe her, those neighbours of ours, particularly the older ones. Fiendish witches. And I – what can I personally do to save my good name? Smelling of the perfumes Night Violets and Maybe, and of the patchouli of the good fairy Laura Ashley, the young *Palisandriia* sets out for the first time on its journey into the world. And as long as our enlightened reader has not yet touched it with his hands and has not drawn far-reaching conclusions, I need to take preventive measures. Why was Flaubert allowed to be candid: *Madame Bovary c'est moi?* After all, if one thinks about it, she has not fallen very low, this Emma. Even as far as her pretentious times are concerned. As Her Highness the Countess of Montenegro, Majorette Moderati, neé Onherback, would justly remark in reference to her: Ah-ah, two lovers, all two of them. And she would laugh wildly straight in the face of the proud Emma. And later, having whipped Emma's entire body with a riding whip, she would call from the street some disgusting indigent vagrants covered with anthological scabs and order them to have their way with the unfortunate one. And watching this curative punishment, she would keep saying with a lisp: Don't you dare, don't you dare to cheat on your husband. Because she lisped. In other words, today, when the horizons of decency are spread much wider than before, two lovers are not only considered not too many: they are indecently few. On the other hand, contemporary society is not yet ready for the accomplishments resembling those of Lope de Vega. And Palisandr, as we know, had outperformed the Spanish dramatist already in his monastic youth. There's no need to mention what happens after this – it's completely tasteless and shocking. And for that reason I, author S, facing my critics, have to cry with a voice in the wilderness the words of this terrible oath: *Palisandre c'est ne pas moi*. Because do I look like a nephew of Beria, a grandson of Rasputin, or at least a hermaphrodite? And do I think that all literature created before me is just a timid effort of the pen? And was I ever employed as a steward in the House of Government Massage, did I work in a troupe of wandering prostitutes, did I seduce widows at cemeteries, and did I hang cats? *Jamais*. Yes, I used to catch and strangle chickens, but who didn't strangle them in those years? Dear barefooted childhood, whither did you gallop on your green crickets? But in order not to appear unsubstantiated, I will present two or three proofs. This is what happened: the chain of happy coincidences and times broke and the weights from the grandfather clock fell on Palisandr's nose. Then, the surgeons inserted in it a platinum plate. And, time after time, whenever he experienced an attack of tick-tock, Palis would click himself on the nose, and the sound of these clicks seemed extraordinarily loud. And I? I don't have anything like that. But even in this case you can only take my word for it because, obviously, I will not allow you to click or just touch. However, there is actually something we can not only touch but even measure. Except that to do so we need to go to M-sk, to the Novodevich'e cemetery and visit a few abandoned crypts. P says that the pedestals in those crypts were irritably high. But even for me, an individual that so disappointed the consul O by his ordinary size, they were, so to speak, just right. The same can be said about the parapets in M-sk doorways: completely comfortable. From this it is clear that Palisandr is not a majestic giant, as he presents himself to us, but almost a Lilliputian. This establishes that P does not equal S. And yet, I still see on the average face of my imaginary reader an expression of distrust. I see it and realize that I do not possess arguments of sufficient weight. And who do I think I am, ultimately, to count on becoming a pleasant exception? Finding myself so helpless, I am calling on the well-wishing critics, asking them to be my witnesses and defenders and to explain to the readers who will judge me that writers have the ability to abstract themselves from the concrete I or Y. Y–X, X–W, W–V. O, amorous carousel of the alphabet! Even turned back you are beautiful. Keep turning. Expressing in advance my gratitude to well-wishing critics, I dedicate to them all parts of this speech, with all their intertextual links. All, except that which I already dedicated earlier to Z. And one of my favourite poems, written by my painfully familiar acquaintance, I offer to everybody else.

What's for me in this name of mine?
What is a name? Mere sound?
A clanging cymbal or a blurry symbol?
My name is Palisandr. I've lived with it for years.
And anywhere I go, we go together.
Sometimes I curse it, but more often praise.
To me, this letter-casting is appealing.
I'm Palisandr. And bearing such a name,
I have a comfortable and pleasant feeling.
We are conjoined and always sound the same.
But then, am I a tree? Forget it.
Likewise, a character that, oddly, was
Named Leo by his loving clueless parents,
Is not a lion. And Peter's not a rock.
And there exists a mass of such mismatches.
Nevertheless, on those rare days when you
Stand lonesome in the calmness of a grain field,
And, having dropped your hands, look all around,
At times things happen that can greatly weaken
Your confidence. A chipmunk runs, no doubt
To tread on you before the nightfall,
A raven flies about –
Perhaps to peck your eyes
Or make its nest delightful.
And then you think, perplexed: 'Who can know?
Perhaps you *are* a tree: It happens so.'

The Key Word of Belles-Lettres

There's a game. The player who goes first has to leave the room. The remaining participants select the name of a person known to all. When the chosen player returns, he asks the other players questions about the qualities of the mysterious subject. Both questions and answers should be metaphorical, picturesque. Dialogues are constructed in accordance with a familiar format. For example: If he or she is a river, then what kind? – the chosen player may ask. If a river – then deep and fast – the other players may answer, thinking about a wise and energetic man. If he or she is a star, then what kind? – asks the selected player. If a star – then twinkling – the other players answer, having in mind a mysterious or changeable character. After questioning all the players and combining all the answers, the first player attempts to guess the identity of the mystery person. The widespread fascination of Russians with this parlour game is the result of a phenomenon well defined by Aleksandr Pushkin: *We, Russians, are a literary nation.* And what do we, Russians, know about Americans in this regard? The oral encyclopedia of anecdotal ethnography teaches us that Americans are a nation of businessmen. Good for them. Every nation has its own path, its own mission, and not everybody has to live in poverty. Someone has to make money to give to the needy. Let the French excel in cooking and flirting, the English in dog breeding and horse racing, the Germans in philosophy and protecting the peace. Let the Spaniards fight bulls and strum guitars in the evening. But the Russians – they should read, write, and play picture games. To each his own. Being a typical representative of my nation, I've been practising literature all my life. I've been writing for as long as I can remember, and for years I was convinced that I would continue to write even on a deserted island. And then I got invited to a

Midwestern college as a writer in residence. I spent about a year there and my conviction was shaken. From a certain point of view, that college became for me a model of a deserted island. Neither in it nor in its environs did I find aficionados of that quite refined literature I pursued. Having lost the customary awareness of my reader's presence, I stopped writing and stood in the middle of my novel as in the middle of Nebraska. I was able to finish the book only after my return to the mainland. Taking into consideration the logic of American individualism, I expect a sceptical reaction: enough; is the attention and support of other readers so necessary, and isn't it sufficient to have just one reader, but the best – yourself? The answer to such a question could be brief. But brevity is good for compiling Latin and Greek aphorisms, while a lecture requires thoroughness. For that reason I will have to begin far away, more precisely – return to the picture game. I have picked two Russian writers. Everyone knows their names, but perhaps not everyone is sufficiently familiar with them. Following the rules of the game, I would compare the writers to two trees from Russian literature. The first is the famous oak from *War and Peace*. We see it through the eyes of Andrei Bolkonskii. At first, this huge old tree seems to us dead and dry, which represents the pessimistic mood of the prince. But spring comes, the oak wakes up to new life, and this symbolizes the spiritual rebirth of the hero. The second tree has the features of a strange hybrid. From the outside it resembles a quivering silvery poplar, although its leaves are sticky like those of a limetree. It blossoms like a St Petersburg geranium or a Siberian rose; in essence, however, it is a poisonous upas tree, disfigured by mistrals, siroccos, monsoons, and other international winds. The first tree could be called the tree of realism, the second – the tree of modernism. In the park of Russian literature they used to grow in the same alley, side by side, but, by the order of the head administrator, the branches of the tree of modernism were regularly chopped off to prevent it from developing new branches and blossoming, while the tree of realism, on the contrary, was encouraged to multiply. All of this would continue even after the death of the head administrator in 1938. Now it's time to name the mystery people. The tree of realism is Tolstoi. The tree of modernism – Dostoevskii. The head administrator, whose name is used today as the name of a park – is Gor'kii. Coming from a family of jacks of all trades, he mixed the realism of Tolstoi with the socialism of Lenin. Having thus become the father of Socialist Realism, Gor'kii declared from his elevated position that literature is no more than an ordinary craft and that anyone willing to do so can learn to write prose, poetry, and plays. This way one outstanding graphomaniac gave birth to a multitude of mediocre ones. The works of epigones and talentless scribblers flooded editorial offices. After difficult transitional years, the number of people who write increased dramatically – noted Osip Mandel'shtam in his article 'An Army of Poets.' The mass shortages of food increased the number of people whose intellectual excitement has a sickly character and does not find for itself an outlet in any healthy activity. The majority of those who write poetry are very bad and careless readers of poetry. Lacking preparation, they are always offended by the recommendation that they should learn to read before starting to write. Not one of them can comprehend that reading poetry is the greatest and most difficult art and that the title of reader is no less honorable than the title of poet. They are born non-readers. End of quote. The most ambitious and pushy among the excited ones forced their way through. They formed the backbone of Soviet literature, determined its second-rate level and its identity. Attached to the Writers Union in Moscow is the Institute of Literary Studies. It also bears the name of Gor'kii. Once a Chukcha, a member of a national minority culturally and geographically related to the Aleuts, decided to enter this institution of higher learning. You should be ashamed – exclaimed the examination committee after finding out that the entrant had not read even one book. Chukcha not a reader, Chukcha a writer, proudly answered the entrant. This would be a good place to mention a popular joke about the entire world being divided into writers and readers. But the funniest thing is that these two anecdotes are funny only to the point at which they become sad. About twenty years ago I heard an interview with Erskine Caldwell. In the interview the author confessed that he read no more than one book a year. Temptation to doubt the sincerity of his words was great: in those years I, a student of journalism, used to read about ten volumes a month. And I succumbed to temptation. Later, after I became a professional writer, I realized that my doubts were the result of insufficient experience. As a matter of fact, the more one writes the less one reads the others. Working twelve to fourteen hours a day on your own text, you are noticeably irritated by the texts of other writers. These texts turn out not only to be uninteresting but also break your concentration, distract you from creative meditation. Rejection of the texts of others inevitably gets transferred to rejection of their authors. Perhaps that's the reason that at parties writers give each other looks that could kill, and in the case of a polemic in a journal, they behave like jackals.

Whatever the reason, this is just a minor problem. The major problem is that as you reread and edit many times your own text, you become alienated from it and lose your intimate connection with it. *What* has been written – is as clear as before. However, to judge *how* it has been written is no longer easy. In other words, you lose the freshness of impressions. The text turns into a thing in itself and becomes blind. And at that moment you need a good reader. A good reader is not just an admirer. He is a well-read, sensitive critic and adviser. He is a reader-friend. Without a good reader there can be no good writer. The creative milieu consists mainly of first-rate readers. In the middle of Nebraska there are no such readers. And those who are on the state's fringes, because of their extreme individualism and disconnection – do not form a milieu. And without a milieu there is no normal literary process because both criteria and the tradition get lost. It is the same tradition that in art plays the role of truth. Is it possible to create something new without tradition, without a collective aesthetic memory, without a compilation of old values? Tradition is the foundation and spirit of art. Only the Almighty creates out of nothing, in emptiness. But the artist, working in His workshop, creates, starting from what's available, what has been worked out by Him and His earlier apprentices. Tradition assures development. The second necessary condition of development, in my opinion, is freedom. It is the light and the wings of art. In Russia, the cultural revolutionaries headed by Gor'kii corrupted the tradition and annulled artistic freedom. As a result, our official literature is as gloomy as the tundra in Chukotka. In America the literary panorama appears happier, but how much? Can I be the judge? After all, here I am an outsider. And, basically, Caldwell is very close to me. He is close in the sense that I have not differed much from him in terms of widening my horizons. In other words, he is close to me not as a writer but as a reader. Waiting for the Nobel takes more and more time and only about half an hour before bedtime remains for reading. Besides, the first fifteen minutes are spent deciding which of the two languages I should choose and the second fifteen minutes which book I should read. After all, even in a small home library like mine there are more books than even a know-it-all guest may imagine. In short, I have time to read just the first phrases. Obviously, this is better than nothing. Particularly when one recalls what importance the classics ascribe to the first sentence. Hemingway used to say that the fate of the rest of the work depends on it. Sometimes he would struggle for days with the first sentence. My favourite first sentence of Hemingway is the one that begins *A Moveable*

Feast. Knowing this subject inside out, I am ready to claim that the sequence of words, 'Then there was the bad weather,' is one of the best first sentences in all of twentieth-century literature. The excellence of the first phrase of *Moby-Dick*, 'Call me Ishmael,' is also amazing. My principle is that the first chord of prose should sound like the first line of a poem. That's why I borrowed the initial phrase of this lecture from a poem of Aleksandr Blok, which begins as follows: 'There's a game. To walk cautiously in . . .' End of quote. The prose written by poets is beautiful exactly because they know how to begin beautifully. Maiakovskii's autobiography *I – Myself* begins with 'I am a poet. This makes me interesting. And this is what I am writing about.' Another Russian poet, Andrei Voznesenskii, starts an essay about his great Spanish colleague in an equally brilliant way: 'I love Lorca.' All the quoted phrases are so uniformly great that it seems that they came from the same pen. Yes, in essence they did. Because their twinkling brilliance is a reflection of the guiding star shared by all the chosen – of God's mysterious spark. To prove that I am right, compare the brilliance of each of those phrases with the brilliance of the first line of the Holy Bible: 'In the beginning God created the heavens and the earth.' In the meantime I will compare the first phrase of a prose work with a note, played by a tuner on a pitch pipe or with a symbolic key that sets the tone of the following music. The first phrase can be called a verbal key to the fortress of form. It is the key that answers the question: by what means? It is the key in the shape of a short word *how*. The shape of this instrument caresses my sight. After all, I come from that literary milieu where *how* is a hundred times more important and more cherished than *what*. Perhaps there are pedants who will not accept on faith my hints and will ask what exactly is *how* and what exactly is *what*. I am not ready to provide precise definitions. On the contrary, in a conversation about what and how I would like to employ a certain vagueness. By the way, vagueness as a way of seeing the world and as a method of representing it lies at the foundation of my favourite movement in art and literature. I am talking, of course, about Impressionism. Possibly the only precise and specific thing that can be detected in the works of the Impressionists is a protest against precision and specificity. It is a protest against the imposed narrowness of norms and rules. It is an escape from the repulsive abode of *what*, embodied in colours and words, into the fantastic celebration of the key word. It is the rising of the young restless soul above barriers. The soul of an Impressionist keeps flying higher and farther. We cannot wait to soar after it; but, unfortunately, we are held back by the anchor of the logos. Therefore, we have to answer for our words, even if we do so vaguely. The conversation about *what* and *how* is an echo of an eternal discussion between materialists and idealists. What was first, argue these philosophers – matter or spirit? Replacing matter with the concept of *what* and spirit with the concept of *how*, we find the formula for our problem. The obvious champions of the latter in art are Kandinskii, Flaubert, Rimbaud, Joyce, Shostakovich, and other idealists. The supporters of *what* are Socialist Realists and Capitalist Primitivists. These are people, working with the topics of the day, choosing the fashionable subjects. Their typical representatives are James Michener and my neighbour Douglas Terman, the author of fascinating novels about nuclear war. These are people who compose their works on the computer and are convinced that the area of their activity is literature. To support my vague reasoning I would like to present a quote from a novel of the first Russian Nobel Prize laureate, Ivan Bunin, *The Life of Arsen'ev*. The creative output of Bunin, whom I dare to consider my teacher, answers the question *how*. And the hero of his novel, a young writer, wants to devote himself precisely to such creativity. I quote from memory: 'I would visit the tavern frequented by carriage drivers, I would sit in its crowded and steamy warmth, look at fleshy red faces with reddish beards, at the rusty and flaking tray on which, in front of me, stood two large teapots with wet pieces of string tied to their lids and handles. Is this an observation of simple folk's life? Not at all. It is an observation of just that tray, of just those wet pieces of string . . . To write! One needs to write about rooftops, galoshes, and backs instead of fighting against tyranny and injustice or defending the unfortunate and oppressed.' End of quote. In the milieu from which I come, in that school, the traditions of so-called art-for-art's-sake are still alive. I am using here the expression *so-called* because by definition art is always for its own sake and there can be no other kind of art. In that school, to write the first draft on a typewriter or on a computer is considered an unbelievable faux pas. Forgive me for being so insistent, but art should be beautiful. And prose – should be refined and superior like poetry. Forgive me, but I doubt that superior prose can be written on a computer. Momentary, newspaper-like prose can. I am not rich enough to buy cheap things, says a good homeowner. And I, says a good prose writer, am not eternal enough to write momentary prose. And I will not write my novels on a computer. It is enough that I have to read computer novels constantly. More precisely, not constantly, but before going to bed. And not novels but their first sentences: 'The first day I did not think it was funny'

(Nora Ephron, *Heartburn*). 'John Joel sat high in the tree, that tall one in the yard' (Anne Vitti, *Becoming*). 'This is the tale of a meeting of two lonesome, skinny, fairly old white men on a planet that was dying fast' (Kurt Vonnegut, *Breakfast of Champions*). 'On the 24th of October 1944, the planet Earth dutifully followed its orbit around the sun as it had done before for almost five million years' (James Michener, *Space*). Limp, grey, and indecisive – these words describe the qualities of the above examples. If an author does not know how to construct the first phrase, one should not expect any revelations in the following ones. I am sorry, but for a maximalist like me, the necessary elements of the initial phrase are sound, search, splash, magic, finesse, and impact. Show me your *how* – a pass to truth, and take away *what*; I will find *what* myself. With these thoughts, I close the book, close my eyes, and fall asleep like the Olympic Chukcha. My dream takes place in the last quarter of the twentieth century. Unbelievable formal experiments took place in the past hundred years in ballet, painting, sculpture, music, theatre, and architecture; the principles, methods, and means of expression were renewed. All of the arts have been reborn and are now appropriate for their time – except literature. Literature is no longer considered a brilliant, sophisticated lady. Sad things have happened to her. In her old age she has started going from hand to hand and ended up on the Hollywood pavement. She has become decrepit and unattractive and subsists on cream of wheat. Nobody sends a limo to fetch her, and as before she rides a pair of bay catafalques harnessed at the dawn of realism before the discovery of electricity and stream of consciousness. And all this takes place in a country, which Gor'kii visited just passing through, where nobody ever chopped off the branches of the tree of modernism and where the Aleuts continue their business as if nothing has happened. Trying to show compassion for the victim, I decide to place an ad in a newspaper. Humiliated and insulted female urgently seeks a sublime, uncommon facial expression. Call anytime. Ask for Literature. I keep running from editorial office to editorial office. But all offices are closed and all doors have the same sign – 'Everybody left to become a writer.' I try to wake up – in vain. Literary nightmares have extremely tenacious claws. Desperate, I force myself to remember some prayer, but instead of a prayer, my mind recalls the first phrase of John. And I keep repeating unceasingly: 'In the beginning was the Word, and the Word was with God, and the Word was God.' And I add every time: 'And will be.'

A Portrait of an Artist in America: Waiting for the Nobel

Eastern sages maintain that at forty a person is still young and should have enough energy and time to begin everything anew. One just needs to reject one's former way of life and totally change one's personal circumstances. The poets in medieval Japan used to do exactly that. Having achieved fame among their countrymen, they gave their possessions away and, in one faded *hitataré*, wandered to another province. There, they assumed different names and found different creative fates. The great practitioners of Christian poetry, Mark, Matthew, Luke, and John, did likewise. After answering the call of the Teacher, they let the dead bury their dead and followed Him. They were following the road of calling. It was a path to the pinnacle of spirituality and, as became clear later, to great literature. It was a path filled with bitterness and deprivations. The Very One, the greatest of the poets that have visited this vale of tears, was also the poorest. Foxes had their holes, the heavenly birds their nests, but the Son of Man had no place to rest His head. Perhaps the poetry of the Christian world, poetry in this most acute sense of the word, in the only sense it can be considered poetry, lives by the Holy Spirit – the spirit of wandering, poverty, self-denial, and self-depreciation. On the Russian Parnassus the presence of this spirit is particularly strong. Here almost everyone is poor. It should be sufficient to mention such famous wanderers as the mad Konstantin Batiushkov, who turned his existence into small change in fifty cities from Tobol'sk to London, or the homeless Velimir Khlebnikov. And the brilliant suicides Vladimir Maiakovskii, Marina Tsvetaeva, and Sergei Esenin don't need any recommendation. However, let's not deal with the extremes. It's not fashionable here. Better, let's return to our Japanese. The optimism of their philosophy has always amazed me, but I never applied the above-mentioned theory to myself. Because an artist is often an idealist, and, as a result, he has extremely weak foresight. Up to the moment when he turns thirty-nine, forty seems to him an unreachable and legendary age. I need to make it to forty, carefree, he keeps saying year after year to his carefree bottle companion in the mirror. And the companion has absolutely no reasons to disagree. And, of course, no *memento mori*, please. After all, the one who creates lasting things is immortal and eternally young. And yet, it happened – I made it. I became a man of legendary age. And, figuratively speaking, the time came to try on the old *hitataré*. Having turned around a few times in this *hitataré* in front of the same mirror, I discovered that the clothes still fit me, but, unfortunately, they had aged not only materially, but also morally. In other words, it was already too late to change my circumstances. About ten years earlier I changed them so fundamentally that the inertia of renewal would last me until old youth. First, from Moscow I went to Vienna, where I exchanged the Russian way of life for the Austrian, and later, I set out for Michigan and exchanged Austrian ways for American. During these travels, I changed three residences, three circles of male and female friends, four dentists, my citizenship, diet, many pairs of shoes and pants, several outlooks on the world, my general attitude to Israel and Vietnam, to Hollywood and Watergate, as well as to feminism and homosexuality. I even changed my name. In Russia, I was Aleksandr, while in America I began to call myself Sasha. In a word, it would be easier to list what I did not change. First and foremost, I remain true to the work I do. I am still writing and there is no end in sight. Emotions experienced in this connection are similar to the feelings of the conductor in Friedrich Dürrenmatt's story 'The Tunnel.' The train enters an ordinary-looking tunnel and cannot exit because the tunnel does not end. It does not ever end and nobody knows what will happen next. Most likely, nothing good. It's not difficult to understand the mood of the conductor: he's truly intrigued. The same thing happens in literature: after you begin, you never know what the result of this deal will be; will there be any result at all, and was it worth it to put on such a yoke? All who write have written about the torments of literary creation. From Hesiod to Hemingway. The latter's friend, Il'ia Erenburg, said that marking the paper with a pen is the most difficult thing in the world. Man is weak in general, but the artist – even more so. Soft, delicate, and sickly, he does not resist when cosmic sorrow weaves a nest in his heart. Visit in your free time a literary salon. Sitting in corners, writers give each other looks that could kill; they communicate with interior monologues and dream about the Nobel Prize. They dream about it for so long that they become completely intimate with the approaching one, and they call it familiarly and tenderly a noble babe, and, occasionally, facetiously – no bells. Gossiping about the family of the inventor the same way as they gossip about their own family, the writers recall that one summer his wife danced with a young teacher of mathematics from the local school. When the engineer learned about this, he invited a notary and added to the text of his last will a postscript: Award no prize for mathematics. Thank God she didn't have anything to do with any *littérateur,* the writers rejoice, otherwise we would have been in trouble. Ah, let it happen as soon as possible! But the Nobel still doesn't come and the writers are as sad as before. Typical victims of existentialism, they complain about their loneliness and alienation, alcoholism and megalomania, and compare the writing of prose to punishment in the mines or the galleys, to the torments of a woman giving birth or of a marathon runner. The essayist Maia Kaganskaia suggested one of the subtlest comparisons. Life alone with the word that had been written, more precisely, with the word being written, is an emigration, she said. It's an emigration from life. When I read these words, I recalled a remark made by Aleksei Tsvetkov during a poetry evening at the University of Michigan. One of those émigrés, who after the years of exile was unable to learn English but had succeeded in unlearning Russian, annoyed, shouted from the audience: It sounds nice, but it's incomprehensible; what are you writing about? I write about death, revealed Tsvetkov. The poet's answer inspired me then to reflect on the nature of creativity. Freud thought that it was unknowable. At least through psychoanalysis. As a scholar, he knew better. In contrast, I, as a writer, feel better. And I feel that the nature of creativity can be learned through practice. It is deadly and one has to pay for the knowledge with the proper currency. For instance – with obols. And if we had to describe in one word the pathos of literature in its natural and greatest manifestations, we could recall the self-destructiveness mentioned earlier. To prove my not entirely original point and to help the fans of comparative literature, I will quote one more master. Everyone who has compared poems written in the West with the real poems written in totalitarian countries, he says, has probably noticed something peculiar: they are not close variants, but two different kinds of the same art. What in the West is a game or at best a confession on a Freudian couch, in the East is still a matter of life and not infrequently death. Western poetry lives mainly on university campuses; the Eastern variety is rather apt to appear in labour-camp universities. In the West the audience of poets consists of other poets (and not always); in the East poetry, at great risks for its author – conquers isolation and alienation. This is the opinion of Tomas Venclova, a Lithuanian poet. Like his compatriot, the Polish poet Czesław Miłosz, Venclova lives in America. The Russian poet Aleksei Tsvetkov also lives here. And Maia Kaganskaia, who writes in Russian, has settled in Jerusalem. Hundreds of prose writers and poets from the countries of Eastern Europe have found themselves in the countries of Western Europe, in the United States, Canada, and Israel. These are the people who have chosen freedom. Creative and personal freedom, so abundant here that its value is often forgotten. Those who were born here receive it for free. But those who were born in imprisonment have to pay for it even here. And a high price as well. Since they were writers, that is, émigrés by nature, by spirit, now they have become émigrés also in the sense of nationality. They are separated from their people, from their native language, from the social milieu they were used to, and, what is most important – from their readers. Not all of them can bridge that chasm. More precisely – almost nobody can. With superhuman willpower one can forget about Nightingales à la Kursk for the sake of Kentucky Fried Chicken. There are many examples of such heroism. But how can one learn to write in a foreign language? And not just to write letters, applications, and articles (although these too), but prose and poetry? Up until recent times, the history of Russian emigration has known only one writer who was able to accomplish this. It was Vladimir Nabokov. And suddenly there appeared one more phenomenon: the pianist Valerii Afanas'ev. Specialists, for example, the violinist Gidon Kremer, think that he plays like a virtuoso. Afanas'ev is a laureate of several international competitions. After one of them, he asked for political asylum in Belgium and, having received it, moved to France. Still giving concerts to make a living, Afanas'ev devotes most of his time to literature. He wrote his first novel in French. The book appeared in Paris and received such critical acclaim that one can only envy the author. And even though Afanas'ev still lives in France, he has written his second and third novels in English. In this connection I will allow myself an excursus into comparative psycholinguistics. Vladimir Nabokov abandoned Russia as a young man. Valerii Afanas'ev decided not to return to his country when he was thirty. Nabokov's nanny was English, his mother, an Anglophile, and the writer himself spoke English from childhood and was educated at Cambridge. Before his emigration, Afanas'ev practically knew neither French nor English. To start writing in English, Nabokov needed twenty years. Afanas'ev's novel *Disparition* appeared six years after the author's disappearance from his former reality. When after a long separation we meet at his place in Versailles or at my place in Vermont, Valerii is sincerely amazed: Are you still writing in this barbaric language? Out of all human vices, snobbism seems to me most appealing. Moreover, in general, the longer one lives in the West, the more one becomes tolerant. And for that reason, as long as Afanas'ev does not stop being amazed, I do not stop explaining to him and at the same time to myself, why I do not appreciate the riches of more elegant dialects. To learn all those things that I can do with the Russian language, I would require exactly as many years as those that have passed since my birth. To switch to another language means to decide in advance to write below one's abilities because it is impossible to master it to the same degree. And, as you know, I am a maximalist, I say to Valerii. Baloney, answers Afanas'ev, I am also a maximalist, but I have mastered it and I am writing. Fine, I say, let's assume that I decided to do it; however, frankly speaking, there are hundreds of languages: which one should I choose? English, of course; after all, you live in the New World. And if I decide to go somewhere else, for example, to the above-mentioned Japan? Then you'll learn Japanese, says Afanas'ev, admiring his *hitataré* from Christian Dior. And these words of his also sound honest. My linguistic idiocy is incomprehensible to him: he is a genius. At the time when I was studying in a school for fools, Afanas'ev went to a special school for wunderkinder. But this doesn't appear to us to be a major difference. What we have in common is much more important. We are the representatives of one generation. We both love Nabokov, Beckett, Joyce, and Borges. We appreciate Márquez, but with some reservations. We have a special feeling for Calvino. In our minds we approve of the experiments of Coetzee. We both grew up in Moscow and received higher education on the same street. Only I loitered around the university and Afanas'ev was close to the conservatory. The street on which all this took place bears the name of a famous literary émigré of the nineteenth century, Aleksandr Gertsen. His closest friend, Mikhail Ogarev, was also an émigré. Another street was named in his honour. Today in Russia there are streets named in honour of Turgenev, Dostoevskii, Gogol', Kuprin, and other writers of the nineteenth century who preferred to live abroad – a long time or permanently. In those years, emigration became in our country a fine tradition. Simultaneously, superfluous men appeared in Russian literature. This name was given to the indecisive heroes, mainly of noble origin, who could not find for themselves a place in society, who did not fit in with their epoch. Nowadays, there are no noblemen in Russia. And in the new

Russian literature there are no superfluous men. They have dissolved into the air with all their problems exactly like the smoke of their duels. Instead of them, there have appeared superfluous writers. They also do not agree, but less with the times than with the regime. Superfluous writers do not fit in the boundaries of ideology. Poor wretches! They have a conscience and cannot be silent. The superfluous writers of Russia are those who choose freedom – in speech and in writing – and, continuing the century-old tradition, depart to the beautiful far away and for a long time. Our country is rich in talents. It has superfluous painters, sculptors, actors, and musicians. They choose the same paths: into silence, into exile, into artistry. The artists of the nineteenth century went to the West in search of wider horizons and more refined circumstances. They were driven by the quest for knowledge and by a hypertrophied appreciation for beauty. The superfluous artists of the twentieth century are driven by art's instinct for self-preservation, and for this reason they flee rather than just leave. They flee from belligerent mediocrity, from a cultural revolution, conventionally named Socialist Realism. Immediately after arriving in America, the Russian artist is enchanted by its beauty, freedoms, and talents. But slowly he begins to understand that even here a revolution is going on. Nobody is sent to the Gulag in its name, as it happened, happens, and for some time will happen in his motherland. In its name nobody cuts off the fingers of bourgeois pianists and violinists, as is done in China. The American cultural revolution, as comrade Stalin would have said, is a revolution of the American type; it is a humanitarian revolution. Tendencies it brings to art are isolationism, a departure from traditional values, the 'washing out' of criteria, and lowering of artistic standards. Its creed is business as usual. Its beloved child is mass culture. In contrast to Socialist Realism I would call it Capitalist Primitivism. The Russian artist in America, as in his own country, has to make a choice: accept the revolution or not. At the same time he must step on the throat of his own song and forget a lot of things he learned in the workshops of Europe. He must forget the lessons of Flaubert, Thomas Mann, Fellini, Bergman, Ionesco, Dante, Kafka, Virginia Woolf, and Proust. He must forget and never ask – himself or others – how it is possible that in the land of Melville, Faulkner, and Dickinson most publications look as if these writers never existed, as if literature flowed backwards – towards Mayne Reid and Fennimore Cooper. To accept the revolution means to forget about the oars and with the smile of a certified fanatic surrender to the mercy of the current. And at the same time, even if one wants to become completely integrated – it is impossible. One of the

Russian artists who accepted the American cultural revolution, and as a result found success in the local movie industry, told me: You cannot even imagine how much you need to sell yourself here in order for them to buy you. But there is freedom, I cheered the compatriot up as much as I could. Not to accept the cultural revolution equals not to give in to the amnesia reigning everywhere and to consider the naked emperor hopelessly naked. That is, to become close to those superfluous artists of America who call themselves the elite, while the respectable public calls them the bohemians. That is, to remain an aristocrat of the spirit and place the responsibility for your future prosperity on MacArthur, Nobel, and other Godots. That is, not to step on the throat of your own song, but to sing it only to yourself, like Salinger. If, after reaching my fortieth birthday, I would finally consider accepting the advice of the Eastern sages, I would become an artist in the first meaning of the word. Thanks to my perseverance I would make up for the lost time in a flash. I would formulate the topic of my first exhibition more or less as follows: Between the Scylla of ideology and the Charybdis of business: the opposition of the Russian creative emigration to two cultural revolutions. Besides the portraits of Baryshnikov, Solzhenitsyn, Rakhmaninov, Shaliapin, Bunin, and Rostropovich, I would present the faces of artists less known, but no less deserving to be shown. The iron woman of our literature, Nina Berberova, would appear here. The sculptor Ernst Neizvestnyi and the prose writer Vasilii Aksenov, who defended creative freedom in quarrels with the mighty of this world, would be here. And the sculptor Oleg Sakhanevich, who in the name of that freedom crossed the Black Sea in a rubber boat. And the poet Konstantin Kuz'minskii, who learned by heart thousands of poems of independent Russian poets and published them here in his multivolume anthology. And the mad painters Vladimir Nekrasov, Oskar Rabin, Vasilii Sitnikov, David Miretskii, Igor' Tiul'panov, and all the masters I mentioned earlier. Plus many others, also called and uncompromising. Following the road of calling, they departed to foreign lands and began new creative journeys. Look at these beautiful, inspired faces, I would tell the viewers during my opening. But I am afraid that not everyone would agree with my opinion. As a matter of fact, according to specialists, my lack of talent for drawing is absolute. Therefore, in order not to advertise this shortcoming, unpleasant for an artist, I would become a conceptualist. My concept would depend on not restricting the viewer's imagination with any frames. Or even canvasses. However, not to be accused of excessive minimalism, I would hammer the nails in.

The Anxious Pupa

To Irina Ratushinskaia
... Everything was going according to plan,
Wasn't it, Lord? Under the cold expanse,
You raved about all lands, confusing fact and fancy.
...
We'd like to know – why we deserve this, God?
Irina Ratushinskaia

What a miss! Instead of being born and growing up in incomparable Buenos Aires, where in place of the expected *¿Como esta usted?* everyone asks *¿Como estan los aires?* and answers *Gracias, gracias, muy buenos*, and where the bike carrier of the paper *Hoy* ostentatiously reads it without a dictionary and in addition rides hands free, while the conductor – an ordinary conductor in a streetcar – recites to his passengers from memory passages from Octavio Paz – that is, instead of appearing among the well-read and sophisticated and becoming a citizen called Jorge Borges... But no, wait a moment – perhaps in Uppsala? In the indescribable Uppsala or somewhere not far from it, in the land of gloomy Gothic wisdom, to be known as professor Lars Bäckström; to be him and in the name of the wondrous Aurora from the famous family Borealis cast with abandon spells called *Svensk poesi?* Or – not to reproach either Rome or Athens – to be born in the incomparable Jerusalem? Oh, the radiant childhood on the Dolorosa street, amid the ascetics and legends! Oh, gods, but why Jerusalem, let's leave it alone until the future calendars; after all, one can appear also not far from there – in unattractive Bethlehem, reeking of falafel, and if not there, then in the once-powerful Afula full of mules or in the hilarious Sodom, and, spending the entire life conversing with friends in the language of the Ecclesiastes, become the master of the Amos Oz guild. In other words, instead of appearing in one of the above-mentioned locations or in some similarly refined and exotic place – you appear and live the devil only knows where – you babble, mumble, speak nonsense, write rubbish, and even fall in love and see visions using the most ordinary Russian – when suddenly, in a flash, you turn out to be nobody knows who, whoever you want, more precisely – simply yourself. O horror! Having realized what had happened, you feel like the victim of an accident – of the concatenation of egotistical circumstances or a similarity in chronology. It feels as if you were entirely covered by cobwebs, as if you were entangled in some sticky mesh, in some weave. Accursed Parcae! Look how I am wrapped up, enpupated. Let me loose immediately. I am offended. Where is your celebrated benevolence? Am I a fly, or what? Do you hear? Apparently, you don't. At any rate – you don't pay attention. Unbelievable. A typical spectacle in poor taste – you joked once in your youth. That is, not you, but they, the others, joked. And you, when you understood the whole ugliness of what had happened, did not feel like laughing at all. On the contrary, entrapped by the dialect given to you a priori, you sank into a chronic despair. And if you smiled at all from time to time, you did it exclusively out of politeness, and even then sardonically. Nevertheless, life was all around you. Trying to fight depression, you followed the instructions written in small print on a flyer – Applicants with weak nerves need not apply – and found yourself a job in a morgue. You started as an orderly's assistant but advanced to a lab technician. Your duties included shaving clients and assisting in autopsies. To state that autopsies are not aesthetically pleasing is hypocritical; it is a pretentious hiding under the cover of a litotes. From the point of view of some humanitarian, an autopsy differs from the aggravated abuse of a deceased only by the keeping of a written record. Nevertheless, this operation caused by death, to use the words of cynics, is performed on all those who die in a hospital. This is a custom sanctified by tradition: exceptions are made only if you know the right people. The poor wretches' lack of any rights resembled your own situation. You were slaves of two contrasting elements. You were a slave of your given language, while the clients – slaves of its lethal absence. Life is banal and evil, you complained to beautiful ladies in parks filled with nightingales. But death is not the solution either. Because even death does not guarantee us free will. Consequently, you used to dedicate to the ladies verses dripping with professional sorrow: In the hall, on the slippery enamelled floor, a skeleton danced through the night, while the distant pale-orange shore radiated an ominous light. The sufferings of a broken talent resonated in the listeners and turned into total adulation. Touched by their compassion, you whispered to them what they expected to hear and received what you desired. Oh, how much balsam one was able to get during those young nights in exchange for the resonant Sesame. And how the lilacs raged on the edges of dawn. And how pink in the rays of sunrise were the ears of cats, implacable like Moirae, who sat like sentinels next to their aquaria guarding their bejewelled fish. Nevertheless, you considered yourself cheated. You wished to find shores where different Sesames were in use. *Ich liebe dich, s'agapo, te amor*, the heroines of your dreams kept saying to you. But dreams occasionally turned into nightmares. The following one, for instance. Pardon me, but where is choice? – you say to someone wearing a mask and a costume resembling the mantle of an inquisitor. You say it passionately, from your guts, exactly as if Dostoevskii were confessing to Freud. There is no choice, he answers coldly and sanctimoniously. But without choice there is no freedom, and without freedom – no happiness, isn't that so? Perhaps, but who told you that you have the right to happiness? The right? I was told that I need no right, that as a moth is born to fly, a person is born to be happy. You are not a person – he replies casually – you are a larva. Well, you protest, how dare you – what a lack of tact – et cetera. In the meantime, his mask falls off. He has the strong-willed face of a usurper, the gloomy and grey eyes of a basilisk, and the unsmiling mouth of an executioner. His tongue quivers and is divided in two, like the iguana's. Or even in three. In four. Endlessly. For pity's sake, who are you? I'm the Unspoken Word. I'm the Word, which was in the beginning of the beginnings. I'm the German yes and in mirror transcription the English I. *Ja* – ay. I – *ja*. I am The One Who Says: I Am. Yes, I am, confirm the champions of universal connections. I am your enemy. I am the whip. I am captivity, misfortune, and a forget-me-not of the valley. I am 'loves me – loves me not.' I am 'if you can live with it, you'll like it, and if you like it, you'll soar.' And having soared above this vale of tears, you'll begin the autopsy of existence, isolating from it the steaming, bleeding essence. Don't feed it to the heavenly birds: they ate their fill of the Fire-Thief's liver. Instead, drop after drop and piece after piece, turn it into living prose. Suffer and work hard. And I'll give you the *stilo* and the wings. Because I'm your language. According to the law of communicating vessels, substances, and states, from such and such a moment dream and reality unnoticeably merged with each other, getting mixed up like things in the house of the Oblonskiis, when just so, without warning and without worries, like some freemason, the wonderful Russian dreamer Oblomov dropped in to show off. He drank, stamped his feet, whistled, cursed, and demanded to do away with barocco and to embrace rococo. He provided an example worthy of the most thorough imitation. However, you weren't admitted to the Oblonskiis, and following in the footsteps of your idol led, frankly speaking, nowhere. Therefore, having abandoned your ambitious plans, you acted according to your language's advice – you suffered and worked hard. All this was happening within the boundaries from a to z and from here to there. Performing on the stage of the world at large, you didn't put to shame the giants of this folk puppet show only because you played minor roles. Instead, you became a wizard of the moment, a virtuoso of the episode. No Olivier could as deftly hand someone a coat, stumble, and overturn the tray. There were more episodes than one could wish for. The entire carnival nakedness of Copacabana could be clad in the costumes of your artistic wardrobe. In your spare time you used to open the revered closet and carefully browse the garments that were hanging there. A sentimental memoirist leafs through the accounts of his own recollections like that – with a dose of melancholy. Besides the lab coat of the embalmer, the following costumes could be seen in your closet: the suit of an office clerk, the uniforms of the circus janitor and the chief of the theatre fire brigade, the vest of a stoker and the frock coat of a chimney sweep, the jacket of a jockey and the apron of a street vendor, a hunter's outfit and the padded jacket of a dog-trainer chewed by his trained dogs, a private's overcoat, and a straitjacket. You treasured the latter as a relic. Paradoxically, that modest garment symbolized your slow emancipation from social and political dogmas. Because in this jacket and no other you set out on your journey to become a Citizen of the World and the Chairman of the Globe. In it, on a Tolstoian cloudy morning, you were taken from the repulsive soldiers' barrack to the institution considered in your motherland the epitome of freedom. The carriage, decorated with red crosses, approached the edge of the square, where the sentries were going through their drills. And, led between the columns of the honour guard, you shouted to the citizens, awakening in them hope and a feeling of pride in their king: Down with rococo and barocco! Long live Surrealism! And in the same jacket seven hundred twenty-nine injections later you stood in front of the high commission. Well, now you probably realize, dear fellow, that you are not Dali? – the army Aesculapiuses asked you. Yes siree, now I am a magical pupa that has grown from the ordinary northern larva. What a magnificent metamorphosis! Look, I am completely transformed. Just like Rodin's Honoré. I am grateful. I feel great. I don't need anything else. And somewhere inside, in my gut, where before I felt a pinch, now I feel endless, more precisely – endlessly cozy. But to tell the truth, I'm still anxious. Was Salvador notified about everything that happened? You have to send him a telegram. *Cito*. It's me, yours truly. I got transformed. And the signature: Your anxious Pupa. Please be so kind and take care of this. Only I am afraid that maestro will not survive this loss. Ach, our faces were so alike. He cries. In our eyes the straitjacket becomes darkened by tears. And in this jacket, as a sign of protest against the conquistadorial politics of late medieval Spain and against Amerigo Vespucci in person, you marched through your unkind city soon after your release. You absconded with this garment secretly. You snatched it from the madhouse in the same way a heroic scout would snatch a banner from the enemy's headquarters. It was a banner of the moral majority waging an undeclared war against the Artist. Having accomplished this heroic deed, you weakened the hydra considerably. However, there was at least one more reason to rejoice. The appropriate document included the long-desired diagnosis: Good for nothing. The basis for the diagnosis: Ravings of a non-entity caused by sluggishly progressing megalomania. And you rejoiced. And you appeared in your jacket among the surviving geniuses of the fine arts and among aesthetes who dared to incite rebellion on crowded squares and in languorous salons. In the hall, on the slippery enamelled floor . . . while the distant light-orange shore . . . Ach, what a jacket it was. In it, you burned your youth as if it were a hole burned by a cigarette. Completely through. What negligence. Isn't it obvious that with such an object one needs to be careful? After all, it is a relic. Remember, in it you eagerly tried to distinguish yourself in your best episodes, playing a bouncer, a swapper of cats for rats, a nude model, an eternal student, and a man of many hats. In it, suffering and working hard, you grew up into a typical representative of your extra-class – the class of people superfluous in their own fatherland. In it, you joined the ranks of the glorious order of Drummers of the Retired Goat, the order of the driven and rebellious, restless and ostracized, seekers of truth and fools for the sake of idée-fixe, whose master is *señor* Don Quixote. A drummer by God's grace, a drummer to the bone, you were a declared enemy of everything that you didn't like. And it didn't matter that because of your enpupated state you couldn't handle the drum. Nobody cared. Instead, you became a famous theoretician of the drum, its brave ideologue. And fighting for the true cause of the Holy Goat, you drummed not with sticks and not against the skin of the drum, but with your heart – against ribs, but with your blood – against your temples and your eardrums, and with your scream – against someone else's eardrums. That's why, on your deathbed, you will be able to say: My heart's a witness, I was a pretty decent God's drummer. So bury me with honours. Only don't go unnecessarily overboard – don't sew a shroud for me. Dress me in my straitjacket – and that's it. In memory of the time when I was, I lived, I fought, and I drummed. And, if you wish – I thought. You thought like a pupa. Like an individual. Like a generation. Like a class. Because there were many of you. Many more than the garments in your mischievous closet. And many more than those episodes. One day you looked back and understood the same thing that Walt Whitman, the overseas dreamer, understood a century earlier. What precisely? That you are multi-faced and populous. There were so many of you, that it would suffice for a mass battle scene in a movie. Even more than for a mass battle scene. It would be enough for a good hecatomb. You realized then that almost everyone from your endless number was enpupated like you – wrapped in the same fabric. And you became horrified thinking about your wretched nation, born in a straitjacket. And its language turned bitter for you. And the prophecy from the visions of the early years came true. Feeling sorry for your language, you embraced its problems and began to love it. It dissolved in your blood and turned into the dust on your wings: in those days you emerged from the pupa and soared. Not as a magical butterfly of Nabokov, but as a gloomy and grey nocturnal moth, carried on the wings of never-ending anxiety. True, it is better to soar gloomily and listlessly than not to soar at all. Following instructions, you started considering yourself a small, but free moth of your native dialect and you made the effort to soar higher and higher. However, in general, language, as before, dragged low, in the dust of the detested valley of tears, or lay prone like a hospital corpse without any rights because the garment that in the ravings of the young non-entity appeared to be the mantle of the Grand Inquisitor was in reality exactly the same as yours and anyone else's – a red straitjacket. And the tedious and uninspired embalmers kept making a mockery of your language, mutilating it. Oh, miserable, helpless, enpupated, and stupefied Russian language, you kept saying to yourself.

And you prayed. O Lord, preserve and bless the dialect we use, since we do not possess any other. Preserve and bless us, its anxious moths that barely hover over the world and appear for brief moments among other languages and people from Uppsala to Buenos Aires. Bless us, gloomy and dull creatures, carrying on our wings the dust of chronicles and alphabets, the ash of apocrypha, and the soot of torches and candles. Bless us and those who are searching for an escape from the straitjackets of their circumstances to soar after us. And those who are not searching. And those who will not soar. Gaze at us and at them. Speak to us in Your noble Esperanto. Give us a sign. Strengthen and edify. Confirm that I am and that it's no longer a dream but reality. And if it's still a dream – wake me up and reveal the truth. Just to me, to a tiny moth. To me – to a bug. To me – to the dust and ash. Whisper into my ear. And through the rustle of a fallen tree leaf, or a manuscript sheet, or a bamboo grove – tell me: why?

The Shared Notebook or a Group Portrait of SMOG

Dedicated to Venedikt Erofeev

Here is a yarn about that how someone, sensitive and sensible, and, in addition, having ears – what for? – to hear? – you must be joking, medic; are we the minions of Selene to grow these oysters for the sake of Ludwig? People of our circle, of our group, need ears to soar over darkness, over dust, above, I beg your pardon, aviaries – so, having ears, and cuddling in the cage of the skeleton – what do you think? – guess! – something so melodious, so melodic, a pure top, something at times dignified by the term guts: to perceive and to believe, and, it seems, to sing – what? So far it's not understandable, it doesn't make sense, it's only clear that somewhere something is maturing, perhaps some kind of a *gazelle*, perhaps a *lalaie* – perhaps to sing precisely it; just like someone who in the extreme din and rumble of the streets, lanes, staircases, tunnels, and other, as the saying goes, trumpets, in principle very hurried and frantic, in their Jericho screams and shrieks, recognized the call, recognized the voice; in a word, the very same individual – how well he hears that voice with his melodic guts, how distinctly. About that. He hears and feels the inevitable. About that. He feels and understands: to him, his. Who could have imagined: about that. About that how – impetuous – all simply movement – a shift to an alternate location – to the outside – one way or another, but precisely as needed, as required, most likely abruptly – isn't it so? – after abruptly pulling fate in exactly the same way as, in case of emergency, there, where it's necessary, where it's customary, someone pulls some insane handle, possibly of the emergency brake, a train or a ship whistle, and a detonator to obliterate silly bridges, bills and banknotes, and various other restraints, including door chains – *vudareski veriga* in Romany – he, being totally consistent, from this time forth acts accordingly: the way it's expected, the way it should be. It makes no difference whether the action is accompanied by the knocking of the train wheels or not; however, having taken with him neither his marmot nor his smokes, travelling light, as the saying goes, he gets off at the first possible *shepetovka:* slag and steam. Remaining sincerely yours, he took flight, as they say, into absolutely foul weather, keeping silent – in order not to rhyme – about the night. Wherever he was – he'd get out of there. He went out, like that incorrigible gambler from Botkin's hospital, about whom it was said: he went out – and that's it; the man was drawn to the place across the street, to the hippodrome, because where else but in the watering hole called The Races, graciously grinning from ear to ear, could he make so many toasts to the Arabian mares that his destiny would gain speed. Whether he went out or got off – it was as if he had trumped it with his guts, as if he had spun the top. You were told that he went out – are you deaf? Blow your Eustachian tubes clean, he was here but left. And only then everything else begins. Then. And only. So let it – on account of anything – just so – let this yarn appear in our mind's dreams and let it be expressed by the fates of our circle, our group, and let it be reflected in the mirrors of our psyches. Yes, yes, it's understandable without words, nothing to argue about; isn't it true that somewhere where it's proper, where it's necessary, it says: it will be reflected? The answer leaves no doubt: it does say so. For that reason it is being reflected – was reflected – in this: the power of the word. Here you have it. Even though in a somewhat unfamiliar way, brokenly, as in the rippled surface of a canal – *canaglia,* why did you shatter our smiles; after all, happiness was so sheltering. Nevertheless, it is apparent that someone from this circle, from this group, someone wearing travel clothes, not flashy, seemingly turned inside out – hurries to catch the streetcar. Cuddling his loneliness. In a valley at a scarlet dawn. Along the alley of a babbling grove. This is Lel', inclined to loveliness, a relative of a simple oil maker. And yet, no, it's not true: he hurries, but not along the alley, not through the grove: he hurries through the deserted places of the outskirts, along the path in the magical grass. Sowing nothing, growing nothing, on his way he picks faded buttercups, marigolds. He picks up and leaves his beloved Krivorozh'e, to use a quote from the mail of the neighbourhood blabbermouths. Mister postmaster, instead of rhyming for no reason with plaster, you'd better seal these useless speeches with thick sealing wax. Don't laugh, paps, nowadays he leaves the dead to the dead, more precisely, he's doing it not on a whim, not for laughs. In these particular early years something special is happening to him. Namely, on the day of becoming aware of the lie, he developed a clear impression that the boulevard was stumbling, the rain was walking on fine springs, and the lamps were casting plywood shadows into the corners. And Dante's shadow, reflected in mirrors – like an echo – had been multiplied long ago. And in general, that man is an artist, in the sense of a poet, therefore – why shouldn't he be getting ready to travel to other places, to reveal himself there in all his impressions and explain all his passions? To wander, particularly on streetcars – better yet on the early ones – this has become appropriate for such seemingly unrefined, unshaven, but in essence terribly volatile, simply explosive beings. Incidentally, it's not important after all that such beings blow themselves up with self-control, using the method of suns, as if nothing were wrong. From the powder's point of view that is even better because it lasts a long time. Relatively forever. Yes, and, by the way, look, the trees are waving their palms: farewell, they disappear beyond. But, characteristically, they cannot exit from the play – here from the play of Parmenides' imagination, out of tune like grandmother's harpsichord. Neither they nor the past epochs can. Neither they nor, letter by letter, Typhon – Electra – Leda – again Electra – Gaia – Rhea – Athena – Phaedra – Helen – do you understand? – nor the telegraph's weeping wires. Neither they, nor the house, constructed by the poet in two strokes. Where the light went out. Where the little window was opened. He built it and soon left it to its own designs. And the front of the carriage coming into view is marked by the long-awaited number. And in the water of the same canal – try to get it – in a rippled, but magical crystal – one can recognize someone else, but also belonging to the above-mentioned group and also quite sensitive, but so far protected by feathered creatures of the celestial spheres – this one, making up his mind to go out for a walk in order not to return ever again – fools fame at dawn. Wrong, what an annoying absurdility: he does not fool fame, but pulls a frame. But definitely at dawn. A window frame, but it's either glued over, stuck, or something. Whatever. It doesn't work. That's not the point. It doesn't open – that's the point. And that's all. And since it is exactly so, therefore he simply steps – steps through the sharp glass directly upward – into the air – into those quiet evenings – in the genre – there is no other genre so beloved – of city romance lightly flavoured by the street. So don't ask how it begins because you know. And if you know – intone, start singing; if you want – howl like a wolf, and if you want – sing silently or hum like a top. Consequently, he steps out and starts singing, and, unharmed, he soars above the rubbish of circumstances, above the nonsense of familial torments and backyard dramas. This young man is moved. To use his imagery for explanation, he is moved approximately in the same sense, in the same spirit, in which Gumilev was moved and touched at the dawn of his execution. He is moved in the spirit of farewell, forgiveness, and disappearance beyond. Having fallen, he gets up. And using stairs filled with something ontological or at least not devoid of it, he ascends. He is planning to return to his cubic content, to his abode, to his cozy familial crypt. To return and discover around familiar places a handful of amazing words, and announce the freedom of soaring. Let him announce. Let him ascend. He still has far to climb – to the fifth. But finally there is a door. Who's there? Yours truly. They open. More precisely, instead of opening, they don't open. They do not. They probably don't want to: that's the reason. Or they want to, but cannot: they're sick or tired. Or just listless. But because the poet keeps knocking, they finally open, although not completely. They open partially. They open slightly, after putting in the chain. But since a poet's path is – blast and smash – no matter whether it is the chain or the *veriga*, he, you understand, breaks it and – is there. Where for some reason they did not expect him. They expected the good son, while the one who dropped in was not very good, not really the anticipated family member who was still beyond the Mozhai, far beyond. This one was the lad from the floor above, the neighbour. Even though he was from the floor above, he also had his problems. He grew quietly, but turned into a capable *smogist*, a wandering mischief maker, so uncontrollable that when he starts having fun, be ready to call the ambulance. The poet is being ridiculed, cursed, and addressed by a malodorous polite plural 'You.' How strange: to the stars – inevitably through the thorns. What a bummer. He enters a room resembling his own and sits down at the harpsichord resembling his grandmother's. And in the music notebook, between the strings of the renowned *Moonlight*: Polina, my polynya: And further – everything else, all the lines. One can see how free they feel there, in this shared notebook. But one can also see the guards arriving with a set of restraints. However, this does not make the poet anxious; this does not make him tense. Because Polina is already on the wing, and, almost a match for the lovely queen, Pugachev, in a second-hand rabbit jacket, in the fashionably new three-corner hat, will soar above the obstacles. In other words, everything that will happen from now on will not be so fatal. And it doesn't matter that some lad living up the stairs, the stairs not devoid of this or that, is being led down and placed in a carriage blatantly shaped like a streetcar. Nothing to be done about it; yes, it happens. It only happens in order to pass. But does it really happen? And at the last moment of endearment he writes in the album of the kind-hearted nurse: The following document is given to the singing Fortune to certify that she is not guilty of anything, since she did not know what she was doing: she was simply singing. And a signature, woven into the acrostic dedicated to Li Qingzhao: Grackles Unbound; Being Art Nouveau, October's Vexing. And someone else among those who were coming was not as impetuous – although he was, to a degree – as he was flighty and restless, and to fight his inclination to fall asleep during all kinds of commotion, he was sometimes inclined to fly wherever his eyes would take him and – having leaned forward – flew precisely there at breakneck speed. Whether like a star or not, but definitely loose, as sure as eggs are eggs. Ask any Hunting Dog: it knows what the tracks of the latter smelled like during the young moons of fugitive time. They either smelled, try as you may, like the soldier's foot bindings or – slightly later – like the cadet's Habanera, or – when – keep this in mind – he retired for good – like a liberated student Polka, like a flying Dutchwoman, a German globetrotter from Povolzh'e, a vulgar Bulgarian, a shivering Siberian, a grumpy Romanian, a turgid Tungus, a finicky Finn, a chewed-up Chud, or a stoker's strumpet. The tracks kept meandering madly, they kept vanishing. But life as an apparition, in the form of a Fata Morgana, pretended to be unconcerned, as if it were not familiar. Not familiar, but strange, revealed by fortune-tellers. And its journeys were long, and its buildings both public and niggardly: each building – nothing to look at, while the streets – copper trumpets. Hence, one should cry out: Be cursed, horns of taxis, odour of omnibuses, and bleating of the exchange cheaters! Be cursed and damned. Do you agree? Only in the house of the brilliantly impoverished in spirit you will find grace. Because only there is the silence to such a degree sailor-like that the speckled mare, whose daydreams are reflected in the Iauzas of our souls, neighs and sews out of it a classy striped sailor's shirt for herself. But at that moment some snake-bearing officials enter the dimension. They're experts. They are cannon fodder Aesculapiuses, cultured and fragrant. Be so kind: honour them by getting up, give them a nod. They will give you a check-up. All in white chlamydas, in burnooses, the officials begin and lose at once. A move. Fine, let's accept the mare, such things happen, but why a sailor's striped shirt? A move. Because every mare wishes to be transformed into an ocean-going zebra. A move. It makes sense, but it won't hurt to ask: How can it neigh, disturbing the sailor's silence so much? A move. But the answer is as wonderful: Don't worry, the mare accomplishes it noiselessly; listen carefully, not even a peep, it's as quiet as at a cattle cemetery. A move. How vivid. A move. Nobody, next to a cradle, would forget horses' skulls. A move. Aren't you a poet, by chance? A move. I am a *proet*. A move. Pro what, sir? A move. Pro such things as a morning and evening twilight, a raven and a turtle dove, hail and rain, and a young female Gypsy dancer with castanets in the thicket of the sandalwood grove for whom we lose everything but our sandals: ringy-dingy. A *proet* is – if you will – a bastard, a mixture of prose writer and lyricist, half this and half that. But what the rascal produces – is *proeziia* of blue blood and pure tears. Basically, tears of amazement, which, when taken in the major scale, back-to-front, or with the inner side of the hide facing outside – must be called endearment. It is the *proeziia* of unobstructed amazism, here, amid the ugliness of this world. And it rings, turning into commandment number one: A singer should amaze being amazed. Hark! What luck, the *gazelle* has grown up. If you please. I will begin, of course, from nowhere, more precisely at random, like an explosion. That is to say, simply all of a sudden, in the middle. And yet, I would like to add a condition: mea culpa. I have a stupid penchant for rhymes. Therefore, do me a favour, forget about them, don't blame me, I am still unable to escape them, wiggle out on my own. And yet in the end I will escape, I will wiggle out. In Tsinandali Valley one day, Dali paints the subject of time: from the pseudo-classic away, the light flows, refined and sublime, and, half-broken in the piano's display, Vertinskii drops a short rime. A move. Wonderful, my dear, you are clearly a whiz: you got refreshed, stronger. You feel adequate. You consider yourself a being within the boundaries of what is proper. As it should be. Amazingly normal. At ease, consider yourself a reservist. Have a happy flight, happy soaring, take care of your oysters. After exiting, you need to turn at the corner, where the wind blows and, pretending that it is not you but someone almost unknown to you, even if he also has an overcoat, a cap with ear flaps, and ears spreading the dust, walk by Dante's puddle that features a flask frozen up to its neck. Up to its neck, on which the wind drones the *doina* of Saint-Saens. And at the ticket booth of the Ferris wheel, without getting baffled because it is boarded up, forgotten, sleazy, and basically – out of season, you should get for yourself in lieu of the farewell a ticket for a streetcar going somewhere. If possible, sir, ride to the twenty-third hieroglyphic, where everything is exemplary. For instance, to Khoroshevo, to the primeval silver forest, to the Penates of the silver youth. In short – away. It will be a streetcar of Gumilev's kind; a car that had started running; a carriage that, while in motion, whistles Griboedov's waltz mixed half and half with some kind of a Persian motif. The express arrives. You board. And all the others are there in the blink. And then everything else begins. Especially – your time. After turning around, congratulate yourself in this connection; no one else is allowed to be cured of it because it has no equals. It befit us, fit us, and agreed with us. For your circle, for the number counted on fingers, it was as appropriate as it was adequate: it was musical. And the hands of its easels were blue for you. And above the streetcar of contemporaneity characteristic of it, having abruptly broken into a swan's cant – into sense – into mind – into originality – and, of course, into greatness – soared the manifesto of amazism. Next station – Vagan'kovo, announced the conductor. But this did not scare you. Do you remember? Everyone was an immortal hero. However, if the group had to select a profile for a commemorative piece of metal, you personally would engrave on it the face of the painter. The latter rode from Verkhniaia Maslovka, bristling up against dogmas with all of his essence and all his attributes – from his beard to his brushes. Even his name was suspicious, gloomy, and looking positively *nedbailo*. As far as his paintings were concerned, they were hung a day earlier in the reading shelter, which you rushed to reach and to begin. It was the highest time for you – by fits and starts – you were expected for so long. Driver, *je ne joue pas:* Begovaia; stop the car right away. Yes, this is it, your old street, waiting every day without holidays, and softly beckoning with tipsy lamps. This is the homeland of your youth, an inevitable vessel. A chalice? A cup? Who cares. A simple hoof print, the trail of running to all the ends, where the beginnings are, the trail full of recollections of youthful trotting races, escapes from wherever and to wherever – just to be a race for the race's sake, the trail of amorous errands, of heated and eternally burning games of catch. And later, having broken away from the orbit of The Races, you ran on the business of your generation. Things were a mess, the sounding brass, not Satchmo, not Dizzy, not Parker, but, for us, they were lip-smacking too and for the park of culture, for Rue Peshkov, they couldn't have been better. You perceived, believed, and in the sounds of that Mongoloid moo you distinguished a voice that knew you. And the voice told you exactly what one should say about such things. It informed you quietly, more precisely, soundlessly. It informed you about the following. But really, what's the use: it doesn't matter about what exactly; it said what it said. It said what was needed. Seemingly just by moving its lips. Just lips, that's all. That'll do. Said, spoke, and you, cuddling the singing, felt that it was the most important one, the one, when there is no other place to go because it's not permitted anymore, it's impossible, it does not make sense; after all, further on is only the darkness of that tunnel, the mad ravings of that trumpet; we've arrived. Conductor, pull your Bickford cord – so it shall be opened onto us. And not later than on a February day in the tear-off calendar – showing the number of the blow-up day – you stepped out. Outside there was a snowstorm. And black ice. And with some kind of buoyancy, light-heartedly, almost the way Botkin used to cite Cicero and Tacitus, the street dedicated to the doctor kept releasing pedestrians and perspectives. But, sensitive and scarred beyond your years, with your entire inner singing – inner howling – and running – you thoroughly sensed every facet of the near future. And of the distant one. And of the inevitable too. *Evoe,* after getting off streetcar number twenty-three, you boarded the other and became yourself again; a man of habit, a man at home. And because the day on the tear-off calendar was lower than the number of the streetcar, and the blow-up day even lower than that, no doubts remained: what remained was to begin. To begin and nothing else. However, to begin almost unexpectedly, in the middle. In the middle of the sixties – in their very midpoint, in their womb, in their guts – to start speaking in a non-human voice and to tell many revelations and yarns. Only calmly. Without excitement. In the manner of the distant suns: as if nothing were happening. Hark: in standard *proeziia*. Of the standard amazism. In short, to blow yourself up, my dear sir, to blow yourself up.

A Mark of Illumination
(An Attempt at Topical Prose)

> I am not writing my autobiography. I consult it
> when someone else's biography requires it.
> Boris Pasternak, *Safe Conduct*

Exposure: A certain man, not lacking specific ambitions and, perhaps, even merits, but later simply named *you* – you discover that you are useless. Deeply disturbed and trying to explain yourself at least a bit or, to be more precise, to explicate for yourself how this is possible, you fatigue your tongue with the words of dejection – you handle their cluster – you create a swarm. You say: I am useless – unnecessary – unsuited. And you think: I've been cheated not only in regard to prospects but also hopes and, what is particularly annoying, it's not clear by whom. However, if you use your speculative faculties more, then, obviously, it is clear. After all, one only needs to squint one's intellect or furrow one's mind and right away the forms of the unspoken image become more distinguishable, sharper, and its existence no longer requires any proof because it turns into a self-evident truth. And when someone says that all this is supposedly nonsense or a phantom, then disagree, speak out. If you are lonely, unsettled, or sad, and someone presents a cheek for you to touch, let's say, with your own, and approximately like that – just like that – as is practised in the best salons of *milonga* – cheek to cheek – whether both of you are killing time dancing or getting over spleen – it does not matter if it is a phantom or not a phantom, even more so that we are talking here about an extremely close, intimate image. On the other hand, perhaps you are not formally introduced, not acquainted yet. So get acquainted: a certain man not lacking specific ambitions; his fate, alias his destiny and his Moira. Just think, the very same. Only don't approach her with inquiries, don't hang over her, pestering her about a confession; why, let's say, she permits herself tactlessness, sarcasm, and wicked smirking. You shouldn't. Elevate yourself above that. In other words – be more humble. And as far as comfort is concerned, find it in something abstract, in some brain exercise like counting aloud. Or recollections. Everybody knows that if the past is onerous, if it weighs one down, brings the malady of nostalgia, and twists the soul into a ram's horn, one has to place it outside the rules of the so-called Mnemosyne – one has to forget it. But first, it is necessary to recall what this past represents, what it consists of, and how exactly things were. Don't rule out that this may help and the level of confusion of your squinted intellect will no longer be so high. Judging by the distribution of events, by the flying of flocks, by the shapes of puddles and the amoebas in them, once, during a feast of diligent and seasoned wordmongers whose ties used to love diamond pins but in recent times tasted ordinary cabbage soup, a conversation started precisely about the vicissitudes of those times. And you, who, on account of the kind of work you did and of your anxieties, were close to this circle and to this feast, you started speaking, excitedly. Why, you said, do you keep making a fuss about your time; to be honest, you have found yourself a lousy subject. It is not only an oar-driven galley and the tool of profit and servility. In addition, it does not have the required refinement of form. And, finally, it possesses feuilleton-like impermanency and banality, as in our works. And you continued speaking. Doesn't it really upset you. Look, if one compares it to eternity mentioned earlier, the result will be a total confusion. Because time is as much less presentable than the latter as reality is less attractive than art. They disagreed with you. One could hear expressions: childishness, nietzscheanism, elementary lack of respect for life. What do you mean – life, you argued with your co-boozers. This mode of bodies' existence is no more than an occasion for a master to show his mastery. More precisely – many occasions, including scores of unfortunate ones – for instance, shattering into pieces – like Pierrot. You are forgetting yourself, they kept saying, how can you label people bodies; in older days for similar insults one was invited to a beheading. Or simply thrown into a lion's cage. After all, we are all people, we are our sole asset, and you – aren't you one of us. One of you, you answered. And together with you, for the benefit of the kindhearted mankind, I am working on the blatantly fast scribbling. Bravo. But as the most talented lyric poet claimed, there is also, you know, art. Besides and despite. And this is absolutely not the same as what you think. It's something else. And there are masters. And I would like to be with them because they depict people only to dress them in weather, and the weather – in passions. There is nothing offensive in such philosophy. To anyone. And the reason for this is that art is supreme because it suppresses the logies: ideo-, physio-, and patho-, and it is cherished – open the quotes – because it is concerned not with man, but with the image of man. And the image of man – as becomes apparent – is greater than man himself – close. But closing the quotes does not equal stopping the development of the idea, since its underground shoot grows through the asphalt of our stagnation without compromising, without holding back, without. One should not try to break down the door left ajar just because the image of some *araucaria, bondonella,* or *vicuña* is larger than these things as such, if they occur at all. And if they don't – there are even more reasons not to do so. It is simply sufficient to note that even though no two people are alike, every one of us, even if we are quite parochial, represents a small fragment of something not human. And resonates with it. And twinkles, whenever possible, to its glory. And rings. And as soon as our images are larger or – after our transfer to the better world – purer and better than we, who are covered with awkward flesh – it appears right there. Art, consisting entirely of separate images, with which it raves and attracts, shouts and keeps silent – is incomparably grander and more beautiful than all of us taken together; it is our guiding beacon. And practically all of us turn around it, naively thinking that we don't. That art turns around us. And that whenever we decide to do so, we will be the same. Like art. But we will not. We'll be lucky if we can keep up with the turning. Zeitnot, zugzwang. The torrential lack of time, the true deficiency of the clock face. And I summarized. What can I say, our time is a chief accountant, a chief god, a pagan idol, which, posing for the master – the rest in quotes – can imagine that it elevates him to its own transitory greatness. Close the quotes. What impudence, though. A mark of exclaiming: exclamation. And my co-boozers argued: no, no. And kept saying: oh, no. They kept saying so because they thought that time – their time – was nobody's fool and that you didn't have the right to ridicule it in their presence. And besides, they said, where did you find such despair. You answered them with a quote. Being not as much a good reader as a good listener, you did not guarantee the precision of the next borrowing and for that reason you unquoted it, unchained, uncorked the expression and supplied it with your own ideas. The result was a long phrase indicating there existed a circle of phenomena that caused suicides, especially in adolescence, and a circle of mistakes made by the infantile imagination, a circle of aberrations and youthful hunger strikes, a circle of *Kreutzer Sonatas* written against *Kreutzer Sonatas*, and, finally, that there is – you approached the essence of the problem – there is a circle of silencing and forgetting of the most illuminated lyric poet of the century, the poet of true ecstasy, and that some of those present have been in this circle for an unpardonably long time, otherwise they would not have asked you: where – question – and would not have said: despair. You were excited, but you were properly rhetorical, and your speech – homage to speech therapists – sounded quite articulate. No one suspected at that moment that in the backwaters of childhood your friends actually called you a Lisper. They called you and you answered. However, you did so not because you liked this nickname so much or because you read in Seneca's work that a sage is immune to injustice and humiliation, but because already from those despicable years onward you were responsive, just, and objective. And since the given nickname corresponded to your position and, more specifically, to the position of the tongue in relation to the palate and lips, not to mention the teeth, not even to hint at them, since usually, the lion's share of the days, they could not be accounted for – the resentment did not keep boiling in your heart and the principle kept turning out to be more essential than bitterness; it prevailed. But from these same babbling years – for the sake of fairness – you yourself began to call both, people and things, by adequate names. You yourself. Without missing even one reason. As you do now. Pharisees, you said to your opponents. The enemy wavered. To solidify your success, you needed to illustrate your thought with a corresponding quote; lack of precision: with a flock of quotes, a full flock. But right there it became clear that all the quotes had run out – so you rushed outside to refill their supply in the storehouse of wisdom, that is, in the *bibliothéque*, which – it was on the way – for some reason always seemed to be old-fashioned, and where – because of the hours of dusk that – as was written on the arbitrary page of the necessary volume – were – again a quote – like sword-bearers of the roses – end the quote – you did not complain about it at all, since hours of dusk were indisputably, truly, sword-bearers of the roses – where – because of it – one could in the blink of an eye become blind and turn either to a hexameter or an oculist, or into flying reptilians. And since the librarian complained that, as he said, the fuses have -out and the candles -down, it became clear that the root of evil had been extracted, elucidated: it was equal to the root of the word *burn*. But even taken separately, *burn* does not burn and does not provide light. Then – because of ordinary necessity, which, if required, overcomes even the total darkness – you continued to page through. Explain: page through a book. And paging through it, you paid attention to the lines you hadn't noticed before. The reason: in comparison with the construction of the other lines the construction of these was uncommonly simple. They were short and invisible in the strong light. The result: you did not notice them, while reading. And here, in the semi-darkness, their modesty blossomed, it shone, and you were illuminated, really. However, no need to get agitated. Because what for; after all, this was not the first time. As far as the meaning of the lines was concerned, it appeared that someone loved someone, went to the Urals, despised everything inartistic, considered himself a person with no talent whatsoever, became a hunter, and returned to the capital. In addition, the lilacs were still in bloom, the summer promised to be hot, September was drawing to a close, dinner time was approaching, colours were moving and coming to a conclusion, art was called a tragedy, tragedy was called by the name of its futurist author, and his soulmate was appearing from beyond the dark river. And in the city you both loved, everything was as in old times: the lights flickered, the snow kept covering it, and not heroes at all but regular employees, coughing and blowing their noses in their handkerchiefs, kept clicking the abaci, crackling their joints, and clanking with the joined cars on the rails. And you became illuminated by the radiance of the syntactic modesty, the same way as, sometime before, the creator of the lines, having returned to the vastness and sadness of his dwelling, became illuminated by the street lights. And one needs to mention that it was the same kind of illumination as when the person illuminated gets illuminated from within, by the non-extinguishable inner light, and becomes, as it were, a lamp, although not visible to everyone, since the light that fills his eyes is visible only to him and to other illuminated individuals, and with it only he and they can see in the night; consequently, they see what they did not see during the day. In short, you were like a light-carrier about whom it is said: blessed is the light-carrier who follows the commandments of his light-carrying fathers: burn thyself, burn brightly. And having become illuminated – you kept reading. And in the night that eclipsed the sword-bearers of the roses, you discovered, while reading, precisely this: that you are useless because you live not your own life, but somebody else's. Exposure,

exposure, a picture of confusion. And so, deeply disturbed and trying to explain yourself at least a little or, to be more precise, to explicate to yourself how this is possible, you fatigue your tongue with the words of dejection, with their bunch, and you construct a string out of them. You say: I am useless – unnecessary – unsuited. You whisper: unrewarded – unsatisfactory – unexpected. And you think. It's amusing but confusing. To admire the lyricist for years, to page diligently and frequently through his works, to believe that almost everyone belongs to the circle that keeps silent and forgets about him, reading instead the works of some wrongly chosen individuals: insensitive and vague, disagreeable and murky; and to do all this so that one day, having looked at his works with a non-extinguishable glance, you'll understand that you also – at least occasionally – find yourself in the same circle and also read the insensitive ones. Because if this were not true, you would have lived and dreamed differently, without confusing your imaginary texts with the texts of the most illuminated one, more precisely, refusing to feed your ambitions by creating variations on his themes and, in any case, without presenting these variations to yourself as original works. And you would not present your wishes as facts, you would not try to convince yourself that you knew the poet personally and that in a short while you would draft memoirs about him based on the fact that both of you used to drop in to a certain house on Ostozhenka and that both of you did it – here is the coincidence – occasionally. You would not. Because the last time he dropped in was before your birth. No, you were not acquainted with the poet. But there were days when you accidentally met some of those, who – without doubt – knew him. That's right: none of them uttered even a peep about it. That was natural because you did not ask them to tell you about him. Let's cut to the chase; you did not ask them about anything at all. You absolutely did not communicate with *them*. But not only out of pride, not just to give them no reasons for thinking that you – unlike them – were not introduced, not admitted to the poet's company, but also because you did not know them either. After all, chance kept bringing you together for a flicker of eyelids – on the street – as pedestrians coming from opposite directions or in a short-distance carriage, where to begin a conversation with strangers is equal to showing bad manners. But if it were really so, if the meetings that actually happened were turning out to be so short that the people encountered were almost indistinguishable from those coming from the counter-direction, and they were mute, how could one recognize that they knew the most illuminated lyricist. Question mark.

Even two. In the analysis of a chess game this indicates an extremely weak move. The only difference is that the move here is not weak, but strong, since the question is justified: how could one. The answer is exhaustive. It is brilliant. Very simply. By the faces. A decent physiognomist has no trouble distinguishing the forehead of a man who personally knows the poet of ecstasy from the forehead of a man who does not know him. You were always a decent physiognomist, and in your meditations you called the sum total of the acquired features characterizing the forehead of a knowledgeable man a seal of involvement. You also provided another, synonymous term: a mark of illumination. But what exactly did these meetings, that knowledge of the knowledgeable yet withdrawn and transitory people, promise you. A question. Nothing. Absolutely. Exclamation. They, their silence, could be useful only in one case. In case you decided to write memoirs about not meeting the illuminated one, about your non-meetings: reminiscences about the lack of involvement, about not knowing. And you should have begun them in the most particular way. You should have revealed right there that you did not know him for long. And to avoid the development of doubts in anyone, you should have clarified everything; you should have given the exact length of not knowing and the dates of this gap; you should have stated: taking into consideration my responsibility before history, I never knew the most illuminated lyricist of the century. I have not known him all my life. And after making such a confession, it would have been completely natural to describe life without the poet of ecstasy, without mutual friendship, without mutual involvement in your fortunes, without walks together, without friendly criticism, without congratulations, without wishing each other a good night, a good year, or simply just luck. Without. Special chapters would contain descriptions of those years when you did not even suspect that you existed in his period, in his dimension. As, by the way, in anybody else's. Then – years of suspicions and conjectures that this entire dimension was invented for a purpose, not for naught, that a given epoch was close at hand, and that someone more ecstatic, more penetrating, and more illuminated than all the other lyricists should be in it. And, even though the others are clearly visible, while he still seems to be absent, it is happening only because it is happening just now, before the actual date. And later, it would be appropriate to say what the circumstances of your first reading of the poet's lyrics were. But since you probably don't remember these circumstances, a completely natural thing for a person belonging to the circle of the lyricist's forgetting, you would have to squint your intellect again. Or furrow your mind. Admittedly, unlike your colleague Coleridge, you don't stick to the differences between these terms, don't juxtapose them. For you, mind, brain, and intellect are like peas in a pod. You would have to furrow, to squint, and afterwards to fork out immediately the lightning bolt of the hypothetical thought. And to create a swarm of hypotheses. And to investigate them. Here's one example. Picture the purchase of some berries, some fruit. The taste of berries, their colour, and the perfunctory reading of the text, printed on the packet. Lack of precision: Not on the packet. On the page of a journal, which the woman vendor rolled up into the packet. It is not important. No more finding faults. The text, printed on the packet, is poetic – these are the lyricist's lyrics. You become absorbed in the reading and sink into a reverie. And the berries spill out of the packet. Exclamation. Never anything like that. No. As our apocalyptic youth put it, you shuffled along. Read: not with a bundle, but with your soul, following the order of consonances – and the colours of passion. Another hypothesis would resonate with a depressing official echo. Your cellmate, a chain smoker, hand-rolled his cigarettes out of people's letters; that is – using messages from the outside. One day he was taken for interrogation during a cigarette break and, staring at his extinguished cigarette butt, you discovered on it a poem signed by an unknown lyricist and copied by someone's involved hand. Whose, remained unclear, since the cellmate did not return. Neither for the butt nor for other things. He did not return in principle. He did not return at all. And when you asked the guards, when would he finally return, the guards answered: *never*. And when the never came, you learned these verses by heart: as a permanent keepsake. And you finished his roll-up: for the peace of his soul. Did it help, did his soul get its peace. A question mark. Go figure. But from that time onward your soul – shuffled – hobbled – sauntered after these and other lines – of the same poet, found later on the outside in secret spots. You would have considered other hypotheses too; however, out of all of them you would apparently have selected the most natural. Precisely here the knowledge would be needed, that is – lack of it, ignorance of those who know. Who are withdrawn. Who are transitory. Having represented them standing, full size – as pedestrians and passengers, bearing the mark of illumination or the seal of involvement – you would continue the memoirs about your own non-involvement with the following statements. Yes, the people were silent, but then came the days when the news about him and the elemental lines of his poems suffused the elements. The elements of the entire dimension. In fact, they simply penetrated it, quenched its thirst, and it seemed that only a pauper dabbling in non-existence could not feel it and not hear what this particular most penetrating and lyrical lyricist had to say. To wake up – to rise from the indifferent – to reject finding a safe haven in the prose of life and in the heavenly vanities – to become involved in some art, even if inappropriately – this was perhaps all that you needed to become suffused too. And you woke up. You rose. You rejected. And in the merciless circle of the populace – in sadness and joy – in messiness and fastidiousness – you dragged your soul after the order of consonances and the colours of passion. And the lyricist was hiding at that time in the suburbs from the rumours and, wandering – here, alas, the quotes are expected; they need to be opened because of custom – following cat's tracks and the fox's, the cat's and fox's tracks – close the quotes – wandering, he considered his position unfortunate. Even now, in view of his simplicity, you cannot completely understand the complaints of the master. You are inclined to treat them as a kind of slyness. It's not possible that he really did not know that a poet of such calibre is not supposed to suffer misfortunes. At any rate – it's not appropriate. He should stand above them by definition. More correctly, because of the definitions of the creative process, craftsmanship, and soul he himself put together in the summer of nineteen seventeen. In the end, if he wants to, he can stop the approach of evil exactly the same way as Gumilev's boy stopped the rain: with a word. And notice that, apparently, with any word, taken directly out of the air: with the cat's, fox's, bird's, or dog's word, the word of Chekhov or Shakespeare. Yes, it is true; the latter requires translation, which, according to the poet's notion, should give the impression of life rather than literature. Well, the teacher's translations are exactly like that, and you are impressed by both his Shakespeare and his Schiller. But not to such an extent that you could be, even for a cigarette butt of evening glow, without him proper, him personally: the one from the time before the war and from the time of the dacha, in a raincoat, spreading oakum and kerosene in the air. Obviously, someone was in love and it was not difficult to discover jealousy. But as is supposed to happen in literary dreams, jealousy seemed to be washed-out and anemic, like the victim of an impressionist. Because it was unclear to what it was related or, more precisely, to whom: to the lyricist, to the Muse, or to both of them simultaneously. And, in addition, there was impatience. And it flared up often. A paradox: the news about the writing of *Werther* and *Valerik*, *The Silver Dove* and *The Golden*

Ass, *Othello* and *Lalla-Rookh* did not cause your impatience. It flared up as a result of much more modest news. For example, the news about a shortage of certain people and about the possibility that the number of those missing individuals equals three; and the children sleep on the porch; and their favourite poplars keep seething under the rain; that at first it appeared as if the bushes of certain thickets were overgrown with ivy, but later it turned out that they were overgrown with hops; and the hay-loft smelled, nostalgically, of wine cork. After all, it was not as much about the factual side of the news, as about what – in the process of prophesying – the messenger kept experiencing. Kept experiencing and announcing. He kept experiencing the illumination. But there is no need to think that by making announcements about it he also placed it in the news. He kept making announcements not about it, but he kept announcing it itself, equalling it with an extraordinary feeling, as pure as that experienced by the Gypsies. And you became animated by this emotion and it inflamed your impatience. If one were to transfer your circumstances to the flatness of a sheet and give you the form of a text, printed on it, one could note that at first it kept burning the margins – on the left, next to the vertical line of caps, and on the right, next to the rhymes, and only then burned through your middle, the inner core with all its caesuras. And the entire surface would flame up. And your letters seemed green like the lungs of smokers. And you kept burning down. And so, in exchange for disappearance, peace was found. But whenever you appeared on a new sheet, your impatience would return. You could not wait to become in every way as penetrating and ecstatic as the lyricist from the Book about Non-Involvement, in order to communicate through writing the unusual feeling. Its shortage in society is acute and glaring. Judging by the faces in albums and on the streets, unfortunately, there are almost no faces truly illuminated, that is, illuminated from birth. You were impatient. The goal had been revealed. It was noble. To remind the world again about the forgotten emotion, to teach it to the world, like a song, using a simple *stilo*. And by doing this, to save the world at the same time. You were impatient. Only the problem of talent worried you. It worried and sobered you up. Would there be enough of it. A question mark. Would there be enough strength to become illuminated so furiously, so passionately, to communicate the emotion to an adequate number of persons, no matter how you counted: to everybody who was alive, to the entire dimension. A mark of questioning. Speech is a bird of very postal qualities: wherever you send it, it will return without fail to the penates of your mind, to the perches of your thoughts, to the ravine of your mouth. Oh my, there's a mouthful of worries about your dove. Periphrasis: from literature, from the dove both lisping and decrepit, there's no escape. The device of repetition: the problem worried and sobered you up: would there be enough talent of the soul, and talent of speech. A question. Mark. The answer was relatively pedestrian, but of a hundred-year vintage, from a venerable New England arboretum. Begin the quote. We never know how great we are: Responding to the call, we could have risen from the fog, and reached the distant clouds. End the quote. Develop the plot. The thought, knocking against the fetters of the invisible quotation marks, seemed even truer because it appeared familiar. The quote, which possessed the power of a prescription with the note *cito*, had something in common with the verse of the German lyricist Rilke in the interpretation of the Russian lyricist; by the way, the latter saw him on a train, when the German undertook his pilgrimage to Iasnaia. Do you remember how unforgettable it was, how much like the nineteen-hundreds and a vacation. So much that Rilke put on that morning a Tyrolean cape. A quote. We have small rows with life's balances, but what's against us seems so bold. If we gave in to the advances of the Storm seeking wide expanses, we would have grown a hundredfold. End of quote. You were even more impatient because there was a distinct possibility that what you were thinking about would come true, the future promised to happen if you just gave in, if you responded. And, of course, if you made use of the experience of predecessors, particularly the experience of self-persuasion or self-hypnosis. After all, before the experts start believing in an artist, he should believe in himself. But even this path is dangerous. Look: how many assertive, bright-eyed individuals were absolutely sure of their own conviction that they were the very tintorettos, sibeliuses, and mao duns, whose coming had been anticipated here for so long, but who were so late in coming. Naturally, this cost them titanic efforts. But the goal compensated for all the means, for all grey matter. Thus, it was even more disappointing that the majority of talents ended up somehow latent and insipid. That's why we value so much the advice of doctors-apathologists: Ask any pharmacist for the pills against apathy. And meanwhile the internist from the verses of your teacher about the unhappy love – which is a sort of apathy – recommends showers and exercise. One can also try to get better through starvation and deprivation. Or through death. Clinical or ordinary. It's miraculous, sir, a veritable resurrection. But that – later, in spare time. And now – now it is better not to ruminate but to create, to act. You were impatient. You kept waiting for spiritual transformation. Having taken the illuminated lyricist for the ideal creator, you actually considered that you would transform into him, that is, assume his position and his role, take his place, even if it were really disastrous: no need to get used to it. Only it would not be appropriate to try mimicry; there is something creepy and servile in this practice. One should not do it; it would be sufficient to simply imagine that he and you are not really the same person – oh, no, a thing like that would contradict common sense – although, by the way, to an extent – to the extent that it is possible and permitted by the rules of good taste – with some tricks and omissions – even exactly the same. Because, why not. A question. One should not be constantly worried about common sense, tremble over it, and make a fuss. Dear god, what does sense have to do with it if we are talking about such a lofty madness as art, which is the lifelong attempt of the master to convince himself that life exists; a futile but beautiful attempt. Yes, even exactly the same. Even whatever. Just to respond and give in. And if the question is put point-blank: to be the same as the lyricist or not to be – the answer will sound ingenious in its unprecedented simplicity: to be and not to be. Simultaneously. That is, being sort of similar to him and having interpreted and fallen in love with the teacher's existence, as if it were your own, to remain not someone else, but yourself. But to remain in such a way that – according to his word – something most perfect – quote – I – am – you – end the quote – would bind you both with every conceivable tie in this world. You were impatient. Then, you responded and gave in. Practising the role became easier on account of the biographical coincidences, even if they were only limited. It's not important, even if they are limited, no need to argue, talents of such calibre are not picky. Of course, there used to be spells of weakness, the bats of doubt used to fly in, but with faith in the reciprocity of the Universe, they should have been unequivocally chased away, condemned to oblivion like the night moths nicknamed Death's Head. Just to respond. And to give in. Even though up to that time you had not attended either the school of sculpture or the State Art-Technical Studios, and regardless of where and when the dacha was rented, regardless of its cost, Skriabin did not turn out to be your neighbour even once. Instead, the school of Morse code kept sending invitations, a jujitsu circle was a magnet, and the institute of rabbit breeding beckoned. And for a number of years, a retired kapellmeister who, while under the influence kept assigning to himself the title of second lieutenant of the smashing suburbs, compensated for

Skriabin as your dacha companion. And while in the composer's works the Russian attraction to being extraordinary manifested itself in the search for the overman, the kapellmeister was extraordinarily worldly-wise, astonishingly fast, sharp, and exceptionally jocular; he amused himself with marsh hunting and cold veal, and through web-footed barking you could hear in his radiant greetings: good morning, good evening, good duckling, and the day is also good; and for approaching slumber he used to wish you a good note. But you did not know notes, your ear turned out to be absolutely unmusical, and your nights kept getting transformed not into nocturnes, but into still lifes of darkness and silence, into speeches without words because you still did not have them, since the future had not come yet. And your memory, fingers, and wrists were unmusical, and if Skriabin turned out to be your neighbour after all, you would have been able to play for him neither nor. And as a result, the composer could not praise you for anything, anything at all. That is, in regard to music, as far as the mastery of the instrument is concerned. But perhaps he would have praised you for something else, like your tact or real neighbourly friendliness. For instance, he'd say: The summer is ending and in the meantime you did not cause me any problems, you did not make any sarcastic remarks; I am certainly grateful to you; you are a good dacha companion; until we meet again; have a nice season break. A hereditary humanist, he would have mentioned this for good reasons, having in mind a show of politeness and a display of attention, but such praise would sound so condescending, so much like charity. No, speaking about praise, it would have been better if the kapellmeister did it, really, it would have been more encouraging. And there really was a kapellmeister. And he really was your dacha neighbour. And that's all. And the composer did not appear in this role. In contrast, one of the neighbours in the city, a recluse not seen by anyone, was famous as a composer, who – according to unconfirmed rumours – lived a few floors above and was deaf, like Beethoven, which – again according to the rumours – did not reflect on his work: after all, he was not an ordinary composer, but extraordinary, one of those bullying maniacs, whose heads and etudes are stuffed with the murders of the most august and with the abductions of their horses and elephants, whose snouts one cannot wait to compare to gas masks. Especially in dream visions. Especially regarding the war between zoos. A typical Ceylon specimen, you caught an African flu in the wind of Europe. Your trunk became congested: you could not clean it by blowing. How sad. And standing with an open mouth in the middle of a vivarium, you are quietly dozing off. And then it begins. The whites are at the gate. And because you are black, like the swans in the pond, you need to come up with a defence. Zeitnot, zugzwang. And as a sign of your respect for the neighbour from above, you invent an Old Indian defence; after all, they say that this chess composer is not young. And it did not matter that according to slightly more precise information, he was rather a checker composer, while according to completely reliable information – an old card cheat. No problem, such things happen; most importantly, he was a composer in principle, a conjurer to the bone. And weren't you forgiving him because of his only shortcoming: an insufficient presence in your field of vision, more correctly, its chronic absence there, the objective non-being. No, after all, not because of that. Instead, you did it because you were also defective in your own way: you had nothing to take to the composer: you did not have the appropriate compositions. And as far as Skriabin was concerned, not as a man, but only as the name of a man, there was no agreement. In the sense that you did not know anyone who would bear such a name. You did not know, but you would have liked to. You tried to find. You conducted a speculative search. You hoped. The lack of Skriabin's name on your horizon indicated its presence outside. And because life, regardless of how hard you try to deny it, is nothing but theatre, that name could have been meaningful. Like in Griboedov's work. Quite possibly, the drama was taking place not farther than Mokhovaia Street and the dramatist used up all of his irony just to make the janitor of the conservatory bear the name of the composer. Complaisant, with a commanding beard and a decent compensation, he regularly cleans the ice from both the sidewalks and the road. The evening is barely there. Scraping, eh – a question mark – a contemplative figure, an unlucky volunteer among the violinists addresses the worker. Yep, scraping, agrees the janitor. And politely adds: With a scraper, sir. Well, fine, keep scraping, says the violinist, that's why you are our Skriabin. And, after opening the case, he takes out the violin. He tunes it. And now the evening is clearly there. The curtain. A complete success. After getting dressed, the viewer leaves the foyer and steps out on the fluffy Mokhovaia, filled with furs. The evening has been served. The plot finds its final development. To the sounds of Chaikovskii, the janitor with a metal number on his chest – janitor Skriabin – scrapes the sidewalk, while the luckless violinist, expelled from the institute, mutilates the Poem of Ecstasy. And even if everything is not like that, you thought, even if the name of the conservatory's janitor is not Skriabin, then now is the time, when someone called Oscar Rabin has appeared, and this sound similarity can be employed instead, even more so because Rabin also used to live in dacha areas; later, he also went to Europe; for a long time, too; and was equally involved in the arts. He was an artist and everyone used to say: Did you see his *Lianozovskie Barracks*. Question. And *A Herring on a Newspaper*. Question. How relief-like. What an eye. He created an entire movement. And in the meantime – to feed himself – Rabin also worked as a scraper or as a watchman. There were many of them all over Russia – Platonovs and Rabins – they kept watch and scraped. And they – after all they too – infused the elements of the entire dimension, the elements of the epoch. And you too. You became infused – you responded – you gave in – you dedicated yourself to Orpheus, to harmony. You started playing with abandon. And many other coincidences occurred. Because, could the playing of the beloved lyricist continue without them. Hardly. And in order not to wait for Moira's charity, you had to trouble yourself with coincidences, but, naturally, in such a way that your involvement would not be too noticeable, first of all to the internal inspection of your mind, called introspection. Otherwise you would have found all kinds of reasons to blame yourself for some insincerity, even if it was not clear in relation to whom. Even if it was not clear, since insincerity – like sincerity – does not have to apply to anyone in particular, does not have to be related to anything, it does not. Because no one can take this right away from it. Even more so because there is absolutely no one to do such a thing. Whatever the case, in order not to distress the introspection, you had to trouble yourself with the coincidences as if you had not noticed the troubles, as if you were looking at them through your fingers. To trouble yourself, but somnambulistically, accidentally, and instinctively. And at the same time – ingratiatingly, cryptically. By the way, such tactics perfectly coincided with the strategy to be but not to be. They coincided and combined. And somewhat instinctively – spontaneously – one day you set out for Marburg. And you arrived. And at the foot of the mountain, on which, covered with moss as before, were the city hall, the castle, and the university – imitating Lomonosov and your teacher, you cocked your head. You cocked it and by so doing you celebrated two anniversaries – in quotes: of two other people's neck muscles. Speaking apropos and honestly, in the lyricist's description this gesture seemed to be exaggerated. It looked as if he mixed up the steep Marburg slopes with the slopes of Zurbagan. Attention to details distinguishes wanderers. Among analogies it is sufficient to recall some hyperbole of Henry

Miller, the pornographer. For example, according to him, the strait between Poros and Galatas is so narrow and the houses on the shores stand so close to the water that the noses of the curious homeowners almost touch the yards of the passing ships. But enough about Hellas: long live Hessen. Exclamation. Thinking dreamily, ideally, in Marburg one should have found the *Kellner,* who on the eve of the reassessment of all values was a friend of all philosophers. And when in the heat of the ordeal the younger brother visited the poet, the Kellner cleverly saved the day by teaching the latter how to drink and play billiards. Nevertheless, it became clear that, after leaving for the First World War, the Kellner returned neither from the First nor from the Second. And, frankly, the brother, but in this case not of the poet, but of the Kellner, and not younger, but older, kept practising in the university tavern as before. And the more he drank, the older he looked, and because of that, towards the evening, when you dropped in to shoot the breeze using scraps of languages, this laconic Esperanto of ignoramuses, the Kellner's brother, also a Kellner, looked like Methuselah and vividly remembered anyone you wished. If Lomonosov then Lomonosov, if Luther then him too: the latter was a distinguished habitué; occasionally he kept conversing with the fiend until past midnight – you could not chase him away; only it seems that later he, that Martin, was shot somewhere beyond the seas. And the Grimms – what about them – brothers like brothers, like us, like everyone, this brother or that. The Kellner's brother also remembered the Russian lyricist, although so dimly that the time came to go home. And even though you did not go through Venice but through Vienna with its sclerotic nostalgia dressed in yellow gaiters and pink riding coats, you set out for the place where you were remembered, if not by the people, then by the streets, if not by philharmonics, then by harmonicas, if not by the horticulture, then by the horizon, and if not by the circumstances, then by spaces. The spaces, where recognition – a quote – used by the trees and fences and all things on earth, when they exist in the open air and not in the mind alone – end the quote – awaited you both. With an involuntary secrecy – secrecy of the eyewitness who sets out to astonish his fellow citizens – you returned to your shared city and lived in it almost unaccounted for – in the form of a soporific splashing life. And following in the steps of the poet, almost by chance, you became a student; you started frequenting the same auditoria of knowledge and corridors of feelings. And you started going to concert halls, museums, and also – to skating rinks. And, essentially, completely without deliberation – spontaneously – you drank the bitterness of the September sky and of tuberoses, the gluten of the slush, the bruises of dawns, and as a blue – no, better, purple – drop you hung from the pen of the Creator, and as a rush-hour passenger you hung from the handles of the means of transportation, noticing the full beauty of carriages, and cramming the schedules of trains or graphics of their movement along various branches. Including the Kamyshinskaia. And you kept your eye on the movement of the storms, admired the dethronement of winters, and kept falling in love. You loved approximately the same women – at any rate from the point of view of shortsightedness – in extreme cases with exactly the same names. And as if by chance, without thinking, you spread your coat for them on the grass. And they – in exactly the same way – without thinking – absent-mindedly, as if they were trees losing leaves in autumn – all kept losing their clothes. And you kept catching fire and going out, burning and thinking in verses. And all this happened not intentionally and not accountably, not. And it mattered little that in the messy conservatory the mossy violins scratched the hearing no more magically than the scrapers and that, burning to commune with Schubert, because of absent-mindedness you became partial to operetta and, as much as it is regrettable to say, got fascinated with another one, but, to be honest, after all, also an Austro-Hungarian, and from time to time you intoned his sparkling 'Silva, bring me some hot bliny.' And it mattered little that the sympathies of school fellows were divided not between Bergson, Shpet, and Trubetskoi, but between three eateries: the one next to Nikitskie Gates, the second across from Rumiantsev's house, and the third in the basement of the history department, usually called a Tube but resembling a morgue. And it was not worth being upset that it did not matter which of those and in what level of prostration one would enter – because the degree to which the silver of the silverware was soiled made it resemble some kind of merciless lead – dull and striking the very soul; the education continued. Take a comparable look from a window of a Zoological auditorium. Make a sketch of weather conditions. Caricature the professorial body. Depict the decameron of the dormitory on a natural scale. And it is not so important and not at all horrifying that the sailor encountered while skating – flared trousers and ribbons, *eniki-beniki*, you drank *Brüderschaft* – came out altogether not like he should have according to the master, since he exhibited no romantic traits, not even one starry feature – but just sincere baseness, cynicism, and wallowing on the bottom. But not of the sea, since he did not serve in the fleet and not even in the flotilla, but was a sailor-lifeguard, here, on the given pond; he was the fisher of the drowned, the hunter of mermaids, the guard of the standing and draining waters, and the drunkard of the mooring. But all this was in summer, and in winters – just so, nothing to do, drunk – that's all; he'd have a few – and then – skating. Finally, it did not matter that the sailor turned out to be really tiny, like the one from the just mentioned children's counting rhyme. He resembled the surrealist Yves Tanguy in the daguerreotype from the Parisian nineteen-twenties: a rebellious genius in a child's sailor shirt, the wise dwarf, however, not with a large, but rather with a terrifyingly small head. To summarize: it did not make – was not worth – was not necessary – did not matter – and was not important. Because, having responded and given in, one cannot be occasionally concerned with isolated blunders and flaws, focus on them. It simply does not make sense. Because if one needs to sustain inspiration, that is, to keep burning at full strength, one needs to do it without a moment's hesitation, without crying about details, and without trying to cheat Fortune. First of all, it will not work. Moreover, total success, a smooth roll down the hill, without corrections, is almost sickening. Not by chance did the teacher insist that success is not the goal. The goal is more a loss, sacrifice, perhaps even the fall, the crashing down into the mud. Blessed is the one who drank to the bottom the cup of his dark days and misfortunes. Drank and rejoiced. Even more so because his circumstances were shaping up altogether quite bearably. And, achieving – God only knew at what price – an extraordinary level of impressions, impulses, and dreams, and at the same time also inspiration, you gradually learned your cherished role, and having learned it you began to live it, be in it, you became, as far as you could judge, a poet. Although how great – you could not tell, exactly like you absolutely weren't able to distinguish victory from defeat. And you thought, what is it: timidity – shyness – some kind of aberration – nyctalopia of the soul. A question mark. And perhaps it is precisely that: the most precious feature of the role, without which the poet dies and gives himself to prose, and the wunderkind at once grows dumb. In other words – isn't this the illumination. A mark, resembling a hook. However, this is also unclear. But whatever this was, the way of life worthy of the student of such a teacher began and continued. In principle, it is described above. With broad strokes. It remains only to emphasize that it was distinguished by a particularly pathetic character of actions and gestures, amusements and creative plans, partings and encounters. And by the personal winged inspiration. And to close the loop of the plot, one needs to mention that the internal illumination, which brought the plot's end, came to you as a result of one of them. Continue: one of the encounters. More specifically: encounters with a circle of the diligent and inveterate. A confession is needed right away. Candidly: encounters with the circle, to which you clandestinely belonged, hiding from the eyes of the Muse and – for some reason – ashamed of your own phrases – probably because they were weak. A regrettable thing: you were a collaborator of hack writers. And time and time again – no, no, we are not talking about the candle – business meetings took place during the day – time and time again the poet's pen – to say it figuratively – was dipped into the common ink, while the neckties – into the ordinary cabbage soup. And gatherings in the name of idleness took place in the evening. Who knows whether this was not the reason that they were called soirées, you thought, when the flow of this fundamental thought was interrupted by shouting. You listened more carefully. The quarrel was about time and it resembled a battle. And then, realizing that all this already happened to you, you started participating. And you juxtaposed time to art and eternity and, particularly, to the eternal nature of art, leaving in reserve the art of eternity and other divine crafts. Having successfully developed the basic figures of speech, you rapidly became aware of the lack of quotes and in search of those you retired into the library's dusk: The lamps had -out and candles -down, explained the employee. I'm not afraid, you answered. And, having turned to your teacher, you became completely illuminated by the modesty of his lines, lines and stanzas, not recognized before. You became illuminated suddenly, spontaneously, almost without being aware that to the east of Cheju-do such a state is called *sátori*, stress on a, and the light-carriers of Flanders joke addressing the light-carrier: carrying the light, carry on. And you kept reading. And reading, you determined that you perished because the following happened: Playing the cherished role, the role of the illuminated himself, you did it wholeheartedly, wholly, with all the reflections of light. Don't blame yourself, by the way, for this jargon, free the dove, the *paloma* of your guttural speech. Coo. Exclamation. You played, as they say, with all the angles, until dawn, carrying enough light for the full *sátori*. It was bright, but, unfortunately, you played too long, got carried away, and got confused. You became illuminated up to the point that you ceased to distinguish not only victory from defeat, but also yourself from the teacher, and his fate – from yours. And you did not make a distinction between your biographies. You crossed the sacred border. And instead of being him while remaining yourself, being without being, following him, but choosing your own way – you tried to be exclusively him. You forgot about yourself, about what was yours, and an irretrievable sum of winters later you turned into someone faceless – into a purposeless nobody, not understood by anyone except cats and foxes. After all, there would have been enough to understand; after all, something really bad really happened, something in the most conclusive sense. Not only did you turn out to be muddle-headed, but you also mixed up everything mentioned before; in addition, you became forgetful. Do you remember – a mark in the form of a hook. The poetry of the most illuminated lyricist inspired you regularly, and yet your inspiration could not find an outlet, did not produce the result. It continued to wander inside you in pure form, in the form of abstractions: uncoordinated rhythms and sounds, ideas and intonations, but there was never enough time to translate them into the language of language. Because, after all, if time is not presentable, if it's feuilleton-like and insignificant, it kind of isn't there. Or is, but insignificantly small. And no impatience can help the misfortune, whether you burn or not. But it was known that another time was approaching, and, waiting for it, you scribbled feuilletons, ate cabbage soup, and saved in your head inspired preparatory sketches, planning to transpose them as soon as. But all your hopes and illuminations suddenly turned to dust. Having illuminated yourself in the semi-darkness of the library with a bright *sátori,* you saw that there is practically nothing to transpose because almost all preparatory materials evaporated from your memory and those that somehow were preserved in it were beyond exposition or transposition, since they were excessively abstract. Not by chance the bird-librarian, dozing off for many thousands of years in the cage nearby, croaked annoyingly: Very abstract preparatory materials. Because it was a prophetic bird and had a dream about your illumination. That's even better. A typical conclusion. And – again – the device of repetition: considerably disturbed and trying to explain yourself a little bit, more precisely, explicate to yourself the essence of things that happened, you fatigue your tongue with the words of sadness. You handle their cluster. You create a swarm. You say: I am useless – unsatisfactory – unexpected. You whisper: unnecessary – unsuited – unrewarded. And you add: unwanted – unclaimed – unfit. And in order to beautify this unattractive list, you stick on the French-flavoured: miserable. Speaking figuratively, as one is supposed to do in theatre – open the quotes – the murmurs ebb: onto the stage I enter – close. You needed a creative pause here. And you wished to find a pleasant oblivion and benevolence. The same way as you kept breathing at sundown into the ear of Fate, pestering her about friendship, now the viewer, the witness of the collapse, keeps breathing in your ear. He keeps breathing like a flock. Like a pack. He is callous and categorical. His wisdom belongs to a bar, the familial hearth, and constitutions, and with roughly the same energy with which the poet of ecstasy tried to arrange a meeting with a certain count – saying: Let me in, let me in, I have to see him – the viewer demands your final monologue. Then say it, vindicate yourself, find consolation in it. Say that if the emotions of your idol infuse this entire century, it does not mean that life – whatever its relationship to the arts would be – is just his, the poet's sister: no, no, the image is close, very close; she is also your sister. And it is not at all mandatory to create anything, to write; it is enough to simply live and witness how someone else writes. To live and to be his inspired admirer. To live and to know that you have an abyss in common, particularly eternity and speech. And doesn't this by itself imply a certain kind of greatness. Even if it is just a limited one. And playing the illuminated critic, haven't you grown a hundredfold to become the very one, the one you dreamed about. And didn't your soul become illuminated by his illuminations. Your. And after getting up, you exit from the library fog into the light of the corridor and the stairs. Stairs and streets. And it becomes amazingly clear that you are alone and that everything around you drowns in total Pharisaism, and that to endure life – regardless of its unprepossessing character – is not the same as to walk, as they say, across a field. And even though, having paged through the poet's books, you have considerably enlarged the number of quotations, somehow it becomes clear – that just like your cellmate who did not come back to finish his cigarette butt, likewise – although for different reason – you will not return anymore to the circle of hack writers. Likewise. Neither to their unfamiliar feasts, nor to Akakii's offices. Apparently, it becomes clear from the gestures. Likewise. After all, some kind of inevitability flickered precisely in them, didn't it. Especially in those you used to loosen your tie as you walked. Likewise – in the sense of never. Closure. A mark of illumination.

An Abstract

When I am asked why I still don't write for the theatre, I defend myself by first indicating that I would like to, but Melpomene does not smile upon me, she is cold, and then adding that I am a dramatist only to the extent to which from time to time I catch – how can I make this clearer – well, don't hide in the back, keep your spirits up, and, incidentally, I recommend that you become passionate about an active way of life, about movement, and, most importantly, that you don't make too much out of it but consider it a special kind of perfect hearing – I catch some conversations, essentially, conversing voices, and on the basis of their motifs, that is, the motifs of these conversations, I create sketches, about two or three pages long, no more, and those exclusively for myself; there's no need even to talk about any kind of staging them; they are too superficial, insubstantial, which is understandable, since their sources are exactly the same; only once did I catch a conversation that turned into a play worth anything at all; to use language in the style of billboards, it's a play for a certain number of human voices, providing testimony about the fate of someone not very stable, someone vacillating, inclined to change places and escape into freedom-loving lyric poetry; isn't he a Gypsy, one would ask; probably, in part, at least in his soul, as is perhaps every real Russian in whose ears this Sokolovian guitar keeps resounding as it did before; and lower: no, whatever you'd say, it's boring in this world without good Gypsy music, ladies and gentlemen, particularly without romances, particularly without the heartbreaking ones; and, incidentally, do you know, which of them is dear to the freedom-loving lyricist more than all the others taken together; I have no idea, name it; a romance about the sad fate of chrysanthemums, about their shrub that in the beginning bloomed and then, alas, when autumn came to the garden for good, finished blooming and wilted; if alas then alas, but what is the reason for the lyricist's special appreciation of this particular piece; the thing is that for him it is a kind of family relic, a musical reminiscence of his grandmother; it's important to mention that she was an inveterate aristocrat of the spirit: she read German philosophers, the British Encyclopedia, fenced a little, smoked, played at the races, made her acquaintance with fashionable practitioners of belles-lettres, critics, and poets, frequently dropped in with Pushkin scholars at Iasnaia, with the Futurists at the Iar, and danced, and sang, and, as far as her appearance was concerned, no need to worry, in her moment she was simply lovely, more precisely not simply, but seemingly by chance, and men used to fall in love with her instantly, but unsuccessfully, because even if she reciprocated, she always did it cursorily, barely, my young grandmother, who kissed your lips *bobeobi*, when the guitar player whom you abandoned wandered through the alleys of the city park and composed his swan song, if I am not mistaken, to sing and dedicate to you as a farewell, and involuntary tears rolled down and dripped on that wilted shrub of chrysanthemums, ach, how cruelly you slighted the troubadour no longer dear to you, but in exchange what a heartbreaking romance was composed about it, the lyricist thinks, growing up; how do you know that he is thinking precisely that; from his own earlier musings, written and oral; in short, he is proud of his grandmother, and he is proud of his other grandmother, the one who lived quietly beyond Siberian blue rivers and, waiting for her husband, made Siberian *pel'meni*, watered Siberian roses, petted her Siberian cat, and regularly went out to the rail embankment to tell fortunes: he's coming – he's coming not, he's coming – he's coming not; and of the grandfather-locomotive engineer who was that long-awaited husband and who kept coming and coming, kept driving his Trans-Siberian expresses; he is proud of him too, and of the grandfather – master armourer who tirelessly cast Tula bullets, one of which probably separated from earth the above-mentioned guitar player; pity, indeed, that everything ended so ridiculously; nevertheless, a free man is free to do whatever he wants; and a little lower: but enough about relatives, let's talk about friends; how dear to him are those with whom in his youth he rushed to live and to feel; so dear that when he thinks how exactly everything was, he becomes withdrawn, pensive; and be assured that he will not forget them ever, of course, or for any reason; and approximately the same can be said about the city where all this took place, about the village where he wrote his first real work, and about the fact that he became a prose writer; and about the river with the village on its shore, and about the plain on which this river flows: he will not forget all that; but no attachment, no friendship, not even respect for the proverbial smoke of the fatherland – not even that – is more important to him than his love of freedom, and – a pause – why did you stop; because I want you to grasp the full gravity of things that are happening; please continue, we already grasped it – and on a nasty and ugly day in his late youth he leaves his fatherland, imagine that; fine, so he left because he felt that it was time to live in a free – no-no, the term fall would not be entirely appropriate here; after all, occasionally a fall isn't aesthetically very pleasing and often ends in absolute disaster – movement; it is time, brother, it is time to live in free and eternal movement, like the great miller from the Wienerwald did, and, travelling around the world, to become a hero of space, rather than of some kind of time, strictly speaking, and if not a hero, then to become simply an eternal student of the globetrotting department, and to continue creating, continue thinking; but Lord, if possible, just don't make this student too poor because poverty deprives wanderings of their lovely charm; I am telling Thee truthfully; and he proceeded as he planned, he proceeded until during his travels his soul got weary, he started longing for his native romances and old friends; therefore, thinking about returning, he appears at the station and buys a ticket, but literally a minute before departure his thoughts begin to run wild and he is paralyzed by total indecisiveness: should he go or is it worth it; and at that moment the narrative breaks off: for some reason the voices have vanished, and since they have not appeared again, my play is not finished; but it does not matter, I calm myself, it does not matter; when Melpomene finally smiles upon me I will concoct the hero's fate, concoct and finish playing; it's the theatre of imagination; look and your vision will clear, you'll soar; I will finish playing and writing the text of the play; in contrast, I think that an abstract is actually not worth finishing; in this case incompleteness is more appropriate than completeness; therefore, hoping that I am not wrong, I dare to dedicate this in many respects autobiographical text to all those who, after reading my books, believed that your humble servant was a writer and elevated him to the rank of Pushkin Prize laureate, and to those who believed in me from the time when I had not yet published anything and had not departed anywhere; my friends, friends of Russian literature, dear ladies and gentlemen, your attention and support are extremely valuable to me; I am grateful to you.

About the Other Encounter

I can tally our encounters on the strings of a guitar, if not a ukulele. Two of them were the result of pure chance. The first – in a bookstore on Allenby. Aleksandr devoted to it one of his city rhapsodies. I am slightly uneasy evaluating this piece; after all, your humble – although at this moment distant – servant is presented there not just as a leading, but as a completely positive character, almost without faults. But I do dare to judge the remaining materials of the collection, in which the essay was included, and at the same time the larger compositions of Aleksandr. Let me share with you my admiration for these texts. I would like to declare them the best examples of this undeniably special kind of belles-lettres that, as I've been suggesting for many years, should be called *proeziia*. They reveal rare merits. For example, the ability to iron out or even reduce to nothing the contradictions between the what and the how. The ability to invalidate, when necessary, the just-mentioned what and to do this while preserving the dynamic equilibrium of the writing. The ability to arrange the narrative space in such a way that the reader won't doubt even for a second that existence is precisely what is happening here and now, on the given page. Whenever we got together, we talked, of course, about these fine points, about abilities, habits, and the writer's intuition. In short – about mastery. However, we also touched in passing upon less sophisticated matters. For instance, that evening, when chance brought us together again – the action took place in a café near Carmel – we were talking specifically about Afula, from where I had just returned. After gulping something refined, I broke into an aesthetic tirade and complained that the trip to the provinces had not worked out because the knights' castle over there was quite uninteresting and the town itself was not much to look at either. Aleksandr responded to my concerns with empathy and proposed to teach Afula a lesson, to subject it to irony, sometimes even bitter, for its lack of appeal, using as a weapon the genre of a biting epigram, preferably in the spirit of Ancient Rome. But why Ancient Rome? – I did not get the idea. It will be more meaningful, said Aleksandr, and besides, Afula rhymes very well with Catullus, particularly when he is put in the genitive or accusative case. What's true is true, but did Catullus ever honour our shores with his presence? – I asked my co-author. It doesn't matter, replied my colleague, since nobody really knows anything about Catullus; there is only speculation and for that reason historical accuracy is out of place here, even more so because we, poets or *proety*, are by definition free, like birds. Since we had the writing instruments with us, we commenced. We worked using the method of *bouts-rimés*. The resulting draft sounded pretty good. However, the necessity of polishing it left no doubts. But then, having looked at his watch, Aleksandr hurried home. We'll polish it later, he suggested, we'll meet somewhere again and polish it. And then I told him: Don't worry; if you don't mind, I'll polish it myself, and in the nearest future. But, as often happens in this vale, somehow it was not possible to bring our common piece to conclusion; somehow there was always something else to do, somehow everything went on like in Nikolai Vasil'evich. And year after year. Then I heard about the evening and realized that the promise given to Aleksandr should be fulfilled without delay. And I acted upon that realization. And it's probably not important, not important at all, that there was such a delay; it's no secret that in the end basically everything will come to pass, everything will turn out, and everything without fail will be heard and settled. But do you know what happened? In the process of polishing, our common thing turned from a general epigram into something diametrically different, into something like a eulogy. I will allow myself to call it precisely that: *A Eulogy to Afula*. I am sending this poem from Venice. It will be read to you by the gracious lady Irina Vrubel'-Golubkina, while sincerely yours Sokolov in the gondola – what do you think, one has to maintain one's reputation, one has to measure up: style is the writer himself – will go in the gondola to San Michele and recite the text to the old man Iosif. I hope that maestro approves of it. After all, he's so friendly with Catullus.

one day to see catullus
i visited afula
and found as many mules there

as wise heads in metula
as sailors in old pula
that's how many there were

since all mules in afula
look so much like catullus
to notice in their lot
his smile oft-likened to a
dull smirking à la sulla
i tried but i could not

thus i had to embrace
what happened what took place
what did occur out there
that being in afula
i didn't meet catullus
but made a poem fair

afula you afula
so loose and spirit-free
while walking with my friula
my mischievous *hatula*

on your streets this catullus
i simply could not see

i'm sitting on a stoolah
deep in despair and pain
you wicked shark afula
why such a trick you'd pull off
you made me such a fool ah
you let me hope in vain

and yet like that abdullah
i praise your mules afula
my praises i'll outline
their fuzz is mystifying
with hunchbacks no denying
they look as if they're flying
they're simply just divine

and though you are not pretty
i offer you this ditty
ah full of mules afula
afula mules so full of
afula swan-like diva
ich libe dich haviva

25 October 2006
Venice

Discourse

To Evgeniia and Viktor

1
Of the kind that, say, somehow, perhaps, this way,
which, essentially, is that way, approximately so,
for this reason or that reason,
in other words, more or less thoroughly,
even if without too much detail:
the details, as everybody knows, come by letter,
in this case in a list, in a special list
to be read during general conversation, to be recited,
and, undoubtedly, to the side,
and not too loudly, apparently *piano*,
precisely, but let's make sure it is
a full-sounding part, let's say,
this and that, this and that, this and that,
and so forth, or like the abrupt cuts in ancient papyri:
etc

2
and slightly below: and that

3
right, the list is sufficiently precise
and, i dare to add, long, with a considerable
number of notes and variations,
and, by the way, i inquire, do you care for theory,

not theory, but the very presence, the very
phenomenon of the counterpoint, understood,
pardon my hegelian leanings, as some, perhaps,
kind of given, as a fact of musical life
and activity, practice and concretism,
and by no means in the narrow sense,
not only in the vocal or, say, instrumental,
in short, do you care for the counterpoint

4
mas o menos, and you, likewise, i do
care for it, but perhaps too carelessly, and you,
i, you know, care for the counterdance, especially
in the form of a quadrille, if i am not mistaken, two-fourths,
do you mean the ballroom dance, no, why, i mean
an ordinary, everyday quadrille, the dance of the simple
but the sincere, continue, i mean a quadrille
of unattractive villages and uninviting suburbs,
where evenings without it are good for nothing, but with it
are impossibly beautiful

5
how passionately you speak,
of course, since i speak with passion,
in a manner bequeathed to us by octavio, sir,
of mexico, this singing firebird,
the glorious and fiery son, ah, mexico, *ay*,
absolutamente, señor, hablo, hablo,
i speak with rapture, i speak above all
about the quadrille of inns and taverns, infused with smoke
and dilapidated, the quadrille often not elegant
at all, but popular, dishevelled,
how properly you speak, how wondrously

6
and, remarkably, all this music,
that is, the conversation, starts and continues so
impromptu and is at the same time so *amabile*
that the number of interlocutors, the quality of their coats
or ponchos, their height, age, education,

connubial conundrums, the structure of their faces
and whose lips had said what was said,
these things don't add up to be important

7
no need to point out that for the same reasons
it's not obvious who all these interlocutors are,
but is it true, don't worry, naturally,
it's true, and if the mentioned talk suggests
some kind of a play, let it suggest a play
for a not very distinct or even for a completely indistinct
number of voices, let it,
one just needs to mention that there are probably many
rather than a few of them, not of them even but of us, since it
sounds not as alien, and, if one listens carefully,
almost affectionate:
of us

8
of us, who are leading this discourse, there are quite a few,
in other words, the discourse is multi-voiced,
and as to the topic, it's no secret that the latter
is surprisingly boundless, and as a whole it's to such an extent
open that, as frequently happens, one
of the voices begins a phrase,
the second continues, and the third or the seventeenth
or whichever number you want
finishes it

9
and if the question is posed: great,
but is everything in order with our speech,
i'm afraid it may be vague, one should answer by saying:
don't be afraid, just believe, our speeches
are obvious and melodious, intelligible
and penetrating, and that's what
we wish for the other voices

10
but if: perhaps it's exactly the way
you just announced, but please consider:

the action of the piece is not developing, it doesn't even have
a starting point, by neglecting the storyline, you openly
short-change the plot, then: esteemed gentlemen,
we are creating here a genuine human document
and you're bringing up some
literary tinsel, don't interfere

11
and slightly below: and do you remember,
do you recall, the list of details mentioned
above, allow me to note that this list itself
is somewhat detailed, i don't disagree,
it's put together with rare accuracy,
interrupting: pardon me for the interruption,
but i'd like to remind you of something at once,
of what, of the fact that the list of this kind
is sometimes called an inventory or a register,
it's called exactly that: a register or an inventory,
an inventory or a register, and some also say:
a balance sheet, a balancing sheet

12
pardon my petty curiosity, but why
do you have to remind me at once and not later,
because later begin various delays
and quagmires, they begin
and continue, distressing and tormenting us greatly,
as if they were not quagmires but wires
of heart-breaking strings

13
strings of some kind, of some instrument from the plucking
pack, let's suppose, of a guitar, if not a cither
or a sitar, let's suppose, but only on the
condition it's a nocturnal and sleepless guitar,
sleepless and merciless, crying to honour
evita and angelita, pepita and rio-rita,
and to salute the friend of their dark-skinned,
sweet-lipped, and teeth-baring youth,
federico garcía, *ay*, of an implacable guitar
crying à la sarasate

14
the condition accepted, *ay*

15
but most unpleasant is the fact that one day
all these 'i'm-too-busy' of yours turn into a total
never because out of nowhere comes someone
to get you and, lo, you are already a figure of uncertain
days and foggy memories, therefore it shouldn't be later,
it has to be at once

16
however, we wandered away from one
essential thing, did you notice
that not only the list of details is fashioned in a very
detailed way, but also the list of peculiarities,
and that, in essence, all the other lists look
wonderful, we did notice, you're right,
inventories to be delivered by recitation
are fashioned superbly, simply *poli oreo*,
which means, approximately: very lovely,
and to express it another way but also
kind of in hellenic:
the lists are filled precisely, as in a pharmacy,
as in thessaly

17
but why are we talking about the hellenic,
after all, it sailed long ago beyond our eyeshot
into the land of no return, poor giorgos, if you will,
and approximately in the same days, his days,
but somewhere at a little distance,
the chaldean and the aramaic used to buzz,
the sumerian and the phoenician used to hum,
and a distinct sensation was born
that these tongues, native to so many
throats and mouths, will never be silent:
no, they became silent just like that

18
intimately: perhaps this is so, but if
we look at the case not from the vantage point of now,
which, when checked, turns out to be at times
the vantage point of blindness,
and not the blindness of a bat at all,
but if we look from the vantage point of eternity,
it seems clear that everything, even that, which went
to rack and ruin and during seven simooms
was scattered by seven samurais,
all this will inevitably get better, will be put together
will be mended again, will return to its merry-go-round,
therefore it's not important what's going on right now,
or yesterday, or tomorrow, but only
what is constant, what is for keeps:
that's important

19
for this reason, even though your hellenic did vanish,
don't forget it, use it regularly to reason
and to narrate, and once tired of hellenic,
switch to latin, you said: latin,
i don't know whether recollections of a distant past
will turn out to be pertinent here,
however, because of the above-mentioned word,
they simply could not help but to surge forth:
latin, how lovely it is, particularly
in its laconic nature

20
but let's do it in order: at first everything is like everyone else's,
nothing remarkable, and only afterwards
it so happens that because
you discover an inclination for it,
consequently, something scholarly
that was erected on cicero street at the corner of tibullus
has a latin leaning, and it turns out that
the time for your mission, the time for admission has come,
go, don't miss it

21

and after arriving, ask in the bureau for a sheet of papyrus
and scribble: in connection with the road
through the thorns straight to the stars, i am at your complete
disposal, do with me whatever you graciously see fit,
furthermore: let the glory of jupiter never fade

22

and while the reply of the directors was making
the desired impression, here and there already resounded:
and autumn, we sense autumn,
but autumn is, in essence, so much a separate song,
there's nothing to subtract or add, or give or take,
and what a suchness, such that it seems
that even the lunar rabbit scrambles to get to his tao,
not to mention that only a rare akakii
will not be transfixed, looking at it

23

it's typical: autumn happens, show that you care,
bare your psyche, don't look away,
comport, try to draw close,
bring her to your lips, make her head spin,
sing in unison, flow together, be liberated
but elegant, smiling but elegiac,
use the solutions of belles-lettres
and against sweat, sweets and rhetorical devices,
including partial and complete silences,
understatements and inconsistencies,
and, of course, repetitions, dear colleague, repetitions,
and in free time, in the pre-dawn solitude,
with dominoes or blocks of the old man palamedes
in young lips, keep improving your articulation, diction,
because, sorry to say, you're lisping

24

the device of repetition: and autumn, and autumn this, autumn that,
and autumn is all around, writing is on the wall, sadness
is in my soul, and gaius, that is, julius, perpetually has to deal

with some miserable thursday or detestable tuesday,
and someone who constantly looks at us like a *lupus*,
this *homo* our mentor *est*,
but at least the windows of our classroom look out at the coliseum,
and if saturday comes after all, we hear
the clinking of armour, roar of animals, screams of the public,
and, thinking of mucius, we add wings to our minds:
let them soar

25
but gradually and at the same time almost suddenly,
it becomes clear that everything in the world already was, happened,
and, after checking, it turns out that everything, alas,
is fuss and languor, as if caused by the strumming of these strings,
o tempora, o, and yet, despite the misfortunes,
latin continues, is studied,
and using the words of the latter about the discourse,
about the way it should be constructed while speaking,
we'll say the following: accurately, correctly

26
and what is remarkable: that this current
discourse of ours reminds us of something quite clearly,
and does it very vividly, *vivace*, at least
from time to time, particularly its list of details,
their register, you remember how it went: let's say,
this and that, this and that, this and that,
and slightly below: and that

27
it's quite straightforward, you'll agree,
and at the same time so elegant that this list,
we have to admit it, completely enchanted us too,
besides, how comforting is the thought that there still exists
somewhere someone who sincerely likes and knows
the business of counting, someone who realizes
that an inventory of any number of things, whether
objects, phenomena, or living creatures,
is possible only by counting them exactly,

after all, that's why somewhere it says:
counting is counting,
inventory taking is inventory taking

28
thus, most likely in the textbook on inventory taking and counting,
it says so in directions how to do them, in the manual, and,
apparently, also in the same place, this: verily, verily i say
unto you: count good and proper, as is required,
be business-like and collected, don't get distracted, keep your
    spirits up
and don't dilly-dally, understand and remember: counting
is the mother of inventory, a sister of a tally clerk, a plus of a cashier,
and a plus of an accountant and a bookkeeper, in sum:
of that arithmetician in the plural

29
of that arithmetician in the plural,
whom one should laud in non-euclidian terms,
except not here, but in some other conversation,
while here let's return to the topic of listing,
of the register reminding us of something so vividly,
perhaps almost instantly,
reminding us about the train schedule
of the southern-scythian railroad,
quickly, basically in the blink of an eye

30
more likely, not about the schedule, but the sketch
of a trip on such a railroad, we read about
in the works of a southern versifier of this noteworthy
century who quite recently, would you believe,
carried by the wind of history, flew,
as the saying goes, away, without a thought,
like some kind of a leaf

31
most likely, a leaf from a tree, dry,
of *demi-saison* lyrics, yes, most likely,

even though the variants are possible: flew like a leaf,
let's say, of an almanac, a tear-off calendar,
flew away like a leaf that carried out its duty,
or like an executive writ, a subscription list, a medical certificate,
flew away like a discarded accounting page
into the infinite distance, and, finally, flew away
like a register, like a list

32
and better yet: it did not fly away, what then, well, it flickered,
seemingly in distances travelled by the railroad, but really
    behind
the unwashed, dull and obviously dim windows
of the antediluvian railroad cars, but our heart,
could our heart ever not cherish them just a little,
enough is enough, try not to doubt it
because it cherishes them adequately, very much,
maybe even too much, cherishes them tortuously,
and so, it flickered beyond the windows very *vivace*,
lively: tá-ta-ta tí-ta-ta, tí-ta-ta tá-ta-ta,
the poet paints vividly, and the landscape

33
and the landscape is flawless

34
and approximately in the same spirit regarding the register,
since about the list of reasons and things
there are, let's say, no complaints, but as far as this
conversation is concerned, it wouldn't be good
to forget that it's not the main discourse itself,
it's only a brief outline of its design,
the main discourse follows and, of course,
will be much more specific, more detailed,
and to get to it is our explicit duty,
and we will get to it, we will get to it,
the last thing we need to understand is
how, properly speaking, to think during the discourse,
that is, in what style, in what key

35
clearing our throat: the selection is sufficiently narrow,
but the choice is, as it often happens, not easy,
since all variants are good in their own way, worthy,
first of all in surges, in what surges,
one can think in surges, in the style of the wind,
not the wind of history, but a simple, ordinary wind,
made of air,
that's first of all

36
it can also be done in the style of a river, that is, with a flow
and at the same time with a few, how to put it, twists and turns
because a river obviously has its twists,
and, finally, scrupulously and accurately, one can think
the way the reeds think

37
in your place, we would have chosen the style of the reeds,
preferably european, and we would never,
as they say, apologize for it, do you, by the way,
imagine how shivery and quivery they are,
thinking on the shores of, let's say, bodensee,
not very distinctly, after all we did not have a chance to
visit the mentioned *see*, and you, we neither,
but then we visited and we discovered
that everything is like that, everything matches:
on the particular *see* the reeds are really shivery and quivery,
and if we judge by their discourse,
they think not just scrupulously,
but scrupulously indeed and at the same time
intoxicatingly slowly because they have
nowhere to hurry at all,
because where should they

38
what probably happened was that the reeds
figured out the most important thing: they understood
that something supposed to happen later,

already happened and ended with creation,
and if we get an impression that
something is still happening, is being created,
it is precisely just an impression,
it's no more than that

39
because all this was once in the future, but
after a while it went by, departed, turned into the past
and exists only in the form of errors or illusions,
and as for the present, since it
slips away without a pang of conscience, hence,
nothing has the strength to exist in it

40
and i understood that since it ended with creation,
it is in its own way perfect and that living creatures
appearing briefly in its milieu, creatures of the bird kind,
and of the insect kind, which, in general,
flutter and flicker all the time,
they are also perfect and because of that too
they are quivery and shivery, shaky and fragile,
and equally lonely

41
pardon my openness but, really,
we are very, very happy that you are not one of those
linnaeuses who, for insects and birds,
just because they have wings,
the latter always and the first often,
finds a common denominator,
finds a single register, woe is us,
there are not a few such mathematicians
particularly among the office workers
ach, how superficial they still are,
how inflexible

42
no, no, you are different, you are awfully sensitive,
we profess our true closeness to you

and you should know: we are not indifferent to the fate of nature too,
and if we go back to the shores, to the reeds,
it will be natural to ask:
what are they thinking about,
would you believe, about everything in the world, it's nice to hear
and what about the discourse, which so far exists
only as a design, it would be interesting to know
whether any progress has been made in this case,
and speaking more concretely,
when and how you hope to present to us
the main discourse

43
we hope to present it without haste,
but in a reasonable time, more precisely, as soon as,
right away, whenever the need for it begins to flicker,
and not afterwards, not waiting for later,
because later, as we noted before,
delays happen constantly, we're tied up by
routine and the prose of life, short-lived events occur,
in brief, there seems to be no time for anything, and when
the discourse is finally presented,
it turns out that now it is worthless
because what is fashionable now is not mindfulness,
considered by the funny know-it-alls like us
the foundation of all truths,
but true mindlessness

44
and precisely these kinds of discourses, not needed
by anyone, will attract attention somewhere:
if you please, here are the discourses not needed
by anyone because they are superfluous, and more:
like some belated *calendulae*
are these discourses

45
but somewhere, not there at all, and from other lips,
and seemingly about something else, but essentially about this exactly,
and in connection with the same: honestly, honestly i tell you:

implacable are the cithers crying in the reeds
of titicaca

46
and the question: wait a moment,
where did you see a connection here,
is answered: because it's not true
that there exist events and things,
phenomena and living creatures not connected
with all the other phenomena and living creatures,
it's not the truth but a lie,
since everything in the world is connected:
whatever you take, is connected

47
and so, therefore, approximately in such
a way, since we're dealing with it,
let me only note that it's connected
so mutually, so masterfully, that it takes
one's breath away, there's not enough air, light, and warmth,
even though this most often does not concern us,
well, you know that better,
and this you should too,
you should

48
and since we're talking about it, in one of the countless
lists of upsetting misprints,
perhaps in the one that from morning to evening
resembles a small brochure,
but in the dusk, as in the cruel dreams
of the barely literate cyclops, turns into a huge
encyclopedia of all possible errors,
with nothing left out, including slips of the tongue, changes of mind,
blunders of memory and imagination,
where they should be discussed in detail

49
although you thought: implacable cithers,
you should consider: non-flammable giraffes,

although you pondered: crying, you should think: blazing,
although you heard: in the reeds of titicaca, you should not believe
and as far as all such nonsense is concerned,
really, don't be sad,
because, actually, there is absolutely
no need to be sad, do you hear,
you better quickly wake up and start laughing,
rise and exclaim:
i don't believe it, fiddlesticks:
in the papyri of limpopo

50
of this kind.

Gazebo

1
So what precisely,
because, perhaps, they did inquire,
that is, asked about, having met somewhere,
what specifically,
probably excitedly, someone unforgettable was saying about finesse,
maybe not changing expression much, but definitely excitedly,
what exactly

2
the man, obviously, was charged with emotions:
apparently, he valued finesse very much,
it seems he admired it, went to the appropriate museums, lectures,
who knows, perchance was a collector,
now and then divined in it the presence of something magical,
some kind of so-called hidden springs, secret strings,
quietly enjoyed its successes,
wished it the greatest good,
chiaro:
none other, but a certain *italos*

3
a child of rubicon,
slightly raspy, but quite delightful street falsetto,
delightful,
or, speaking as in a gondola, simply *celeste*,
in his youth,

wandering from *vagants* to *sänger*, he crossed the rhine
and with the watch,
first with the third, then with the fourth,
the watch of these currents and bends,
heart-enchanting armoured knights, with eyes like anjou *gris*,
he kissed it, mischievous, at a round-the-clock hole-in-the-wall,
gibber-jabbered, staged live tableaux,
sang vocalises and arias,
and at dawn,
gazing at his surroundings,
sensed germany as harmony
and settled on the elbe,
and became harmony's *doctor honoris causa*, ignited the balls, and
  hired a major-domo,
but having no luck in a particular sphere,
he often thought in a minor key
and his ad announced:

4
a certain *italos*,
smiley, middle-aged, bachelor,
will establish a lofty relationship with a *frau* of good repute,
preferably zoftig,
though he's concerned he has little experience in such
because for years he has endlessly made music:
on the clavichord,
on strings,
served as a conductor,
published several volumes of refined compositions:
ask in the music store next to the conservatory,
there's a sale on right now,
and there leave a letter for maestro scandello

5
and epistles and *rendez-vous* followed,
and one lofty relationship led to another,
but here,
the talk turns to the fact that no longer than once upon a time he was
  approached and asked:
colleague,

where is it most correct to create graceful compositions and, in
    general, finesse,
and he replied:
finesse, you should know, must be virtuosic,
and it's most correct to create it in arboretums,
moreover, in pre-dawn ones,
at any rate, for me,
and, by the way, to touch upon its aspects too,
both mentally and verbally

6
and he said:
complete darkness there makes you anxious and almost gives you
    goosebumps,
particularly in those whimsical kiosks called in some countries
    gazebos,
particularly if one touches upon and creates not solos but more or less
    for voices,
give it a try,
only don't forget to show them respect,
otherwise they'll get upset and become silent

7
and they wondered:
but what's so correct about it, pardon us, if there's so much anxiety,
and he answered them, the envious and fearful:
the more anxiety – the more virtuosity

8
in other words, if this is so,
why not exit, like in one of his *canzoni*,
wondrous *canzoni alla napolitana*,
singing it silently on the way,
la-la-la-la, let's say,
why not step out, *donnerwetter, in den geliebten garten*

9
and though not right away, not right now,
not before putting something on, buttoning something up,
clicking for some reason with a clasp or a stick-pin,

which, somehow, always lay and will forever lie on the
  same lowboy,
but at the very end, in the proverbial final analysis,
to step out after all, right,
and let the doubts die down,
the one walking down the alley of anxiety towards enlightenment
  salutes you,
outer gloom

10
and walking, walk,
and at the very threshold of the gazebo give your name, explain the
  purpose of your appearance:
say, i dropped in to touch upon some aspects of finesse and, in
  general, to converse,
and why here,
because nowhere else, wherever you'd cast,
in this case your mind's eyes, wherever you'd toss them,
only here it's *so* appropriate to touch upon such things,
since you don't even know *how* appropriate it is to touch upon them
  here,
and having entered, to be there and also:
to converse and touch upon

11
however, not loudly,
unquestionably, one should not make noise, don't you agree,
naturally, sir,
in this genre people communicate in a quiet babble, in a murmur,
and more:
don't censure the boldness of the plot trick,
after all, i appeared here not only as, and even not as much as, a
  troubadour,
but as a messenger,
i appeared to inform you that in the expanses of the beloved
  oikoumene flows the speech
in which your and our theatre,
that is, this shack, this kiosk
perfectly rhymes with the striped hoofed creature of the
  tropical lands

12
indifferently:
what-what, hoofed,
passionately:
you didn't misunderstand, sir, hoofed,
even if, perhaps, not cloven, even if,
instead, as a certain professor would exclaim, what harmony, listen
    carefully:
zebra – gazebo,
gazebo – zebra,
what's true is true, first class harmony,
as in the best homes of the acropolis in the time of citizen pericles,
and to the side:
murmuring metaphorically, not just harmony but a whole
    harmonium,
the chorus, giggling sardonically and also to the side:
if not a full philharmonic,
or a complete phillumeny,
or felinology *à tout prix*

13
by the way, you know what,
and if you don't – then know:
that this consonance, exactly as that dialect and all the public that
    converses in it,
and the space, where that public lives,
are, apparently, not important here,
'cause essentially all of them aren't present in the real thing, they
    don't play any role in it,
well, if this is so, that's, frankly, even better,
let's compare them in this connection to the four virtual ephemerides,
that flickered in the troubadour's mind just to mark their non-
    participation in our drama,
let's, why not, no problem,
and, having compared,
let's follow them with our eyes and forget them,
forget them and notice right away
how it starred up, isn't it so,
don't worry, more precisely, it's not your concern,
it starred up just the way it did

14
you forget yourself,
we are here to engage in a comparative contemplation,
it is a serious colloquium,
you were invited to play the role of a specialist in questions of the heavens,
but instead of fitting in, you're distant and impolite,
we request that you share your opinion,
yes, objectively, it starred up,
but how
does this phenomenon appear subjectively,
personally to you

15
it appears simply hard to believe,
you sound vague, provide more details, particulars,
i'll be delighted:
above our garden it starred up holy moly, like that time,
when you needed neither a pension nor a *pince-nez*,
and the haughties of your staircases and streets wore such platforms, such hoodies, such jackets
and in their pockets – letters from captivity, and *aqua vitae*,
and smokes, and knives,
and on the nicest nights,
recoiling in the risky *pas* of inconsolable *fado*,
they whispered that it starred up to a 't'

16
babbling more briefly,
above the garden,
above this all-common garden, where our conversation is going on,
above the arboretum of our voices,
there, i dare say, it starred up exactly so:
as in those whispers

17
and after a pause,
which in its elegance resembles a caesura in the music of a virtuoso:
don't you wish, in this connection, to have a talk about finesse,

finesse in this glorious sense,
in which it inflamed the valiant buttadeus

18
wandering thinker, rebel, chimney sweep,
he trumpeted about it from roofs and troubadoured
 from cornices,
he knocked inspired at any door
and, finally, the biographer notes, knocked himself out:
so be on your radiant, milky way, enchanting roamer,
cut down by authorities for lunacy and ravings on art

19
let's begin from the latter, if nobody objects,
i am hoping you are participating,
with pleasure,
but what art are you essentially concerned with,
so concerned you offered to talk about it so suddenly
that you didn't even have time to introduce yourself,
which, of course, reveals your highly impulsive nature,
but also forces one to wish you a bit more polished manners,
i'm respectfully sorry, i'll say my name right away,
say it, and i'll say mine

20
they say their names, introduce themselves,
a sound is heard which makes one think they popped it,
to your health,
ditto,
after the first, they get drunk at once and continue drinking:
to our encounter,
to blossoms of carnations and assignations,
to politeness betwixt people,
to the welfare of their majesties,
and more broadly: to all things wonderful and refined,
including art,
in which, again, everything, as in chekhov's proper man,
should be powdered and pleasant

21
and for you personally,
what do you mean, for me,
is it personally pleasing
what exactly,
getting acquainted,
you surprise me, what a strange attitude,
it's not simply pleasing for me,
it's simply delightful to meet you,
the feeling's mutual,
now you see how well we match,
perhaps quite soon we'll become good friends,
and for that reason all the more i wouldn't want you
to think that the deficiency of your manners bothered me at all
and that i agreed to converse only out of politeness,
just not to offend you by my refusal,
no, no, i haven't developed any ifs about you,
and i agreed to converse without any hidden or second thoughts,
exclusively because of my love for the subject,
id est – for the art mentioned above

22
blows his nose

23
and if i was able to convince you,
we only have to set the program right,
just straighten the vector, the course of the discourse,
that is, let's finally disengage,
more precisely, engage in something definitive,
and even more precisely, define
about what kind of art exactly we'll be conversing here,
what kind specifically

24
let's think about it purely logically, à la lobachevskii:
since it starred up, it's clear:
out of all arts it's best to touch upon the art of accounting,
i'll be honoured, count me in,

but touching upon the art of accounting, one must ponder the question
of the art of simple listing,
speak more clearly, you're mumbling

25
i'm saying that a successful accounting of things or living beings
is impossible without a careful listing of such,
and those who want to do it appropriately,
insert their names into a register or a list,
and, doing so, intentionally or accidentally list them:
say, first this, then that

26
and that accountant who creates the list on quality paper,
sets the margins, follows the spacing,
numbers the columns and inserts in them most carefully information about the accounting items,
acts properly, as is required

27
and, wishing to encourage him, you say when you have a chance:
i value your lists,
reread them often,
and think that they follow all the norms of accounting practice,
you are extraordinarily scrupulous,
please accept my thanks

28
and, proud, but modest, he'd remark:
we're trying, we have to, otherwise – kaput,
after all, for some reason it's written somewhere: when accounting, account

29
and it's reasonable to think
that it's probably written in the same place where it is written: when listing, list

because listing is the mother of accounting,
plus the sister of all the workers of high arithmetic in the world

30
so, if you're not busy, here's a tale about one of them,
who, in modest suspenders and as if nothing were wrong,
as if he didn't feel that in a short while our comfortable now would
    ebb away, would pass,
and another now, foul and unfamiliar, and without special joys,
    would arrive,
he bravely serves at the desk of various benefits,
bravely, but quietly,
he serves, but isn't servile,
and doesn't make too much of himself or of his courage,
only occasionally he remembers and smiles in his heart:
i am an arithmetician

31
in the words of the quarterly report, he's devoted to the company:
he's usually there before it's light and at the same time – a specialist of
    flexible profile,
he de jure works as an arithmetician,
but de facto is more active as an inspector, cashier, paymaster,
or, finally, a bookkeeper,
stays 'til late, leaves the section last, and, leaving,
unfailingly turns off the lights:
here and there,
there and everywhere

32
only the lamp of outside illumination is left on,
and this lamp, firmly fixed to the façade,
is sometimes called a control lamp,
this lamp, as a certain spectator would say,
extracts the entrance door from the darkness

33
an accidental spectator, a passer-by,
moreover, definitely not from here,
a visitor from the realm of true tenderness, from the shores of oyashio,

perhaps the same who earlier was the best gaffer in the theatre *noh*,
but somehow,
admiring the cinder of a chinese match,
experienced himself *dunwu*,
fell into *wu wei*,
and found a job as an ordinary spectator from a window in a *go* club

34
and he would say:
it extracts as it should, not sparing the candelas,
from the darkness, he would say,
from the complete outer gloom,
which we're never able to measure or comprehend,
he'd say this to someone also random,
encountered or passing by,
if he didn't know that the uttered can't compare with the hidden,
with the unspoken

35
therefore take into account,
that this control lamp,
extracts the entrance door with the schedule of payments,
which, in turn, reveals that on second wednesdays and fourth fridays
benefits are disbursed to just widows,
and you, obviously, understand why they are called so,
we understand:
they are called so because their husbands didn't return from just wars,
having died on their battlefields the death of the fragile

36
unfortunately, the benefits are rather small,
and sometimes, acknowledging their receipt,
one of these women suddenly gets upset and tells the arithmetician
    playing the cashier
that she would like to ask,
is there really no possibility to increase her benefits

37
then the cashier:
ask the inspector,

and the inspector:
go to the bookkeeper,
and the bookkeeper:
inquire with the paymaster,
and he:
woman, talk to the arithmetician

38
and the arithmetician,
in his past a sea gypsy and, in general, a wee bit of a romantic,
gives her a talk that just wars happen too often,
the number of just widows keeps growing,
and there is no possibility whatsoever to increase the benefits
    of them all,
and to increase the benefits of only one or a few just widows
would be unjust to all the others

39
but at the same time he
personally thinks one should not despair at all,
should not despair, but do exactly the opposite:
should hope, *esperar*:
he crammed esperanto in bouzouki bars of piraeus,
in *trattorias* of taormina and rimini,
in *tangerias* of la plata

40
and advises:
on days of your distress do not abandon hope,
nourish it, cherish,
and like a swallow that builds its abode out of clay,
exactly like that,
steadily,
build your dream that with time the times will change, look better,
they'll be hard to recognize,
and because the number of just wars, and hence, also widows, will
    diminish,
consequently, there will be fewer concerns,
the treasury will catch the next wind,

and on account of the saved resources,
all benefits will be increased forever

41
and the woman does not abandon hope,
she nourishes, cherishes it, she preserves it and builds her dream,
and, asked about her health,
she replies she feels much better than, perhaps, it seems,
more precisely,
as if she were not a widow at all,
not a widow, but almost like a bird,
even if, you know, not very nimble,
with an awkward walk, with an incoherent fate,
it doesn't matter, don't be woeful, since a bird after all, a bird,
an unexplainable bird

42
but hark,
somewhere between the second wednesday and the fourth friday,
    another now begins:
the space that meditated in the style of barocco,
switches to sirocco:
everything becomes washed out, unclear, and seemingly optional,
and when approximately the same widow visits roughly the same
    desk,
relatively the same arithmetician informs her that since the day,
when she came there the last time,
the times have changed,
do sit down

43
they changed, but for some reason not for the better at all,
and those wars,
which earlier were considered completely just,
now are considered just, but not completely,
and the widows,
whose unlucky husbands did not return from these wars,
they, unfortunately, also,
for that reason their benefits were not increased, but decreased,

and from now on she should neither nourish nor cherish
the hope that they will be increased some day,
but should abandon it, say farewell, leave it alone
and should live without it any way she can

44
and the woman abandons hope,
says farewell to it forever,
and does not build a dream of anything,
and asked about her health,
she complains that she's not well and somehow cannot recognize
    herself in a mirror,
apparently something is wrong with her face,
and in general, admittedly, she's not the same

45
and when she's told:
for pity's sake, haven't you been the same, identical, just yestreen,
what caused such decadence,
such a lack of faith, if you will, in the way and the image,
you should come to our club, to our chats about the
    benefits of *tao*,
really, why wouldn't you,
we contract with mentors from beneath the heavens:
mainly hermits, geezers, but they would probably make
    you stronger,
decide, you'll be issued a seasonal membership,
and the woman:
don't make me laugh, what do i need their heavens for,
if i'm no longer a bird

46
then who are you,
and she says: o-la-la,
who'd believe you're so well preserved you're still near-sighted, not
    far-sighted,
and where are your celebrated oculars, that is *pince-nez, monsieur,
mille pardons* for the jab, but clamp it on and you shall see,
don't be shy, even now you probably look good in it,

when you wore it before, you reminded me of an acquaintance from
    the realm of first joys,
of the early, unforgettable encounters,
but perhaps this is not interesting at all,
no, no, why not,
don't pretend, my distress doesn't move you at all,
as before, you are concerned only with your own

47
nevertheless, imagine: a zoologist,
a beacon of the national live autopsy,
vivisector, as they say, by god's grace,
a trustee of various menageries and *kunstkammern, privatdozent,*
became famous for his open experiments on bonobos,
little imps, really, mischief makers, but then how *charmant,*
basically just monkeys, but how much more distinguished,
and, actually, he himself was an *imposant,* debonair, a sight to behold,
and what a sharp wit,
and what a dancer,
and how smoothly he harmonized on the *triangolo,*
and on various other instruments

48
but why are you silent,
why don't you ask how we became us,
is it really not interesting,
or perhaps you simply pretend indifference,
you want me to become even more despondent and inadvertently
    entrust to you all my secrets,
including the most immodest,
what a pretender you are

49
we got acquainted sort of by accident, while kissing,
to say it more properly, on the occasion of kissing in the church,
after the easter all-night vigil,
we kissed, got confused, like kids, should we laugh or cry,
and for some reason we went to a *pied-à-terre* right away,

right away, in a blink,
to tell the truth, in the carriage we were still timid, we held back,
but as soon as we arrived,
i wasn't even able to think,
and would you believe:
simply until the daybreak, until the byrdes,
we became, as you see, good pals,
we were friends, drove, as a loving couple, to various salons, to the
    ballet,
we frequented séances, trotting races, dog shows,
and everywhere he was recognized, praised,
everywhere he was applauded,
the studentry kept exclaiming: *vivat privat*,
ladies made sheep's eyes at him, offered pearls and curls, wired
    billets-doux,
oh no, i was not nervous at all,
why should i,
they didn't deserve much respect, scumbags,
and there were no reasons, after all

50
and on the eve of the trinity
some of them come and say that he is not very faithful to me,
he enjoys, they say, delights somewhere on the side,
and i tell them:
don't say such filth, we are always together until the byrdes,
and they:
we don't say until the byrdes, we say from the byrdes until the late
    frühstück,
if not to the gaol's cannon, which cuckoos you know what

51
and i:
in our *pied-à-terre*,
and they:
no, dearie, are such gals permitted to enter such lodges,
they're his bonobabes, no matter how you spin it,
therefore, in vivaria, miss, their shenanigans go on in vivaria,
so they say, and meanwhile make faces and ape around

52
and later, already on the stairs,
they looked back, and as if to comfort me:
don't be too upset, thank god he's not experimenting with gorillas:
after all, they're so shaggy, so clumpy,
one can't pick all the fleas,
can't comb them all out,
bonobabes seem much cleaner, much finer,
noble ladies, you could say

53
and i wrote to him:
farewell, don't look for me, how could you,
but when they stuck him in the house of grief and the city paper
    called him *privat*-primate,
i wore myself out, exhausted myself in prayers,
and right in those days
some zeppelins came out of the blue,
bombs went boom-tara-doom,
as it turned out, the war began,
many warriors appeared:
they kept walking and having fun,
and one officer came by and instantly became my zoologist:
mobilization, you know, an edict here, an order there,
as you see, they conscript even the most handicapped,
perhaps you're unaware,
but out of our half-insane folk who do know some do-re-mi,
the fresh musical battalions are formed,
and justly so: the old ones are extremely tattered

54
as for me, i got shaved into a tambour class,
i tamboured about the camp, but soon snared a promotion, imagine:
i became a bassoon-à-piston of the guard,
attached to the imperial wind harmonists' staff,
here, look, what decorative galloons, aren't they pretty,
however, don't take it wrong,
the hour had struck, more or less:
we're all dispatched to the front, to the orchestral pit of the trenches,
thinking of it, to the ensemble of funeral songs and pandemonium

55
and experiments,
who will continue your most precious experiments,
there will be no more experiments, bonobos got evacuated homeward,
it's marvellous, tropical over there,
while in our place, in our here, chilled to the bone,
everything is so shamelessly crumpled, faded,
and to such an extent inhospitable,
and hopes are simply spectres,
and since i am in all respects truly alone,
i would consider it a great kindness if you could wait for me at least a little

56
and then it started blowing, storming like crazy,
the snow literally glued my eyelashes together,
we were definitely supposed to hurry and without delay
take shelter in a relatively warm building:
we are running,
we run into some church,
we light two candles,
read from the book of hours,
we are quickly married
and, dispatched to his post post-haste,
my spouse promised me that he will never get lost, perish,
that he'll return with the rank of tambour major

57
but they only returned to me his *pince-nez* in a special package stamped 'fragile,'
and despite this it broke into pieces:
they shook it up in their reckless carriages, thrice-damned automedons,
so clamp it on, clamp it, that is, yours,
create a little déjà vu for me, please be so kind,
i will be endlessly grateful to you,
what,
you still can't find it,
you don't have it,
you dropped it during guard duty,

don't tell me tall tales,
you left it, in a rush, at some *demimondaine*,
didn't you

58
in that case come closer,
in that case look me straight in them,
in those once dearest to you,
in those,
as you endlessly assured,
mesmerizing emeralds,
they did not fade at all, right,
only now they have a completely different construction, examine,
they seem to be glued together from sections of *pamplemousse*
    or *citron*,
zoologists call such eyes compound,
so what kind of bird am i,
when i'm the most genuine green-eyed fly, not needed by anyone in
    the world,
and she leaves right away,
she leaves quite instantly,
period

59
how lucid and true all this is, my captain,
especially as far as the instant is concerned,
because many a thing passes exactly like this,
in one veritable *momentum*, i would say, in one stroke:
it either leaves right away,
or vanishes right away,
it begins to be absent and actually continues to be:
this or that, subject, object,
some circumstance, feature, a slice of continuum,
a limb chopped off at full gallop, a piece, if you will, of fate,
let's say, the entire youth

60
there's no problem, when it's abstract, concerns somebody else,
so-and-so good for nothing,
who, perhaps, even had a high rank,

but, most likely, served casually, fought without inspiration,
did not receive wounds or decorations, shirked duels,
and, in this variant, one may involuntarily ask,
involuntarily, but softly, as if in passing:
is something like that proper,
is something like that appropriate for a commissioned officer,
claro que no, que nunca,
so now let him drool for this on his frilly bibbie,
to pity him or feel sympathy for him makes no sense
and no sense will be in stock soon:
he let himself go – serves him right

61
well, and if precisely not somebody's, but *vice versa*,
if it vanished practically without reason,
if what got lost was the youth of strictly personal use,
also known as the youth of special purpose,
fanned, more or less, as the songs say, by the glory of military and
    amorous *peripeteias*,
the spirited, tenacious, savoury, and furious youth,
in a word, specifically yours,
then, a question arises, what happens

62
then the results are extremely nasty,
feel remorse or mount your horse,
yes, you'll bite, you'll bite your bit, you piebald loin,
and despite all your genuine self-esteem,
you will hurt it in every possible way,
tormented

63
that is, it would seem, well what then, if it's so,
vanish, melt away, fly where your eyes take you, and this and that,
why cry over spilled milk, chin up,
perhaps without all this it's simpler, freer,
but no, it doesn't work that way,
because wherever you'd look,
this or that only flies away from the field of external vision,

but not from the internal, not from *memoriae*,
not from the bundle of, pardon my agitation, flabby nerves

64
in short, call the scribe and dictate: *c'est fini*,
because of the fate of certain us, who are still visible,
keeping in mind that the main points established above depart to this
    cozy vale
only to remain in some sense:
that is, to remain in our plexuses and spin their nets, and gnaw, and
    wring,
and twist us with despair endlessly

65
therefore, as you see, i hear you, you're not alone,
i also know how to read the wind of sorrow, my dear dove sire,
and in regard to that instantly departed, suddenly vanished widow,
i understand everything distinctly and dare to think that your elegy
    about her,
obviously, if this is an elegy,
and, obviously, it is an elegy, even if without rhymes,
and if not an elegy after all, it doesn't matter, absolutely not,
since every composition can be called simply a thing,
and as a result your thing or, if it's more convenient, this
    watchamacallit
terribly wakes up,
more precisely, shakes up the entire past in me,
all my fibres

66
but in concert,
at the same this, which, apparently, furtively ticks and tocks,
it appears very sophisticated,
and no need to add, delicate,
delicate and even slightly translucent,
like a precious venetian bauble, i swear,
which in the light literally morphs colours and glows,
and if it doesn't have rhymes,
don't be concerned:

rhyme-weaving, with the exception of perhaps anniversary verses,
does not befit our rank anyway
and, in general, is from the evil one

67
in sum,
your report found its port, my captain,
everything about the earthly and the divine is absolutely sincere,
only it creates a slight impression that in the period you announced
there is, i would say, a certain commability

68
you've got it, commander,
the story of the given lady is not completely finished,
but shouldn't we have a puff first,
bosnian, i won't refuse, their smoke's just what the medics ordered,
now listen:
sometime in those same days, our combined semi-cavalry orchestra
was ordered to don winter garb and move to other positions,
we immediately covered up and set out using the british manoeuvre:
without saying goodbye to anyone,
and because the postal units, excuse my *quodlibet*,
were already partially disunited, and partially destroyed,
afterwards i had absolutely no news about her

69
nevertheless, i regularly dream
that whatever happened to that unfortunate widow also happened to
    mine:
it sort of turned out she got so upset by her misfortunes
that she transformed into a real fly,
and that this fly, mind it, is my widow,
not visited by humbly yours for long because of constant battles,
she flies to the desk of benefits and, seemingly to spite someone,
keeps dancing some kind of *sarabande*
on the glass of lampshades, window panes, and human spectacles

70
and what is peculiar:
that i had this vision for the first time on the eve of our fatal raid:

thinking soberly, it was a prophetic dream,
but at the time it appeared to me no more than a chimerism,
after all, besides, as they say, an entry in the book of wedlocks,
we were tied by a relationship of such a kind,
it would be simply silly to think that something
could separate us for real, that is, for a long time,
while forever would be completely bizarre

71
and yet, because of this fly,
because of its distasteful dancing,
i got horribly frightened for my wife and for our future together:
i woke up, wanted to calm down with arpeggios:
it didn't work,
my guarneri is clearly in a bad mood, can't be tuned:
probably, says my adjutant, from humidity,
after all, he says, fog's all over the place

72
i admit i don't fancy late festivities, and cavalcades even less,
who needs them, really,
after all, at night, even during the merriest war, it's better to sleep
    than play the hero,
but not knowing what to do with my insomnia
and how to avoid even greater despair, i woke up the pipers:
friends, angels,
why don't we take a ride at this bleak hour down the enemy's
    fortifications
and delight him with a concert of heart-rending music,
and:
march-march through overgrown water-meadows,
march-march

73
and as long as, blasting the radetzky, we pounded the hooves in
    the dale,
everything was going *très bien*,
but as soon as we started galloping up and down the knolls playing
    in memory of elise,
imagine, the same elise whose gallic grandmother

was first a confidante of lacaille, then clairaut,
and later turned the head of the young lalande,
needless to say, *mademoiselle* was dizzy from stargazers,
and so, as soon as we started playing for elise,
the fog dissipated,
and the night turned to be as moonlit,
as chopin's *nachtstück* in c-minor,
opus, if i am not mistaken, twenty something,
and it's finished,
we were discovered and:
with shrapnel, with shrapnel
and so mercilessly, unceremoniously,
do you remember, old pal bassoon, our disappointing demise

74
jawohl, captain,
only what is disappointment in comparison with the musician's bravery,
which we all, without a doubt, demonstrated,
starting with you and counting from that minute,
when, prancing in front of the staff tent, you passionately called to us:
my six-winged lads, let's trot with god's help,
and you yourself trotted first, trumpeting

75
and trumpeting
we trotted after you,
we trotted and harmonized in the name of the motherland,
to more gracious times and refined manners,
and all this turned out so valiant,
that, perhaps, there are almost no regrets,
both you and we,
utterly unexpectedly,
ended up so riddled

76
alas, gentlemen,
death on the line is sometimes unattractive,
but i must remind you that our wars,

whatever the accounting civilians maintain, are truly just,
and, most importantly, they are arranged so humanely that, having
 fallen,
we are reborn, like some phoenixes, for *vita nuova*,
for new battles

77
for instance, after this casus with the shrapnel,
i had that absurd dream again,
and, looking for an escape from despair,
i woke up quickly, swiftly evaluated the situation and instantly gave
 an order:
anchors a-weigh,
lay the course – to the roadstead,
force the enemy's galleon to *abordage*

78
however, as soon as we left the harbour,
the scalawags opened a squall of fire,
and an exploding shell demolished our captain's bridge
 right away,
and i, a captain far above the third rank,
and without false modesty, at that moment,
not even a captain, but a most genuine admiral,
i was thrown up to the birds and instantly
not just entirely dismembered,
but divided into tiny bits, into microbes,
more precisely, not all of me, but most of me,
with the exception of my head:
it,
as i saw with some kind of side-sight,
it,
wildly blinking and wincing, apparently from pain,
it
rolled down the foredeck and fell, poor thing, overboard:
how embarrassing

79
and again i had this vision:
that my widow, my fly-*frau*, with wings in disgusting specks,

keeps dancing now a *sarabande,* now a *tarantelle* on the glass of the
   same benefits' desk,
and the arithmetician,
the arithmetician could not care less,
since, in essence, why would he, frankly:
abaci in his hands,
although they are not abaci anymore, but a kind of maracas,
and *assa* can be heard, *assa, ai-da-ne-ne,*
because, as is aptly noted somewhere in la pérouse,
sea gypsies, nowadays impulsively called by other nations
filibusters and arithmeticians of fortune,
are dance-loving, gentle, and cordial folk,
and their souls are diamonds, the suit of diamonds,
if not hearts

80
this is mentioned in his *notes on the spare fore topgallant*
standing on the arithmetician's table next to his ledger
and a manual *how to become a true accountant,*
which claims that only he can become a true accountant
who, taking into account living beings and things,
lists them carefully

81
pause

82
in voices of people who keenly feel the beauty of the moment:
look,
the end of the quote coincided with the end of darkness,
morning has hatched,
it's getting light quickly,
and at the same time it becomes clear that about art,
and about finesse in general
absolutely enough was said,
at least here, in our resonant multi-voiced garden,
in this exquisitely aged gazebo

83
so permit me to bow and take my leave,
as they exclaim beyond the oder, *cześć,*

hold on, have you visited our parts too, *pan* matathias,
i wandered there, excellency, i did, and, doing so, learned the idiom,
you sound simply perfect, i suppose you've got dedication,
    enthusiasm,
but, I wonder, why would you, a free man of the levant, need our
    slavic abracadabra,
well, why not, sir,
if you want to roam like a human being
and be shown concern and respect, you'd better know languages:
the tongueless guest won't get the best bed

84
i have to admit i am a little bit envious:
after all, you're an exile unbound by any borders,
while for me
the path to my fatherland has been forbidden for so many years,
and, you know, it seems to become more and more blurry,
i don't grasp clearly what is going on there and how,
don't worry, beyond the oder everything is like it should be, *pan* ogiński,
that is, proper, like beyond the bug:
the fields, permit me to say, are sad, the highways – dusty,
but then how crusty is the *szlachta*,
and the middle class is, essentially, hyper:
all have inflammation of polishness, a bellamania of speech,
at the same time, all hurry somewhere, meet and part every moment
and you just hear all over:
cześć, cześć

85
and somewhere beyond the pechora,
where nearly always there's absolutely nothing to rush to,
they express themselves with much greater respect:
it's been, you know, a great honour to chat,
while beyond the rubicon, in the land of universal nonchalance,
in parting, if they utter anything at all, it's only the casual *ciao,*
and no more, so be glad

86
therefore, so long,
i wish you everything most wonderful,
drop in at any time, we'll talk,

only keep in mind that the treaty of eleven eleven, eleven hundred
    eleven,
signed between the troubadours and arboretums represented by their
    voices,
is still in force,
is still talking to us in its courteous vers libre

87
it is talking and relates to all of us
who are the voices of the above-mentioned these and those
and a legion of others,
possessed and called, enchanted and winged,
as well as their muses, their musics, and their musical instruments,
and other
beings and things that eternity would be too short to list

88
it relates to us, talking about finesse,
relates to us, and at the end of its last, eleven hundred eleventh song,
reminds us in a whisper:
well, so we agreed:
henceforth, from the break of day to the earliest stars
about finesse – not a sound.

Philornist

1
Arrepentios,
advised the unsightly one in something drab,
with pleats or ruffles,
like some kind of *peplum,*
appearing in rooms

2
she stooped, wafted decay,
and as to her eyes,
they were dark orbs,
and they were inclement, they grieved,
reproach flickered in them

3
but go on, go on,
it's not worth it,
resembling a sensitive instrument from the ranks of the stringed,
to get out of tune and freeze in minor nuances,
if only just because
such nuances have been worn out and buzzed around too long,
and mainly – don't proffer any comfort

4
much more exciting
is to think about her way of communicating,
or rather, her method of conveying thoughts to you,

transporting them,
in short, about the fact that she spoke silently,
as they say, not with her mouth, but fibres,
or, as is written in pamphlets about the other-worldly,
electricity of *chakras*,
emanations of *kundalini*

5
arrepentios,
she used to say, appearing in rooms and halls,
in halls and rooms of a certain museum,
in their enfilades,
the museum where lollygagged
the one who records all this here
or rather not here but there,
in the virtual continuum

6
how come,
are the writing accessories absent,
no, they're present,
but the gliding of the lead or nib over paper,
that is, the sound of the gliding
has always brought to his mind gnashing of teeth,
and thus saddens him deeply

7
moreover, he's not too fond of his handwriting:
since it's so out of the ordinary
that he still cannot get used to it,
get used to, not to pay attention to it
and stop recognizing himself by it every minute,
like a bird by its flight:
aha, it turns out, that's the character i am

8
of course it turns out,
and what did you think,
you must have thought that no,
that in no way,

but why,
no need to nourish illusions,
you are precisely like that
and, excuse my uncanny candour,
none other

9
'cause what other kind
of a character can you be,
if your latin script resembles a woodlouse,
and cyrillic – a scolopendra,
however, both are trying to mimic
nothing else but the feathered kind

10
and not simply,
not even simply the feathered,
but the kind
that possesses nearly the most praiseworthy features,
über, as they say, *alles*,
flying, in the squint of the meticulous philornist,
i.e., bird lover,
if not with the swiftness of the wild pigeon,
then at least of the kestrel, of the saker,
with circafalconian, colleague,
with circafalconian

11
and conversing in the same key,
that is, using parts,
several, so to speak, roles,
one has to note that the result is more harmonious,
because the years
in the given version incline not as much to prose,
as to fine drama,
which, without saying, is wonderful,
since partaking in such art,
even if abstract,
is worth a lot

12
but what is not wonderful,
apparently, is the fact
that, in general, these years treat us quite unkindly,
you're right,
the years don't have the slightest respect for us,
more precisely, they absolutely don't show us mercy:
they wrinkle us and do other things,
consider, they mock us,
even though, pondering from their position,
then why not, really,
since they don't care,
aren't they the free gryphons
or, let's say, *vetalas*

13
it would be fine if they only mocked the flesh,
the flesh, come what may,
well, to hell with it,
ignoble and annoying,
but no,
they make fun of the gentle *prajna*,
after all, precisely they
fill the mind's vessel with the clouding weed

14
so stop splitting hairs in fear,
is its twilight a token of death,
because what else really
could its twilight be,
it's becoming nearsighted, night-blind,
and more and more often can't imagine something,
    remember,
something like some dates,
someone's manners and features,
even if cherished before

15
and from time to time
it seems to hear squeaks of the coming catafalque,

dirges of its sad reckless driver,
and is constantly tormented by questions,
which cannot be cured,
trouble,
it was, people laugh, a mind,
and became a never mind

16
and because of this *casus* –
casus of the chronic mind clouding –
the next instalment brings the roles
and parts not very clear,
and even not clear at all

17
no problem,
happiness, sir, lies not in clarity,
in what then,
in ensuring
that the filament of the plot is not broken,
and the action,
captivating and educating,
goes on irrepressibly and smoothly,
and conventions of various kinds are almost invisible

18
almost,
because not to notice them at all
will not be possible, try as hard as you may,
exactly as it will never be possible
to get rid of them, to reject them,
since it is, after all, theatre

19
and theatre,
as every gertrude knows,
is, exactly, theatre,
is, naturally, theatre,
is, indisputably and undeniably, theatre

20
well, come in,
feel at home or as you wish,
only don't anticipate the coat-room,
either coat-room or foyer,
or snack-bar, or boxes,
or other outmoded tangibles such as stage or props

21
they're absent:
not needed
because in the given space
the performance is not for the public, but exclusively for oneself,
even more so because the public is also not required

22
you lucky dog,
you found yourself in the institution named after immanuel k,
in the theatre of pure reason,
which, inspired, keeps silent all over the *mahashunya*

23
repent,
advised the unsightly one in something drab,
appearing in the halls and rooms,
repent,
she spoke with her *kundalini* to you and others in the museum,
which, of course, was not strange at all

24
what do you mean,
what, in essence, was not strange,
her *kundalini*,
one just needs to specify, from whose point,
in whose, to inquire in slovenian, *pogled*,
or, if you like, for whom it's not strange

25
apparently, for the one

who besides emanations discerned the sense of the phenomenon,
who understood,
why this gaunt *señora* does not express herself using her mouth,
what, strictly speaking, is the deal,
while the deal, in general,
was in the centre of europe

26
in other words, i understood, i discerned
because i was quite attuned to it, sensitive,
and were also attuned those,
zusammen with whom you lollygagged,
your co-workers

27
why are you asking,
what do you need it for,
aren't you by chance an adherent of a theory
of equality of all minds and perceptions in the world,
no, no, they did not discern,
refinement, figuratively speaking,
did not happen to be their cup of tea

28
and if you think that something
linked or made me close to those people,
then nothing of the kind,
we no more than bowed to each other,
and besides the space of presence
we shared only the epoch's brief moment

29
its circumstances
you distinguish so clearly even now,
particularly such and such,
the same,
which the latter kept lending you so furtively,
so casually
that they seemed personally yours

30
so clearly
that you're again becoming quite agitated, spirited,
proud of familial ties, bonds,
slenderness of your anubis-like wrists, joints,
graciousness of nature,
construction of beloved constellations,
cut of pants,
you maintain a reputation, show off,
pour forth finno-ugric jokes,
black sea parables,
you whistle monteverdi, verdi,
you cite petipa

31
and how sharp in your mind are circumstances of the place,
more precisely, not circumstances, but contrivances,
here: furnishings of these halls and rooms,
where all this was happening

32
you recall either all the *mobilia* together
or *pezzo per pezzo,*
starting with the antique
slate tabula for official notes,
and ending with the stool
that figured on the glassed-in balcony,
was nicknamed by you the stool of balcony repose,
and, not to censure the other pieces,
was exemplarily stable, comely, gainly,
constantly ready for services
and encouraging them with its entire stance

33
and you used them with no hesitation and regularly,
however, at an untimely time,
even if so,
consider something mitigating:
as soon as i used them,
right away,

probably thanks to the stool's positive energies,
right away my ability to discern sharpened,
and somehow everything became particularly clear

34
but why are we going on and on about furniture,
it's almost boring,
you know, i'm not such an avid amateur of it,
at least not like some others,
hold on,
what did it do to deserve your disapproval,
after all, by and large, it's so comfortable

35
i don't disagree,
those fleeting joys that this matter instils,
as a human being, i find not too shabby,
however, maybe not as a citizen of the world
or a subject of a long-distance special,
but simply as a bit of a drifter,
i am bugged by its apparent earthbound, humdrum nature,
its surrender to the prose of life

36
but look what happens:
once they're immanent,
i am, of course, talking about the above characteristics,
once these characteristics are immanent to furniture,
and this is exactly so,
then they are, in principle, unchanging and inescapable,
and to make an example of them, annoy them with lectures,
i don't consider right:
showing off this kind of cleverness would not serve
the interests of common sense

37
in short, enough, enough about furniture,
because about furniture we have said absolutely enough,
at least here,

or herein,
which is, perhaps, more refined

38
precisely like that lu lun,
whose second name was yun yan,
would have inked to otomo tabito,
if he only knew his address:
compare in spare time:
'herein,'
'here'

39
and, most likely, would add:
stay healthy,
everything most marvellous to you,
good bye

40
greetings, my friend,
the other would answer,
i'll tell you a story

41
one time in summer,
enjoying tea next to the palace baths,
near the weeping willows,
the emperor and i accidentally lost ourselves admiring them
and the habits of the *takumidori*,
which wove nests in their hollows

42
at the same time we were so permeated
with the charm and sorrow of these trees,
that we also became slightly saddened, dropped our hands
and gradually gave in to the thought
that 'herein' is, perhaps, more refined
than 'here'

43
and then,
four moons later,
having discovered, strolling in the park,
that our willows had almost completely lost their leaves
and that the last *takumidori* had flown away,
we, without agreeing beforehand,
yielded to its continuation and said:
yes, yes, for some reason more refined,
but how much,
is it a lot

44
most likely no, not much,
more refined, essentially, only a bit,
just slightly,
that is approximately as much,
as 'here'
is sharper and smarter

45
will we see each other again,
how severe is the sea that separates us,
so farewell

46
farewell,
in response would have inked lu lun
whose second name was yun yan

47
in one word,
the unsightly one's way to communicate through *kundalini*
was not surprising:
the vigilant intuit,
you discerned that she's observing the vow of silence,
finding herself at the time
in a shelter for destitute widows,
whose husbands

had not come back from alien motherlands,
had not returned from some campaigns

48
some campaigns of such a kind as those,
you thought,
which for a long time had been called crusades,
and, in the opinion of historians of human games,
were particularly popular in the epoch of high *preferans*

49
and you thought:
then, in this enviable fragment,
all the past without exceptions and entirely
was considered glorious,
and the present – luminous and joyful,
and to the password: *all play,*
you gave an excited and instantaneous reply:
and all win

50
and later, as if out of spite,
came the era of the wretched, thrown-in,
despised,
but, unfortunately, global, blockhead

51
and then the honourable, honest players became distressed,
they experienced confusion and affront,
while the dishonest and the wicked rejoiced,
they started to cheat more than before,
which resulted in a regular mishmash,
kings became to such a degree stupid
that they ordered everything base to be lifted up
and everything lofty debased

52
and they downgraded those crusades to clubscapades,
declared them unjust,

they allowed sixes and other rags
to bully publicly the veterans and the memory of those,
who, in essence, returned,
but were chased away,
since they were not recognized

53
'cause they appeared with different features,
resembling heavenly byrdes,
and they flew into their homes,
and by their looks and calls
they announced it was them,
that they had returned,
but their wives
and even mothers did not believe them
and tried to convince them, looking askance:
you are not them,
they are not birds,
and exclaimed: *va via,*
and shouted: *fuera, a kysz*

54
and they flew away not to return anymore,
and remembering them,
people said they died the death of the quite valiant,
but sufficiently weak of flesh,
or, as the chronicler expressed it,
supremely fragile

55
it would seem like quite an epithet,
but no,
looking through the manuscript,
the crowned censor,
considered the best stylist of the fatherland,
made a note on the margin: *style,*
and was so gracious
he offered right there his own variant:
they died the death of the fine

56
glory to you, your highness,
your saying,
having the most gallant characteristics,
transformed the entire page,
flooded it with the same light,
the light, permit me to say, of genuine preciousness,
which later enlivened the name of the museum

57
museum named after you,
museum,
erected in our capital according to your instructions and plans,
museum,
in which hundreds of winters later
a sentinel appeared in the mornings,
and an interlocutor of your portraits on the walls,
admirer of your way of being and your style of ruling,
so you thought, appearing

58
an expert in the four noble truths,
and wines,
and tobacco products,
slightly angular, ectomorph,
you were a conscientious master of a pair of bay
brogans from rangoon,
procured at the dawn of your ardent europassion,
a *troika* suit of madapollam, grey,
and a skewbald
arkhaluk from dzaudzikau,
performing the duties of a coat,
while the role of a decent head covering
played a liver beret à la che
from borneo

59
ah, how they all, most likely, waited for you that spring
in the establishment of a dark-skinned gentleman in fatigues,
thrift-store owner

and concurrently commander of the entire legion
of steadfast tins of the guard

60
he commanded,
gramophoned marches,
marched on,
honoured himself as a marshal,
demanded to be addressed by his full name:
sese seko nkuku ngbendu wa za banga,
even though his colleagues and habitués of the flea market
called him familiarly by his family name:
mobutu,
our glorious fellow mobutu,
our brave old chap

61
they waited, and their waiting was rewarded,
and after trying them on,
you saw that they were made literally for you,
and decided to acquire them

62
that is, you literally shod, dressed yourself,
and they covered you up as well as they could,
they looked quite elegant,
they fit you,
they evoked a feeling of friendliness,
one sensed that among you, for you,
harmony would happen indeed,
everything would work out

63
and having paid, you acquired them,
rejoicing, you filled with them your portmanteau,
clicked your heels,
started walking in the direction of your domicile,
and in them precisely
you've been appearing since then in the museum

64
you appeared in this museum just because
you were employed there,
or, as was said before, lollygagged,
you lollygagged in the museum of fine,
is it true,
true,
however, not arts, but beings

65
large numbers
of dried-up organisms were stored there,
skeletons, stuffed animals, and plaster casts,
and what was your position there

66
you were a sentinel,
you kept order in the room
with the above-mentioned balcony
and a view of the horizon and the suburbs

67
if you will,
you were a man on duty at the exposition,
which was located in that room,
the exposition of those
who breathe with tracheas and undergo metamorphosis

68
the same,
whose number of orders,
according to some sources, reaches almost forty,
and of species almost two million

69
and here,
here one needs to mention
that the representatives of many species
are very harmful
and they are being exterminated,

but their number is constantly growing,
while the number of useful species, in contrast, diminishes:
it's a true paradox

70
and did you pay attention
to what degree dissimilar
are the specimens collected here,
right, sometimes even too much,
but because each has
a body divided into a head, thorax, and abdomen,
and the number of legs of every one
inexorably equals six,
and almost every one possesses wings,
they are all members of one class

71
sic, on call in the class of invertebrates
of the arthropod type you lollygagged,
a sentinel in the room of insects
you were there

72
and what is remarkable:
that you were the sentinel in that room as part of your duties,
but when you stepped out on the balcony
and sat on the stool of balcony repose,
and looked for long through the fragments of semi-transparent
    stained glass,
then absolutely spontaneously
you were also becoming a sentinel of space

73
which appeared multicoloured, rainbow-like,
but quite often
seemed to be an area of utter losses and sorrows

74
and all of them
gathered there in the form of anxious, quivering birds,

and if you got attached to it like to a brother-in-the-endless-now,
in the eternal 'here' or 'herein,'
then why is it so surprising

75
so take a look,
how many things at this particular point
happened, coincided, and got tangled up:
while europe,
shaking the surplus of her flabby cheeks on rail-joints,
was rolling back, to *akmé*,
and in *kursaals* and parks
waltzes and *rokambol'* were played again,
your best feelings,
including the feeling for the refined,
were becoming clearer and sharper,
and the feathered ones to you
were becoming dearer, more cherished

76
what a pleasant transformation:
if during the first museum phase
you were a not-yet-serious bird lover,
a little later – almost serious,
after which – serious to a certain extent,
and further – considerably, quite considerably,
then – fully and indisputably,
and now in front of you stands a perfect, complete bird lover,
and, obviously, a committed bird-gazer

77
and as far as the relationship with space,
thinking to welcome, encourage it at least a little,
from time to time you mentally
sent it an aerial kiss,
or gave it an imaginary smile,
or imaginary curtsy

78
and for these invisible signs of compassion
it treated you with intoxicating openness,
and, seeing it, your gaze became literally gaping,
gaping and motionless,
gaping and elegiac:
like in the scenes of leaving,
in episodes of forgiving

79
moreover, the visitors were so tactful,
that neither by questions,
nor wishes of good whatsoever,
nor by the sounds of their influenzas and colds
did they hinder your meetings

80
only the unsightly in drab,
appearing on sundays,
tediously *kundalinied:*
repent or you'll be sorry,
since it was probably you
who personally killed all these fine ones

81
well-mannered museum-wise
you replied in accordance with the occasion:
silently and in good castilian,
which you studied at some point in a lyceum
with a latin bent

82
señora,
you kept courteously silent,
allow me to assure you that in the extermination of the creatures
whose remains are presented in this *kunstkammer,*
i am not involved,
the creatures are killed by people of a special mould:
scientists, experts

83
and i –
you do see who i am:
an ordinary guardian,
which, really, somehow does not tally with anything
and, in general, is ridiculous,
after all, your humble one is decently gifted,
his vocation is to observe the feathered,
to show compassion, worry about them,
to believe in their lofty and mysterious purpose,
and, finally, just simply to admire them

84
he, allow me to put it this way,
is an inborn, innate philornist,
who feels miserable in the insect room,
what a sad contradiction,
you'll agree

85
don't fall into despair,
you discerned the soundless answer,
because these winged insects,
aren't they in their own way birds

86
in their own way, undoubtedly, *señora*,
you projected then onto her,
in their own way, absolutely,
accept my assurances

87
having accepted,
she'd leave the museum,
by her stature and gait
and her haughty smile resembling the one
whom the gondoliers of the adriatic waters
so deftly celebrated in one of their erotic *arioso*

88
la-la-la-la, they sang,
la-la-la-la,
ragazza piccola mia

89
we are talking, of course,
about the venetian marsh bittern
botaurus stellaris,
relatively small, woeful,
but at the same time quite a graceful heron,
whose grey plumage morphs into purple

90
and do you remember, my friend,
how in the light of the waterfront lamp,
carnival fireworks,
a torch,
or, perhaps, a beacon
the scales on her feet opalesce

91
and more precisely not how but with what,
isn't it with mother-of-pearl,
and rather, not mother-of-pearl,
but, let's say, some tourmaline

92
and what,
why wouldn't they,
for what reason,
if something opalesces somewhere
then with mother-of-pearl for sure

93
not for sure at all,
a thought
is a bird, flying all by itself,
if tourmaline then tourmaline

94
and if mother-of-pearl after all,
there's nothing you can do,
therefore, think:
well, with mother-of-pearl

95
it's completely logical,
and yet a blunder crept into the given recollections:
considering the sources of light,
you did not include in their listing
the match of our *cicerone*,
a swarthy smoker from the island of san michele

96
he struck it as soon as he cast off,
cast off and struck it,
and the scales on the feet of the one
who stood on the sand spit,
started glimmering and changing colours,
and, the dead ringer of celentano,
our *cicerone* began to light up,
struck it – and began

97
in brief, include it, include,
after all, a match, burning in darkness,
is unbelievably fine,
and also typical,
and without it in our transitory landscape
we will be clearly missing something,
apparently, exactly it,
yes, we will

98
in other words,
once in the evening,
having dropped us at the door of a *trattoria*,
he received his *obolus* and cast off right away,
cast off and struck it right there

99
and this entire instant, when he was lighting up,
the scales on the heron's metatarsals
glimmered and shimmered,
and, having lit up,
our celentano said to us quietly:
ciao,
and we answered respectfully:
arrivederci.

Notes

On Secret Tablets

(p. 3, line 7–8 from bottom) **Aleksandr Sergeevich** – Pushkin, Aleksandr Sergeevich.

(p. 3, line 7–8 from bottom) **What was Aleksandr Sergeevich doing in the country in the winter** – a reference to the opening line of Pushkin's 1829 poem 'November 2' ('2 noiabria'): 'Zima. Chto delat' nam v derevne?' (Winter. What shall we do out in the country?).

(p. 3, line 6 from bottom) **Ivan Sergeevich** – Turgenev, Ivan Sergeevich.

(p. 3, line 6–7 from bottom) **how fair . . . how fresh were the roses** – a reference to Turgenev's 1879 poem in prose 'Kak khoroshi, kak svezhi byli rozy.' Turgenev mentions that he remembers only this line from some poem he read long ago. The author of the original line is Ivan Petrovich Miatlev, who used the expression in his 1834 poem 'Roses' ('Rozy'). Interestingly, the same line was used in 1925 by Igor' Severianin in his poem 'Classic Roses' ('Klassicheskie rozy').

(p. 3, last line, to p. 4, top line) **do you respect me** – a popular Russian saying 'ty menia uvazhaesh'; used when someone refuses to have a drink or to continue drinking.

(p. 4, line 8–9 from top) **by the lacquered packaging overstuffed with mind-boggling rubbish** ('s primeneniem lakirovannoi tary, zatovarennoi umopomrachitel'noi trebukhoi') – a possible paraphrase of the title of Vasilii Aksenov's 1968 novel *Overstocked Packaging Barrels* (*Zatovarennaia bochkotara*).

(p. 4, line 6 from bottom) **belles-lettres** – in French, literally, beautiful or fine writing; in other words, all artistic forms of writing: poetry, prose, drama, and essays. In Russian, Sokolov often employs the word *slovesnost'*, derived from *slovo* (word), but usually translated in English as 'literature' or 'writing,' even though it could be more precisely rendered as 'word craft' or 'word knowledge.' To distinguish it from 'literature' and avoid a neologism or a descriptive term, belles-lettres is used here.

(p. 4, last line) **Gorky Park** – a popular best-selling novel by the American writer Martin Cruz Smith (1981).

(p. 6, line 6 from top) **Petra Nikolaich** – colloquial forms of the first name and patronymic of Petr Nikolaevich Krasolymov, Sokolov's acquaintance from the hunting preserve.

(p. 6, line 16 from top) **peace and freedom** – a quote from the last stanza of Pushkin's untitled 1834 poem, beginning with the words "'Tis time, my friend, 'tis time' (Pora, moi drug, pora).

(p. 7, last line) **it'll rip out our sinful tongues** – a reference to Pushkin's 1826 poem 'The Prophet' ('Prorok').

In the House of the Hanged

(p. 10, line 5 from top) **more famous dissident** – see Avvakum Petrov, Archpriest.

(p. 11, line 8 from top) **brainless Panurge's herd** – a reference to the 1532 French novel *Pantagruel* by François Rabelais, in which one of the characters, Panurge, buys a sheep from the merchant Dindelaut and, in revenge, makes it jump off a cliff. All the other sheep stupidly follow the first and tumble to their death. The French expression is *mouton de Panurge*.

(p. 12, line 16 from top) **white ticket** – a document attesting to one's discharge from the military service or a postponement of the draft.

(p. 13, line 19 from bottom) *Jedem das seine* – to each his own (each gets what he deserves), a German proverb made infamous when the Nazis placed it above the entrance to Buchenwald.

Having Discovered It – Opened It Wide – Given It Wings

(p. 14, line 13 from bottom) **locusts and wild honey** – a reference to a phrase from the Gospels (Matthew 3:4; Mark 1:6) describing John the Baptist's diet in the wilderness. Today, the phrase 'pitat'sia akridami i dikim medom' (to eat locusts and wild honey) is used to describe someone subsisting on meagre amounts of food.

(p. 14, line 4–5 from bottom) **sluggishly progressing repressions** – a parodic paraphrase of the term 'sluggishly progressing schizophrenia' or 'sluggish schizophrenia' (vialotekushchaia shizofreniia), introduced in Soviet psychiatry by Andrei Snezhnevskii and often used in diagnoses of dissidents. The vague definition of the term made it possible for the Soviet authorities to equate any form of political dissent with mental illness.

Palisandre – C'est Moi?

(p. 16, title) *Palisandre – C'est Moi?* – Am I Palisandr? (French).

(p. 16, line 2 from top) **OM** – Olga Matich.

(p. 16, line 2 from top) **AB** – Alexander Boguslawski.

(p. 16, line 2 from top) **DJ** – Don Barton Johnson.

(p. 16, line 2 from top) **AZ** – Aleksandr Zholkovskii.

(p. 16, line 2 from top) **AT** – Aleksei Petrovich Tsvetkov.

(p. 16, line 13 from top) **Post mortem** – after death (Latin).

(p. 17, line 16 from top) *glintwein* – the Russian word for German *Glühwein*, spiced hot wine or mulled wine.

(p. 17, line 20 from top) **police tea** – an expression from Osip Mandel'shtam's 1930 collection of essays *Fourth Prose* (*Chetvertaia proza*). Here, it refers to the morning hangover, when the interlocutors do not want to eat anything, and the only thing they can stomach is a cup of weak, watery tea.

(p. 17, line 13 from bottom) *stanitsas* – Cossack administrative units consisting of one or several settlements.

(p. 17, line 13 from bottom) *kishlaks* – winter settlements of the nomadic tribes of Central Asia.

(p. 17, lines 4–5 from bottom) **the beautiful simply must be majestic** – a quote from Pushkin's poem '19th of October 1825' ('19 oktiabria 1825').

(p. 18, line 4 from top) **Leonardo** – da Vinci.

(p. 18, line 6 from top) *largo* – very slowly (Italian).

(p. 18, line 8 from top) **painfully familiar acquaintance of mine** – Palisandr, the hero of Sokolov's novel *Palisandriia*.

(p. 19, lines 18–19 from top) **Tolstoi's death** – The consul is not very accurate in his dates. Tolstoi died on 7 November 1910, according to the Julian calendar (Old Style), and the armed insurrection in Petrograd took place on 7 November 1917, according to the Gregorian calendar (New Style). Sokolov was born on 6 November 1943 (New Style).

(p. 20, line 19 from bottom) **Night Violets and Maybe** – in Russian, Nochnaia fialka and Byt' mozhet, popular brands of Soviet perfume.

(p. 20, line 14 from bottom) *Madame Bovary c'est moi* – I am Madame Bovary (French).

(p. 21, line 6 from top) *Palisandre c'est ne pas moi* – I am not Palisandr (French).

(p. 21, line 12 from top) *Jamais* – never (French).

(p. 22, line 5 from top) **What's for me in this name of mine?** – the poem, written by Palisandr, is a response to, and a continuation and development of, Rimskii-Korsakov's romance to the 1830 poem by Pushkin 'To the Album' ('V al'bom'). Pushkin's initial line, 'Chto v imeni tebe moem?' (What's for you in this name of mine?), is based on the famous words of Juliet in Act II, scene 2, of Shakespeare's *Romeo and Juliet*: 'What's in a name?'

The Key Word of Belles-Lettres

(p. 24, line 15 from bottom) **upas tree** – for Russian readers, this immediately brings to mind the 1828 poem 'The Upas Tree' ('Anchar') by Pushkin.

(p. 24, line 14 from bottom) **international winds** – the words mistral, sirocco, and monsoon sound foreign to Russian readers and in the text symbolize international influences on Russian literature.

(p. 25, line 15 from bottom) **funny only to the point at which they become sad** – compare the line 'Vse eto bylo by smeshno, kogda by ne bylo tak grustno' (All this would be funny, if it weren't so sad), from Mikhail Lermontov's 1840 poem 'To A.O. Smirnova' ('A.O. Smirnovoi').

(p. 27, lines 7–8 from top) **There's a game. To walk cautiously in . . .** – the opening line of Blok's untitled 1913 poem.

(p. 28, lines 18–19 from top) **I would visit the tavern** – an imprecise quote (the order of sentences is reversed) from Ivan Alekseevich Bunin's *The Life of Arsen'ev* (*Zhizn' Arsen'eva*, 1933). Compare: 'On Moscow Street I stopped into a cabbies' tearoom and sat in its hum of voices, crowdedness, and steamy warmth, watched the meaty, scarlet faces, the reddish beards, the peeling, rusty tray on which there were two white teapots with moist cords joining their tops to their handles . . . an observation of the people's daily life? Not at all – it is just that tray, that moist cord!' (192) and 'To write! Yes, I had to write about rooftops, about galoshes, about backs, and not at all in order to "fight tyranny and violence, to defend the oppressed and destitute"' (191). These quotes are from *The Life of Arseniev: Youth*, translated by Andrew Wachtel (Evanston, IL: Northwestern University Press, 1994).

(p. 29, line 16 from bottom) **pair of bay catafalques harnessed at the dawn** – a reference to and a paraphrase of the title of a popular romance, 'A Pair of Bays' ('Para gnedykh'), a free translation by A.N. Apukhtin (1840–93) of Sergei Donaurov's (1839–97) poem in French, 'Pauvres Cheveaux.'

(p. 29, line 10 from bottom) **Humiliated and insulted** – an allusion to Dostoevskii's 1861 novel *Humiliated and Insulted* (*Unizhennye i oskorblennye*, also translated as *The Insulted and Humiliated* or *The Insulted and Injured*).

(p. 29, line 9 from bottom) **uncommon facial expression** – a quote from Baratynskii's 1830 poem 'The Muse' ('Muza').

A Portrait of an Artist in America: Waiting for the Nobel

(p. 30, line 6 from top) *hitataré* – the formal court dress of a samurai (Japanese).

(p. 31, line 6 from top) *memento mori* – remember that you're mortal (Latin).

(p. 33, line 18 from top) **Nightingales à la Kursk** – a jocular reference to the nightingales from Kursk, considered the best singing birds in Russia. The quality of their singing was legendary and in the 1860s one bird could cost more than 150 rubles, enough money to buy two cows and two horses.

(p. 34, line 19 from bottom) **wunderkinder** – literally, wonder children (German) – child prodigies.

The Anxious Pupa

(p. 37, line 10 from top) *¿Como esta usted?* – How are you? (Spanish).

(p. 37, line 11 from top) *¿Como estan los aires?* and answers *Gracias, gracias, muy buenos* – the inhabitants of Buenos Aires (literally, Good Airs) instead of asking, 'How are you?' supposedly ask, 'How are the airs?' and answer, 'Thank you, thank you, they're very good.'

(p. 37, line 12 from top) *Hoy* – Today (Spanish). A popular daily newspaper in Buenos Aires (also known in its web-based version as *Diario Hoy*).

(p. 37, line 6 from bottom) *Svensk poesi* – Swedish poetry (Swedish).

(p. 37, lines 2–3 from bottom) **but why Jerusalem, let's leave it alone until the future calendars** – a reference to the phrase 'Le-shanah ha-ba-a b'Yerushalayim' (Next year in Jerusalem) said at the end of the Passover Seder.

(p. 38, line 11 from bottom) **litotes** – rhetorical device of understatement, implying the opposite meaning. In our example, 'is not aesthetically pleasing' could be replaced with 'ugly' or 'disgusting.'

(p. 39, line 13 from top) *Ich liebe dich, s'agapo, te amor* – 'I love you' (in German, Greek, and Spanish).

(p. 39, line 4 from bottom) **Fire-Thief** – Prometheus, who stole fire from Zeus.

(p. 39, line 2 from bottom) *stilo* – pen (French).

(p. 40, lines 2–3 from top) **getting mixed up like things in the house of the Oblonskiis** – a reference to the second sentence from Tolstoi's *Anna Karenina*: 'Vse smeshalos' v dome Oblonskikh' (Everything got mixed up in the house of the Oblonskiis).

(p. 41, line 5 from top) **Rodin's Honoré** – Auguste Rodin's monument to Honoré Balzac.

(p. 41, line 9 from top) *Cito* – quickly (Latin).

(p. 41, lines 17–18 from bottom) **sluggishly progressing megalomania** – see note to 'Having Discovered It,' p. 149.

(p. 41, line 2 from bottom) *señor* – mister, sir (Spanish).

(p. 42, lines 1–2 from bottom) **Oh, miserable, helpless, enpupated, and stupefied Russian language** – a paraphrase of 'o velikii, moguchii, pravdivyi i svobodnyi russkii iazyk' (oh great, powerful, righteous, and free Russian language), from Turgenev's famous 1882 tribute to the Russian language, 'Russian Language' (Russkii iazyk), in his *Poems in Prose* (*Stikhotvoreniia v proze*).

The Shared Notebook or a Group Portrait of SMOG

(p. 44, line 3 from top) **Dedicated to Venedikt Erofeev** – the dedication to Erofeev, author of the acclaimed *Moscow to the End of the Line* (*Moskva-Petushki*), is Sokolov's acknowledgment of the important role of Erofeev in the development of Russian postmodernism and his general importance for modern Russian culture.

(p. 44, line 14 from bottom) ***gazelle*** – a genre of Persian poetry, *ghazal* (Turkish *gazel*, Spanish *gacela*).

(p. 44, line 14 from bottom) ***lalaie*** – a genre of Persian lullaby (sometimes spelled *lalaei*).

(p. 45, line 2 from top) ***vudareski veriga* in Romany** – the Russian word for 'chain,' *tsepochka*, in contemporary Romany pronunciation, bears the stress on the first syllable rather than on the second. Since this cannot be rendered in English, in translation the Romany expression (literally, 'a chain of the door') is used.

(p. 45, line 6 from top) **his marmot** – a reference to Beethoven's song 'La Marmotte' (1792), with lyrics by Johann Wolfgang Goethe. Goethe's poem, featuring the French phrase 'avec que la marmotte,' was about children from Savoy who, in hungry years, travelled around Germany to make some money. They carried with them trained marmots and entertained the wealthy by singing and having the marmots perform tricks.

(p. 45, lines 7–8 from top) ***shepetovka*** – the name of a railroad station made famous by Nikolai Ostrovskii in his 1936 novel *How the Steel Was Tempered* (*Kak zakalialas' stal'*). Lowercase is used here because the name should bring to mind a generic train station and generic laconic exchanges between railroad workers.

(p. 45, line 11 from top) **Botkin's hospital** – a famous hospital named for Sergei Petrovich Botkin; it is one of the leading health care facilities in Moscow. The hospital was founded and financed in 1908–10 by Koz'ma Terent'evich Soldatenkov.

(p. 45, line 14 from top) **The Races** – (in Russian, Bega) a bar located near the racetrack, on Begovaia Street.

(p. 45, line 15 from top) **toasts to the Arabian mares** – a reference to popular vulgar jokes about lieutenant Rzhevskii, a rogue and a womanizer famous for his sexual exploits and for his habit of comparing women to horses.

(p. 45, lines 20–1 from top) **in our mind's dreams** – an allusion to *Sny razuma* (Mind's Dreams), a series of Nikolai Nedbailo's surrealist paintings.

(p. 45, line 13 from bottom) *canaglia* – a scoundrel (Italian).

(p. 45, line 12 from bottom) **happiness was so sheltering** – a paraphrase of a quote from Pushkin's *Eugene Onegin* ('and happiness was so possible, so close'). The entire sentence in Russian depends on sound similarities (*kanal – kanal'ia, iskoverkal – koverkotovo*), rendered here with slight differences in meaning, but with close sound similarities: canal – *canaglia,* shatter – sheltering).

(p. 45, line 9 from bottom) **Cuddling his loneliness . . .** – the entire fragment is based on the euphonic similarities of the words used and the name of the SMOG member Vladimir Aleinikov.

(p. 45, line 3 from bottom) **Krivorozh'e** – Krivoi Rog, the place where Vladimir Aleinikov grew up.

(p. 46, first line) **Don't laugh, paps** – a quote from Aleinikov's 1964 poem 'The Moral' ('Moral").

(p. 46, line 4 from top) **the day of becoming aware of the lie** – a fragment of the first line of Aleinikov's poem 'The Moral.'

(p. 46, lines 5–7 from top) **the boulevard was stumbling, the rain was walking on fine springs, and the lamps were casting plywood shadows into the corners** – quotes from Aleinikov's 'The Moral.'

(p. 46, lines 7–8 from top) **And Dante's shadow, reflected in mirrors – like an echo – had been multiplied long ago** – a quote from Aleinikov's 1981 poem 'But the Primordial Light' ('No svet iznachal'nyi').

(p. 46, line 12 from top) **on the early ones** – perhaps an allusion to Pasternak's 1943 poem 'On Early Trains' ('Na rannikh poezdakh').

(p. 46, line 18 from top) **the trees are waving their palms** – a quote from Aleinikov's 'The Moral.'

(p. 46, lines 15–16 from bottom) **Where the light went out. Where the little window was opened** – quotes from Aleinikov's 1964 poem 'When in the Province Poplars Are Sick' ('Kogda v provintsii boleiut topolia'). 'The little window' in the Russian original is *fortochka,* a ventilation window that opens independently from the window in which it is installed to allow just a small amount of fresh air to enter the room.

(p. 46, line 8 from bottom) **absurdility** – a neologism rendering the Russian neologism *nesurazka*.

(p. 47, lines 18–19 from bottom) **they did not expect him** – a reference to the title of a famous painting by Il'ia Repin, 'Ne zhdali' (1884–8).

(p. 47, line 16 from bottom) **was still beyond the Mozhai** – the expression 'zagnat' za Mozhai' (to chase beyond the Mozhai) means to send one to prison or into exile.

(p. 47, line 13 from bottom) *smogist* – a member of the SMOG group.

(p. 47, line 7 from bottom) **Moonlight** – Piano Sonata no. 14 in C-sharp minor *Quasi una fantasia*, op. 27, no. 2, otherwise known as the *Moonlight Sonata*, is one of the most celebrated works by Beethoven (1801).

(p. 47, line 7 from bottom) **Polina, my polynya** – a quote from Leonid Gubanov's famous 1964 poem 'Polina.' Polynya is a hole in the ice or an area of open water surrounded by sea ice.

(p. 47, lines 1–2 from bottom) **in a second-hand rabbit jacket** – a reference to Pushkin's 1836 novel *The Captain's Daughter* (*Kapitanskaia dochka*), in which the hero rewards Pugachev for saving him from a snowstorm by giving him his rabbit jacket. In addition, it may be a reference to Gubanov's 1963–4 poem 'Pugachev.'

(p. 48, lines 10–11 from top) **Grackles Unbound; Being Art Nouveau, October's Vexing** – to create the acronym of the last name of the poet Leonid Gubanov, Sokolov changes the famous title of Aleksei Savrasov's 1871 painting 'Grachi prileteli' (The Rooks Have Come Back) into 'Grachi Uleteli' (The Rooks Have Flown Away). To render the acronym in English, the rooks are replaced by grackles, a related species.

(p. 48, lines 17–18 from top) **Ask any Hunting Dog** – a reference to Canes Venatici, the Constellation of Hunting Dogs, situated right under the handle of the Big Dipper.

(p. 48, line 15 from bottom) **Fata Morgana** – a mirage or illusion that appears as a result of light reflecting differently in air of different temperatures.

(p. 48, lines 12–13 from bottom) **journeys were long, and its buildings both public** – references to fortune-telling terminology; in Russian, *dal'niaia doroga* and *kazennyi dom*.

(p. 48, line 11 from bottom) **copper trumpets** – a reference to the expression 'proiti ogon', vodu, i mednye truby' (to walk through fire, water, and the copper trumpets), used to describe an individual who has overcome many difficult trials. Here, 'copper trumpets' are a metaphor for life's tribulations or the hectic and noisy life of the city.

(p. 49, line 4 from top) **sailor's silence** – (in Russian, *Matrosskaia Tishina*) – the name of a Moscow street and, by association, of the high-security prison and a mental hospital located on the street, the prison at no. 18a and the hospital at no. 20.

(p. 49, lines 7–8 from top) **Nobody, next to a cradle, would forget horses' skulls** – a quote from the Russian translation of the 1936 poem by Garcia Lorca 'Gazelle of the Flight' ('Gacela de la Huida'): 'ni hay nadie que, al tocar un recién nacido, olvide las inmóviles calaveras de caballo' (Nor anyone who, upon touching a newborn, forgets the immobile horse skeletons).

(p. 49, line 9 from top) *proet* – Sokolov's neologism for a writer who elevates prose to the level of poetry.

(p. 49, line 13 from top) **ringy-dingy** – (in Russian, 'lamtsa-dritsa') refers to the first part of the last line in all the stanzas of a popular 1920s song 'Shel tramvai deviatyi nomer' ('The Streetcar Number Nine Was on Its Way') that spawned many variants. The first stanza is given here with a rhymed English translation: 'Shel tramvai deviatyi nomer, / Na ploshchadke kto-to pomer. / Tianut, tianut mertvetsa, / Lamtsa-dritsa, gop-tsa-tsa.' (In a streetcar, nine in number, / someone found eternal slumber / People drag the one who died, / Ringy-dingy, what a ride!) For Russian readers, that nonsensical, onomatopoeic line immediately brings to mind an image of a streetcar, so important in this text.

(p. 49, line 15 from top) *proeziia* – Sokolov's neologism created from *proza* (prose) and *poeziia* (poetry).

(p. 49, line 18 from top) **amazism** – in Russian, *izumizm* is a neologism created by combining the verb *izumit'* (to amaze) and the ending, *-izm*, known from other art movements and styles.

(p. 49, line 18 from bottom) **mea culpa** – my fault (Latin).

(p. 49, line 3 from bottom) *doina* – a type of poetic or melancholic Romanian musical tune style with a well-defined rhythmic pattern and common musical phrasing; doinas can deal with such topics as love, adventure, nature, and fate.

(p. 50, lines 1–2 from top) **a streetcar going somewhere** – a reference to the 1919 poem 'The Streetcar that Got Lost' ('Zabludivshiisia tramvai') by Nikolai Gumilev.

(p. 50, line 2 from top) **twenty-third hieroglyphic** – the twenty-third letter of the Russian alphabet, the letter *Kh*, here alludes to Khoroshevo. By a strange coincidence, the number of the streetcar operating on Begovaia Street was also 23.

(p. 50, lines 3–4 from top) **primeval silver forest** – a reference to Serebrianyi Bor, an island on the Moscow River adjacent to Khoroshevo-Mnevniki. The island lies across from the terminal point of the Khoroshevskoe Highway. It was a playground of the silver youth and one of the most prestigious dacha locations in Moscow.

(p. 50, lines 6–7 from top) **Griboedov's waltz mixed half and half with some kind of Persian motif** – Aleksandr Griboedov, author of the 1823 verse comedy *Woe from Wit* (*Gore ot uma*), was murdered by the Persian mob at the Russian embassy in Tehran, and he is also known for composing two popular waltzes, one in E minor and one in A-flat major.

(p. 50, line 13 from top) **hands of its easels were blue** – a reference to Gubanov's 1964 poem 'Polina' or to its fragment, published separately as 'The Artist' ('Khudozhnik'): 'na golubykh rukakh mol'berta' (on the blue hands of the easel).

(p. 50, lines 17–18 from bottom) **positively *nedbailo*** – the Russian expression *sugubo nedbailo* (positively nedbailo) is nonsensical, as it depends solely on the strange appearance and the sound of the painter's name. Since the name ends in o, it resembles Russian adverbs; etymologically its meaning may be associated with the Polish *niedbale* (carelessly) and *niedbałość* (carelessness).

(p. 50, line 14 from bottom) *je ne joue pas* – I don't play (French).

(p. 50, line 14 from bottom) **Begovaia** – the street adjacent to the hippodrome (also the name of a metro station opened in 1972); the Furmanov Library on Begovaia was where the first public performance by the members of SMOG (on 19 February 1965) as well as subsequent exhibitions and gatherings of the group took place.

(p. 50, lines 13–14 from bottom) **stop the car right away** – a quote from Gumilev's 'The Streetcar That Got Lost.'

(p. 50, line 12 from bottom) **softly beckoning with tipsy lamps** – a reference to a song by Gleb Gorbovskii, 'When the Tipsy Lamps Are Swinging' ('Kogda fonariki kachaiutsia kirnye'), popularized by Vladimir Vysotskii, but with the change of the word *kirnye* into *nochnye* (of the night).

(p. 50, lines 10–11 from bottom) **a simple hoof print** – a reference to the Russian folktale 'Sister Alenushka and Brother Ivanushka' ('Sestritsa Alenushka i bratets Ivanushka'). In the tale, Alenushka warns Ivanushka not to drink water from a hoof print in the ground; his disobedience leads to his transformation into a little goat.

(p. 50, line 5 from bottom) **sounding brass** – (in Russian, 'zveniashchaia med") a reference to *1 Corinthians*, 13:1.

(p. 50, line 4 from bottom) **not Satchmo, not Dizzy, not Parker** – a reference to the three famous jazz trumpet and saxophone players: Satchmo (Louis Daniel Armstrong, 1901–71), Dizzy (John Birks Gillespie, 1917–93), and Charlie Parker Jr (1920–55).

(p. 50, line 3 from bottom) **Rue** – Street (French). In the original, Sokolov says 'Peshkov Street' to make the name of the real Gor'kii Street sound unfamiliar to the Russian readers. Therefore, in the English translation, 'Street' was replaced by 'Rue.'

(p. 50, lines 1–2 from bottom) **sounds of that Mongoloid moo** – a reference to the Russian rock group Zvuki Mu (Sounds of Moo).

(p. 51, lines 9–10 from top) **pull your Bickford cord** – a Bickford cord is a detonating cord developed by Ensign-Bickford Company of Connecticut and universally used in the mining industry. In Sokolov's text, it metaphorically indicates the cord in the streetcar that a conductor pulls when he needs to tell the driver that passengers will be getting off at the next stop and that the door should be opened.

(p. 51, line 12 from bottom) *Evoe* – in classical antiquity, an exclamation used during celebrations of the gods, for instance, Jupiter or Bacchus.

A Mark of Illumination

(p. 52, title) '**A Mark of Illumination**' (*Znak ozaren'ia*) was written to commemorate the 100th anniversary of Boris Pasternak's birth (1890). The essay makes extensive references to Pasternak's autobiography, *Safe Conduct* (*Okhrannaia gramota*), and to his poems. Moreover, it is a poetic tribute and acknowledgment of the importance of Pasternak to Sokolov's own art.

(p. 52, line 5 from top) *Safe Conduct* – the title of Boris Pasternak's autobiography (1931), quoted here in Beatrice Scott's translation: *Safe Conduct: An Autobiography and Other Writings* (New York: New Directions, 1959). All further references to Pasternak's autobiography refer to this edition. When necessary, Scott's translation has been revised to render the words of the original more accurately.

(p. 52, line 5 from bottom) *milonga* – music and dance that originated in the Rio de la Plata region early in the nineteenth century and by the 1870s had become extremely popular in lower-class neighbourhoods. By the 1890s, it had blended with the tango, despite some rhythmical differences. Today, the word *milonga* is also used to denote a place or an event where the milonga and the tango are performed.

(p. 53, line 11 from bottom) **nietzscheanism** – a slightly derogatory term indicating that one is blindly following the philosophy of Nietzsche.

(p. 53, line 5 from bottom) **invited to a beheading** – a paraphrase of the title of a famous 1935–6 novel by Vladimir Nabokov, *Invitation to a Beheading* (*Priglashenie na kazn'*).

(p. 54, lines 3–4 from top) **they depict people only to dress them in weather, and the weather – in passions** – from *Safe Conduct*, 33.

(p. 54, lines 7–9 from top) **because it is concerned not with man, but with the image of man. And the image of man – as becomes apparent – is greater than man himself** – from *Safe Conduct*, 59.

(p. 54, lines 13–14 from top) *araucaria* – a South American or Australian coniferous tree resembling the pine.

(p. 54, line 14 from top) *bondonella* – an extinct genus of marine arthropods, the trilobites that lived between 530 and 524 million years ago.

(p. 54, line 14 from top) *vicuña* – a wild ruminant of the Andes, related to the llama and alpaca.

(p. 54, line 13 from bottom) **Zeitnot, zugzwang** – international chess terms, meaning 'time trouble' and 'a compulsion to move' (from German).

(p. 54, lines 9–10 from bottom) **can imagine that it elevates him to its own transitory greatness** – from *Safe Conduct*, part II, sect. 17. The entire sentence about time is missing in Scott's translation. Cf. page 99.

(p. 55, lines 4–5 from top) **circle of *Kreutzer Sonatas* written against *Kreutzer Sonatas*** – from *Safe Conduct*, 57. Pasternak refers to *The Kreutzer Sonata* (*Krejtserova sonata*), one of the most famous short stories by Tolstoi, written in 1889 and, in its turn, referring to Beethoven's *Kreutzer Sonata*. Tolstoi's work is an argument for the ideal of sexual abstinence and a profound description of jealousy.

(p. 55, line 10 from bottom) *bibliothèque* – a library (French). In Russian, Sokolov uses the old-fashioned stress in the Russian word *biblioteka*, on *o* rather than on *e*; here, to create a feeling of something old-fashioned, the French word for the library is used.

(p. 55, lines 4–5 from bottom) **like sword-bearers of the roses** – a quote from Pasternak's 1913 poem 'Hours of Dusk' ('Sumerki').

(p. 56, line 16 from top) **the summer promised to be hot** – from *Safe Conduct*, 118–19.

(p. 56, line 17 from top) **September was drawing to a close** – from *Safe Conduct*, 120.

(p. 56, lines 17–18 from top) **colours were moving and coming to a conclusion** – from *Safe Conduct*, 78.

(p. 56, line 19 from top) **tragedy was called by the name of its futurist author** – from *Safe Conduct*, 116 (here with small changes to render the meaning more precisely). This is a reference to the 1913 play *Vladimir Maiakovskii: A Tragedy*.

(p. 59, line 15 from top) **not with a bundle** – a reference to a line from the famous late nineteenth-century prison song about a run-away exile 'Vagabond' ('Brodiaga'): 'tashchilsia s sumoi na plechakh' (he shuffled, carrying a bundle on his shoulder).

(p. 60, lines 13–14 from top) **following cat's tracks and the fox's, the cat's and fox's tracks** – a quote from Pasternak's late (1956–9) poem 'The Shadows of the Evening Are Thinner than a Hair' ('Teni vechera volosa ton'she').

(p. 60, line 2 from bottom) **there was impatience** – compare with 'attacks of chronic impatience' in *Safe Conduct*, 33.

(p. 60, last line, and p. 61, first line) ***Werther*** **and** ***Valerik***, ***The Silver Dove*** **and** ***The Golden Ass***, ***Othello*** **and** ***Lalla-Rookh*** – references to famous works of Goethe (1787), Mikhail Lermontov (1840), Andrei Belyi (1909), Apuleius (2nd century), Shakespeare (1603), and Thomas Moore (1817).

(p. 61, line 8 from top) **hay-loft smelled ... of wine cork** – a reference to a line from the poem 'There Was' ('Imelos'') from Pasternak's collection *My Sister – Life* (*Moia sestra – zhizn'*, 1922).

(p. 61, line 15 from bottom) **Book about Non-Involvement** – a reference to Pasternak's novel *Doctor Zhivago*.

(p. 61, line 9 from bottom) *stilo* – pen (French).

(p. 62, lines 7–8 from top) **We never know how great we are** – Sokolov quotes the Russian translation of the first stanza of the untitled poem No. 1176 by Emily Dickinson and refers to its words later in the essay. Dickinson's original is slightly different: We never know how high we are / Till we are called to rise / And then, if we are true to plan / Our statures touch the skies.

(p. 62, line 12 from top) *cito* – quickly (Latin).

(p. 62, line 15 from top) **Iasnaia** – Iasnaia Poliana, Tolstoi's estate and the place where the writer is buried.

(p. 62, lines 17–18 from top) **Rilke put on that morning a Tyrolean cape** – from *Safe Conduct*, 13.

(p. 62, lines 18–20 from top) **We have small rows with life's balances, but what's against us seems so bold. If we gave in to the advances of the Storm seeking wide expanses, we would have grown a hundredfold** – Pasternak's translation of Rilke's 1902 poem 'Der Schauende' ('The Man Watching'). In Robert Bly's English translation, the fragment reads as follows: 'What we choose to fight is so tiny! What fights us is so great! If only we would let ourselves be dominated as things do by some immense storm, we would become strong too, and not need names.' See *The Rag and Bone Shop of the Heart: A Poetry Anthology*, edited by Robert Bly, James Hillman, and Michael Meade (New York: First Harper Perennial Edition, 1993), 298.

(p. 62, line 4 from bottom) **recommends showers and exercise** – a reference to Pasternak's 1928 poem 'Twenty Stanzas with a Foreword' ('Dvadtsat' strof s predisloviem'): 'Poprobuite gimnastiku i dushi!' (Try exercise and showers).

(p. 63, lines 17–18 from bottom) **I – am – you** – from *Safe Conduct*, 140.

(p. 63, lines 9–10 from bottom) **night moths nicknamed Death's Head** – a reference to a song, 'Recollections' ('Vospominaniia'), by the poet, composer, and singer Izabella Kremer (1889–1956).

(p. 63, lines 2–3 from bottom) **kapellmeister** – the director of a choir or an orchestra; a choirmaster (German).

(p. 65, line 19 from bottom) **Like in Griboedov's work** – a reference to Griboedov's verse comedy *Woe from Wit* (*Gore ot uma*), where the names of many characters are meaningful.

(p. 66, line 5 from bottom) **of two other people's neck muscles** – from *Safe Conduct*, 48.

(p. 67, line 6 from top) ***Kellner*** – waiter (German).

(p. 67, line 9 from top) **how to drink and play billiards** – see *Safe Conduct*, 81.

(p. 67, line 19 from top) **Luther** – Martin Luther and the brothers Grimm are mentioned in Pasternak's 1916 poem 'Marburg.'

(p. 67, lines 8–10 from bottom) **used by the trees and fences and all things on earth, when they exist in the open air and not in the mind alone** – from *Safe Conduct*, 139.

(p. 67, line 5 from bottom) **in the form of a soporific splashing life** – a combined quote from Pasternak's 1917 poems 'How Soporific Life Is' ('Kak usypitel'na zhizn'') and 'My Sister – Life Is Splashing Out Today' ('Sestra moia – zhizn' i segodnia v razlive').

(p. 68, line 7 from top) **Including the Kamyshinskaia** – continuing references to the poem 'My Sister – Life Is Splashing Out Today': 'kogda poezdov raspisan'e Kamyshinskoi vetkoi chitaesh v puti' (when you are reading on your way the schedule of trains on the Kamyshinskaia line).

(p. 68, line 14 from top) **all kept losing their clothes** – a reference to Pasternak's 1949 poem 'Autumn' ('Osen''): 'Ty tak zhe sbrasyvaesh' plat'e, kak roshcha sbrasyvaet list'ia' (literally: You throw off your dress the same way a grove throws off its leaves).

(p. 68, lines 19–20 from bottom) **also an Austro-Hungarian** – a reference to the Hungarian composer Imre Kalman, the author of the operetta *Silva* (1915).

(p. 68, line 18 from bottom) **Silva, bring me some hot bliny** – a slightly altered quote from a song 'Dunia (Bliny)': 'Dunia, nesi (davai) bliny s ognia' (Dunia, bring the bliny from the fire). The song was popularized by the singer and performer Petr Leshchenko (1898–1954).

(p. 68, line 15 from bottom) **Rumiantsev house** – the Lenin Library.

(p. 68, line 5 from bottom) ***eniki-beniki*** – a popular Russian nonsensical counting rhyme: 'Eniki-beniki eli vareniki, eniki-beniki klyots(k), vyshel malen'kii matros' (*Eniki-beniki*, they ate dumplings, *eniki-beniki, klyots(k)*, a tiny sailor came out).

(p. 68, line 4 from bottom) **Brüderschaft** – literally, brotherhood (German); used in an expression when agreeing over a drink to switch to the familiar 'you.'

(p. 68, line 3 from bottom) **according to the master** – a reference to Pasternak's 1919 poem 'A Sailor in Moscow' ('Matros v Moskve').

(p. 70, line 9 from top) **And time and time again** – a quote from the penultimate stanza of 'Winter Night' ('Zimniaia noch''), a poem from Pasternak's *Doctor Zhivago* (1957).

(p. 70, line 13 from bottom) *sátori* – an individual Enlightenment (Japanese), or a flash of sudden awareness, the spiritual goal of Zen Buddhism.

(p. 70, line 7 from bottom) *paloma* – dove (Spanish).

(p. 71, last line, and p. 72, first line) **the murmurs ebb: onto the stage I enter** – a quote from Pasternak's poem 'Hamlet,' the first poem at the end of *Doctor Zhivago*.

(p. 72, lines 12–13 from top) **the poet's sister** – a reference to Pasternak's *My Sister – Life*.

(p. 72, lines 10–13 from bottom) **you are alone and that everything around you drowns in total Pharisaism, and that to endure life – regardless of its unprepossessing character – is not the same as to walk, as they say, across a field** – a combined quote of two lines from the last stanza of Pasternak's 'Hamlet'; the last line is also a Russian proverb ('zhizn' prozhit' – ne pole pereiti').

(p. 72, lines 4–5 from bottom) **Akakii's offices** – a reference to Akakii Akakievich Bashmachkin, the hero of *The Overcoat* (*Shinel'*) by Nikolai Gogol'. In the story, Akakii is employed in a government office, where he mindlessly copies documents.

An Abstract

(p. 73, lines 7–8 from bottom) **this Sokolovian guitar** – the title of a popular song about the Sokolovs, a famous Gypsy guitar-playing dynasty performing at the Moscow restaurant Iar.

(p. 74, line 15 from top) *bobeobi* – a reference to Velimir Khlebnikov's 1909–10 poem 'Bobeobi Were Sung the Lips' ('Bobeobi pelis' guby').

(p. 74, line 19 from top) **chrysanthemums** – a reference to a popular 1910 romance 'Chrysanthemums Finished Blooming' ('Ottsveli khrizantemy') by Nikolai Ivanovich Kharito and Vasilii Shumskii.

(p. 74, line 16 from bottom) *pel'meni* – a popular Siberian delicacy, a dumpling stuffed with seasoned meat.

(p. 75, line 4 from top) **smoke of the fatherland** – a reference to the Latin saying 'dulcis fumus patriae' (the sweet smoke of the fatherland), popularized in Russia through the works of Derzhavin and Griboedov.

(p. 75, line 13 from top) **miller from the Wienerwald** – a reference to the first song from Franz Schubert's cycle *The Beautiful Miller's Daughter* (*Die Schöne Müllerin*), 'Wandering' ('Das Wandern'): 'The miller's joy is wandering . . . '

About the Other Encounter

(p. 77, lines 6–7 from top) **genitive or accusative case** – in Russian, Catullus is *Katull*, which in the genitive and accusative cases becomes *Katulla*.

(p. 77, line 13 from top) *bouts-rimés* – (in French, *rhymed endings*) are poems created by matching several end rhymes. One variant is created by two or more people, with one person writing a line and giving it to another person to write a second to rhyme with it, and so on. A more popular variant of *bouts-rimés* involves writing a poem to a set of rhymes assigned by someone else.

(p. 77, line 19 from top) **somehow it was not possible . . .** – a reference to one of the most celebrated stylistic devices of Gogol': the use of the vague or indeterminate expressions like *kak-to* (somehow).

(p. 77, line 19 from bottom) **Nikolai Vasil'evich** – see Gogol', Nikolai Vasil'evich.

(p. 77, line 6 from bottom) **style is the writer himself** – a paraphrase of 'le style c'est l'homme même' (style is the man himself), from George-Louis Leclerc de Buffon's *Discours sur le style* (1753).

(p. 78, fourth stanza, line 3) *friula* – in the poem, an invented name of a cat based on the similarity of its sound to the name of the region Friuli-Venezia in Italy. Incidentally, a real female name Friula can be found as early as in the eighth century (Friula Perez Duque de Cantabria).

(p. 78, fourth stanza, line 4) *hatula* – in Hebrew, a female cat.

Notes

(p. 79, last stanza, line 6) **ich libe dich** – in Yiddish, 'I love you.'

(p. 79, last stanza, line 6) **haviva** – in Hebrew, 'well-loved' or 'beloved'; an equivalent to 'honey' or 'darling' in English. This word has been added in translation for rhyme and for its euphonic closeness to Tel Aviv.

Discourse

(p. 80, line 2 from top) **Evgeniia and Viktor** – Evgeniia Diurer and Viktor Erofeev.

(stanza 1, line 6) **come by letter** – a phrase used in telegrams to indicate that the details will be explained later, in a letter.

(stanza 1, line 10) *piano* – softly, quietly (Italian).

(stanza 3, line 7) **hegelian leanings** – see Hegel, Georg Wilhelm Friedrich.

(stanza 4, line 1) *mas o menos* – more or less (Spanish).

(stanza 5, line 3) **octavio** – see Paz, Octavio.

(stanza 5, line 5–6) *ay, absolutamente, señor, hablo, hablo* – oh, absolutely, sir, I speak, I speak (Spanish).

(stanza 6, line 3) *impromptu* – without special preparation, extemporaneously (French).

(stanza 6, line 3) *amabile* – amiably, pleasantly (Italian).

(stanza 13, line 9) **federico garcía** – see García Lorca, Federico.

(stanza 16, line 8) *poli oreo* – very beautiful (Greek).

(stanza 16, last line) **thessaly** – in the Russian original, Sokolov uses the word Attica, because it sounds similar to the Russian word for pharmacy – *apteka*. To render the euphonic similarity between the two words, Thessaly is used because it will be as easily recognizable by the reader as Attica.

(stanza 17, line 3) **giorgos** – George (Greek).

(stanza 18, line 8) **simooms** – sudden (but short-lived) dry, hot, and dusty winds common in North Africa and the Middle East.

(stanza 22, line 8) **akakii** – a reference to Akakii Akakievich Bashmachkin, the hero of the famous 1843 short story 'The Overcoat' by Gogol'.

(stanza 23, line 2) **bare your psyche** – in the original, Sokolov paraphrases the expression 'ne chaite dushi' (dote on it, lavish attention on it), converting it to 'ne chaite psikhei.' To render this word game at least partially in English, I paraphrase the expression 'bare your soul.'

(stanza 24, line 3) **gaius, that is, julius** – see Caesar, Gaius Julius.

(stanza 24, line 5) *lupus* – wolf (Latin).

(stanza 24, line 6) **this *homo* our mentor *est*** – this man is our mentor. A playful reference to the famous Latin saying 'Homo homini lupus est' (Man is a wolf to man).

(stanza 24, line 10) **mucius** – see Scaevola, Gaius Mucius.

(stanza 25, line 5) *o tempora, o* – oh the times, oh (Latin); the beginning of the famous phrase 'o tempora, o mores' (oh the times, oh the customs) from Cicero's *First Oration against Catiline*.

(stanza 26, line 3) *vivace* – lively, fast (Italian).

(stanza 31, line 2) *demi-saison* – in-between seasons (French).

(stanza 32, line 10) **tá-ta-ta tí-ta-ta, tí-ta-ta tá-ta-ta** – a slightly altered quote from Maksimilian Voloshin's 1901 poem 'In a Train Car' ('V vagone').

(stanza 44, line 5) *calendulae* – (singular *calendula*), a genus of annual or perennial plants (commonly called marigolds) in the daisy family Asteraceae.

Gazebo

(stanza 2, line 9) *chiaro* – it's clear (Italian).

(stanza 2, line 10) *italos* – an inhabitant of the land of Italy.

(stanza 3, line 4) *celeste* – heavenly (Italian).

(stanza 3, line 6) **wandering from *vagants* to *sänger*** – one of the characters, Antonio Scandello (see Index), travels from Italy to France pursuing various careers related to music. *Vagants* (or *vagaunts*) were originally simply wanderers but later the term was used to describe wandering students, poets, minstrels, bards, actors, and even painters. *Die sänger*, singers (German), known in medieval times as Minnesänger and Meistersänger, are mentioned here to indicate the final destination of Scandello: Germany.

(stanza 3, line 7) **and with the watch** – a reference to the famous German song 'The Watch/Guard on the Rhine' (Die Wacht am Rhein), written in 1840 by Max Schneckenburger and set to music in 1854 by Karl Wilhelm.

(stanza 3, line 10) *gris* – grey (French).

(stanza 3, line 18) *doctor honoris causa* – an honorary doctoral degree bestowed upon individuals for their special achievements (Latin).

(stanza 4, line 3) *frau* – woman (German).

(stanza 5, line 1) *rendez-vous* – meetings or meeting (French).

(stanza 5, line 8) **finesse, you should know, must be virtuosic** – a paraphrase of 'prekrasnoe dolzhno byt' velichavo' (the beautiful must be majestic), a line from Aleksandr Pushkin's poem '19th of October 1825.'

(stanza 8, line 3) *canzoni alla napolitana* – Neapolitan songs (Italian).

(stanza 8, line 6) *donnerwetter, in den geliebten garten* – darn it, in the beloved garden (German).

(stanza 9, line 7) **doubts die down** – a quote from a popular song, 'Doubts' ('Somneniia'), also known as 'English Romance' ('Angliiskii romans'), written in 1838 by Nestor Vasil'evich Kukol'nik and set to music by Mikhail Glinka.

(stanza 9, line 8) **the one walking . . . salutes you** – a paraphrase of the famous Latin expression 'morituri te salutant' (those who are about to die, salute you).

(stanza 9, line 9) **outer gloom** – a paraphrase of the expression 'outer darkness' from the Gospel of Matthew (8:12).

(stanza 10, line 2) **and at the very threshold of the gazebo** – 'I na samom poroge besedki,' a quote from the popular 1898 romance 'Gate' ('Kalitka'), with lyrics by A.N. Budishchev and music by V.I. Buiukli.

(stanza 11, line 9) **oikoumene** – a term originally used in the Greco-Roman world to refer to the inhabited earth or inhabited world.

(stanza 12, line 15) **phillumeny** – a hobby that includes the collecting of things related to matches: labels, boxes, covers, matchbooks, and holders.

(stanza 12, line 16) **felinology** – the study of cats, from the Latin *felinus* (feline) and the Greek *logos* (word, science).

(stanza 12, line 16) *à tout prix* – at all costs, at any cost (French).

(stanza 15, line 5) *pince-nez* – a style of spectacles, popular in the nineteenth century, which are supported without earpieces, by pinching the bridge of the nose. The name comes from the French words *pincer*, to pinch, and *nez*, nose. Modern pince-nez made their appearance in the 1840s, reaching their peak popularity between 1880 and 1900.

(stanza 15, line 6) **haughties** – a neologism formed from haughty, corresponding to Sokolov's neologism *spesivitsy* formed from *spesivyi* and *spes'*. The English neologism has an additional phonetic similarity to the word hotties, quite appropriate in the context.

(stanza 15, line 7) *aqua vitae* – water of life, a medieval name for alcoholic beverages (Latin).

(stanza 15, line 10) *pas* – step (French).

(stanza 15, line 10) *fado* – a type of popular Portuguese song and dance dealing with destiny or fate.

(stanza 20, line 7) **to blossoms of carnations and assignations** – a drunken slip of the tongue replacing the expected 'to the blossoming of nations.' 'Assignations' here denote paper currency.

(stanza 20, line 13) **should be powdered** – a parodic paraphrase of the famous sentence from Chekhov's play *Uncle Vania:* 'V cheloveke dolzhno byt' vse prekrasno: i litso, i odezhda, i dusha, i mysli' (Everything in a man should be beautiful: his face, his clothes, his soul, and his thoughts).

(stanza 21, last line) *id est* – that is (Latin).

(stanza 30, line 10) **i am an arithmetician** – a parodic paraphrase of the title of Norbert Wiener's 1956 book, *I Am a Mathematician*.

(stanza 33, line 4) **theatre *noh*** – the name derived from the Japanese *nō*, meaning 'talent' or 'skill,' Noh is very different from Western theatre. Noh performers are simply storytellers who use their visual appearances and their movements to suggest the essence of their tale rather than performing their roles. A Noh drama presents a visual metaphor or simile rather than action or storyline. The spectators know the story's plot well and they come to the theatre to see how the performers' movements and words reveal the symbols of and allusions to Japanese history and culture.

(stanza 33, line 7) *dunwu* – a sudden enlightenment; an important principle of Zen Buddhism. It was formulated by Dajian Huineng (638–713). Its goal is to direct the consciousness towards grasping true reality. The overcoming of illusions requires long effort, and during this time, one's vision of the world is flawed. When one finally reaches the correct vision, one suddenly comprehends reality in all its wholeness and fullness.

(stanza 33, line 8) *wu wei* – in Taoism, knowing when to act and when not to act. *Wu* may be translated as 'not have' or 'without'; *wei* may be translated as 'do, act, serve as, govern or effort.' The literal meaning of *wu wei* is 'without action,' and its aim is to achieve a state of perfect equilibrium, or alignment with the Tao. There is another, less common meaning of *wu wei:* 'action that does not involve struggle or excessive effort.' In this instance, *wu* means 'without' and *wei* means 'effort.' However, *wu wei* also can be interpreted as simply 'non-action,' a state, when, for example, one simply sits on the meadow, while the grass around grows without any involvement of the person sitting there, making it an ideal 'non-action.'

(stanza 33, line 9) **spectator from a window** – in Japan, after the retirement of a devoted employee, an employer may create for him a position called a 'window man.' Such an employee is required only to sit and do nothing and the fact that he is 'employed' (and visible to everyone) is a testimony to his employer's success and status.

(stanza 33, line 9) *go* – a strategic board game for two players. It originated in China more than 2,500 years ago, and although it is not known exactly when the game was invented, by the third century BC it was already a popular pastime. The early game was played on a board with a 17×17 grid, but by the seventh century, boards with a 19×19 grid had become standard in Korea and Japan.

(stanza 34, line 8) **uttered** – compare with the famous line from 1829 Fedor Tiutchev's poem, 'Silentium': 'mysl' izrechennaia est' lozh'' (the uttered thought is a lie).

(stanza 39, line 4) *esperar* – to hope (Spanish).

(stanza 39, line 5) **esperanto** – a universal language invented by the Polish oculist and philologist Ludwig Zamenhof (1859–1917). The name of the language is based on the Spanish word for hope – *esperanza,* a testimony to Zamenhof's hope that his language will help bring about world peace.

(stanza 39, line 6) *trattoria* – tavern (Italian).

(stanza 39, line 7) *tangeria* – a club or restaurant where tango is performed (Spanish).

(stanza 45, line 5) *tao* – Taoism asks each person to focus on the world around him or her in order to understand the inner harmonies of the universe. It is a system of thought heavily centred on meditation and contemplation. The Tao surrounds everyone, and one must listen to find enlightenment.

(stanza 45, line 7) **beneath the heavens** – a traditional name for China (*Tian xia*). The other name variants include Under the Heavens, the Celestial Empire, and the Heavenly Empire.

(stanza 46, line 5) *mille pardons* – a thousand pardons (French).

(stanza 47, line 4) *kunstkammern* – chambers of art and curiosities (German). The *Kunstkammern* were the predecessors of museums and housed various objects, ranging from works of art to human fetuses and exotic species of fauna and flora.

(stanza 47, line 4) *privatdozent* – a title given in some European university systems, especially in German-speaking countries, to someone who pursues an academic career and holds all of the formal qualifications (doctorate and habilitation) to become a tenured university professor.

(stanza 47, line 5) **bonobos** – (s. bonobo) *Pan paniscus* (often called the Pygmy or Dwarf Chimpanzee), is a great ape and one of the two species making up the genus *Pan*. The bonobos have relatively long legs, pink lips, dark face, tail-tuft, and parted long hair on their head. A popular perception that bonobos are a matriarchal species that engages in uncommonly casual sexual practices is questionable; however, research indicates that they are female-centred, more peaceful than chimpanzees, more egalitarian, and do have a much larger sexual repertoire. The bonobos are endangered and are found in the wild only in the Democratic Republic of the Congo.

(stanza 47, line 6) *charmant* – charming (French).

(stanza 47, line 8) **an** *imposant* – impressive, imposing (French). In Russian, it is a neologism because it is used as a noun rather than an adjective (*imposantnyi*); to duplicate this in English, the word is preceded by an article.

(stanza 47, line 11) *triangolo* – a triangle, a percussion instrument (Italian).

(stanza 49, line 5) *pied-à-terre* – a temporary lodging (French); literally, foot to the ground.

(stanza 49, line 18) *billets-doux* – love letters (French); literally, sweet letters.

(stanza 50, line 7) *frühstück* – breakfast (German); literally, early piece.

(stanza 57, line 3) **automedons** – the word derived from the name of Achilles' chariot driver in the *Iliad*, Automedon.

(stanza 57, line 12) *demimondaine* – a woman of the demimonde, a prostitute (French).

(stanza 58, line 9) *pamplemousse* – grapefruit (French).

(stanza 58, line 9) *citron* – lemon (French).

(stanza 59, line 4) *momentum* – moment (Latin).

(stanza 60, line 10) *claro que no, que nunca* – it's clear that no, that never (Spanish).

(stanza 60, line 11) **bibbie** – a bib.

(stanza 61, line 5) *peripeteias* – reversals of fortune, turning points, adventures, peripeties (Greek).

(stanza 62, line 3) **loin** – a singular form derived from the biblical plural 'loins,' corresponding to the Russian *ud* (from *udy*).

(stanza 63, line 8) *memoriae* – memories (Latin).

(stanza 64, line 1) *c'est fini* – it's all over; it is finished (French).

(stanza 66, last line) **from the evil one** – a quote from the Gospel of Matthew (5:37).

(stanza 67, line 5) **commability** – this nonsensical neologism indicates that the story of the widow is not finished, has been suspended. Sokolov uses a word play ('v . . . tochke est' kakoe-to zapiataistvo'), referring to the period (*tochka*) and creating a neologism, *zapiataistvo*, related to *zapiataia* (comma). To preserve the word play at least partially, in English the word is coined from comma and disability.

(stanza 68, line 10) *quodlibet* – a musical composition in which several well-known melodies are combined, either simultaneously or, less frequently, sequentially, for humorous effect. It can also refer to an amalgamation of different song texts in a vocal composition. The speaker jocularly misuses the word, having in mind a quip or a pun.

(stanza 69, line 8) *sarabande* – a Spanish dance in triple metre with a distinctive rhythm.

(stanza 70, line 4) **chimerism** – a neologism formed from the word chimera.

(stanza 72, line 3) **the merriest war** – the expression derives from the epithet given by Peter the Great and his contemporaries to his 'play' soldiers, *poteshnye voiska*. In English, the common translation of *poteshnyi* is merry, even though it can also mean 'mock,' as in the *poteshnyi gorodok* (mock fortress) that Peter constructed to train his merry soldiers, or 'just for play' (therefore, not serious, not real).

(stanza 73, line 1) **radetzky** – the *Radetzky March*, op. 228, is a march composed by Johann Strauss Sr in 1848. It was dedicated to the Austrian Field Marshal Joseph Radetzky von Radetz.

(stanza 73, line 2) *très bien* – very well (French).

(stanza 73, line 3) **in memory of elise** – a reference to Beethoven's famous 1810 bagatelle in A minor, *Für Elise*.

(stanza 73, line 7) *mademoiselle* – miss (French).

(stanza 73, line 10) **the night turned to be as moonlit** – a reference to Apollon Grigor'ev's 1857 untitled poem that later became known as a popular song 'Two Guitars' ('Dve gitary'), with many variants.

(stanza 73, line 11) *nachtstück* – night piece (German); here, a reference to Chopin's 1836 *Nocturne in C sharp minor*, op. 27, or to the *Nocturne No. 21 in C minor*.

(stanza 74, line 1) *jawohl* – yes sir (German).

(stanza 76, line 6) *vita nuova* – new life (Italian).

(stanza 77, line 7) *abordage* – positioning the ship alongside another one to board it (French).

(stanza 79, line 2) *frau* – wife (German).

(stanza 79, line 3) *tarantelle* – a popular southern Italian folk dance accompanied by tambourines; from the town of Taranto, where it originated.

(stanza 79, line 9) *assa* – a Caucasian exclamation used during a dance to applaud and encourage the dancers to go on, show their skills, and enjoy themselves.

(stanza 79, line 9) *ai-da-ne-ne* – a popular line in the choruses of many Gypsy songs.

(stanza 83, line 2) *cześć* – an informal expression used both as 'hi' and 'bye' in Polish.

(stanza 83, line 3) *pan* – mister, sir (Polish). The proper vocative is *panie*, but many Russians use the nominative form, *pan*.

(stanza 84, line 9) **the fields . . . are sad** – ('polia pechal'nye'), a quote from Turgenev's 1843 poem 'A Foggy Morning' ('Utro tumannoe').

(stanza 84, line 10) *szlachta* – Polish nobility.

(stanza 84, line 12) **a bellamania of speech** – a neologism indicating the ability of the Poles to express themselves beautifully and profusely.

(stanza 85, line 6) *ciao* – bye (Italian).

(stanza 86, last line) *vers libre* – free verse (French).

Philornist

(p. 123, title) **Philornist** – the author's neologism for a bird lover (in Russian, *filornit*). In English, a similar neologism has been created to resemble entomologist, lepidopterist, etc., even though in the 16 June 1886 edition of *The Oxford Magazine* we find the word philornith.

(stanza 1, line 1) *Arrepentios* – repent (Spanish). The use of this imperative form indicates that the speaker is from Spain; in Latin America, the common imperative form would be *arrepiéntanse*.

(stanza 1, line 4) *peplum* – the Roman equivalent of the Greek *peplos*; a kind of woman's tunic, made of a tubular cut of fabric, folded inside-out from the top about halfway down, draped into loose folds, and held at the shoulders by pins.

(stanza 2, line 3) **dark orbs** – in the Russian text, Sokolov uses two different words for eyes – 'glaza' and 'ochi.' The latter word is archaic and is most often used in poetry and songs, as in the famous romance 'Dark Eyes' ('Ochi chernye'). The addition of the word 'dark' in the translation creates a reference to this romance and allows me to avoid the repetition of the word 'eyes.'

(stanza 4, line 8) *chakra* – a Sanskrit word that translates as 'wheel' or 'turning.' It is related to wheel-like vortices, 'force centres' or whorls of energy permeating, from a point on the physical body, the layers of the subtle bodies in an ever-increasing fan-shaped formation. Rotating vortices of subtle matter, chakras are considered to be the focal points for the reception and transmission of energies. Seven major chakras or energy centres (also understood as wheels of light) are believed to exist.

(stanza 4, line 9) *kundalini* – a Sanskrit word literally meaning 'coiled.' In Indian yoga, a 'corporeal energy' – an unconscious, instinctive, or libidinal force lies coiled at the base of the spine. It is envisioned as either a goddess or a sleeping serpent; hence, in English it is translated as 'serpent power.' The Kundalini resides in the sacrum bone in three and a half coils and has been described as a residual power of pure desire. Kundalini energy is nothing but the natural energy of the Self, where Self is the universal consciousness present in every being, but prevented by the mind from free expression. Therefore, self-realization, enlightenment, nirvana, and awakened Kundalini are all the same thing, and can be achieved by self-inquiry and meditation.

(stanza 5, line 4) **enfilade** – in architecture, a suite of rooms formally aligned with each other; the doors entering each room are aligned with the doors of the connecting rooms along a single axis, providing a vista through the entire suite.

(stanza 9, line 4) **scolopendra** – a genus of many centipedes of the family Scolopendridae.

(stanza 10, line 5) *über . . . alles* – above all (German). A reference to the famous first line of the German national anthem, 'Song of Germany' ('Deutschlandlied'), with the music written by Joseph Haydn in 1797 and the lyrics added in 1841 by August Heinrich Hoffmann von Fallersleben.

(stanza 10, line 7) *i.e.* – an abbreviation of the Latin words *id est* – that is.

(stanza 10, line 9) **kestrel** – the name of several species of birds from the falcon genus, *Falco*, characterized by the brown coloration of their plumage. Kestrels don't build their own nests but use the nests of other species. Unlike their relatives the sakers, they adapt well to the conditions of modern life.

(stanza 10, line 9) **saker** – *Falco cherrug*, a large species of falcon, 47 to 55 cm in length with a wing span of 105 to 129 cm. Considered endangered, the saker is protected and flourishes today in Hungary.

(stanza 10, line 10) **circafalconian** – a neologism (in Russian, *okolosokolinnaia*) to describe a speed approximating the speed of falcons.

(stanza 11, line 6) **prose** – a paraphrase of Pushkin's 'leta k surovoi proze kloniat' (years incline one to austere prose), from *Eugene Onegin*, chapter 6, stanza 46, line 5.

(stanza 12, line 12) **gryphon** – also griffin or griffon, a legendary creature with the body of a lion and the head and wings of an eagle.

Notes

(stanza 12, last line) *vetala* – a Sanskrit word denoting a vampire-like being in Hindu mythology. Vetalas are immaterial spirits inhabiting corpses and burial grounds and have the ability to fly in search of new hosts.

(stanza 13, line 6) *prajna* – in Sanskrit, wisdom, mind, or consciousness.

(stanza 16, line 1) *casus* – an extraordinary case, event, occurrence, occasion, circumstance (Latin).

(stanza 19, line 2) **gertrude** – a reference to Gertrude Stein and to her famous and often paraphrased statement, 'a rose is a rose is a rose.'

(stanza 20, line 3) **coat-room** – a reference to the saying 'teatr nachinaetsia s veshalki' (theatre starts with a coat-room), attributed to the famous stage director Konstantin Stanislavskii.

(stanza 22, last line) *mahashunya* – in Sanskrit, 'great emptiness,' 'supreme void,' or 'great vacuum,' the depths of the universe from which everything springs and to which everything returns. Beyond all comprehension, it is the sum total of omnipotent, omniscient, omnipresent, and always perfect Spirit.

(stanza 24, line 5) *pogled* – opinion, view (Slovenian).

(stanza 25, line 4) *señora* – lady, woman (Spanish).

(stanza 26, line 4) *zusammen* – together (German).

(stanza 30, line 4) **anubis** – Greek name of a jackal- or dog-headed god associated in Egyptian mythology with mummification and the afterlife. The narrator imagines his wrists to be as narrow as those of Anubis.

(stanza 30, line 9) *finno-ugric* – a group of languages in the Uralic language family. Unlike most of the other languages spoken in Europe, they are not part of the Indo-European family. The best-known are Hungarian and Finnish.

(stanza 32, line 1) *mobilia* – furniture (Italian). In the Russian text, the author uses the English word, unfamiliar to Russian readers. Therefore, in the English translation, this and subsequent English words or expressions are replaced with foreign ones.

(stanza 32, line 2) *pezzo per pezzo* – piece by piece (Italian). In the original, the English phrase is used.

(stanza 32, line 9) **gainly** – in Russian, *ukliuzh,* a neologism formed from *neukliuzhii* (ungainly); in English, the same thing is achieved by cutting off the negative prefix.

(stanza 35, line 5) **long-distance special** – the narrator applies railroad terminology to his life and character.

(stanza 38, line 2) **yun yan** – a reference to an ancient tradition that an educated person (usually a male), besides his family name and given name, also acquired another name, *zi*, commonly translated as 'courtesy name' or 'adult name,' when he became an adult (at about age 20). In the case of Lu Lun, Lu is his family name, Lun his given name, while Yun Yan is his courtesy or adult name.

(stanza 41, line 5) *takumidori* – in Japanese, a 'carpenter bird,' or woodpecker.

(stanza 47, line 4) **intuit** – as a noun, the word is a neologism in both Russian and English.

(stanza 47, line 9) **motherlands** – the author creates a word play on the expression 'vernut'sia v svoi palestiny' (to return home, homeward), changing it to the oxymoronic 'ne vernulis' iz chuzhikh palestin' (did not return from alien motherlands).

(stanza 48, last line) *preferans* – a popular Russian card game, invented in the nineteenth century and in English called preference. In Russian, 'vysokii preferans' is a word play on the expression 'vysokii renessans' (High Renaissance); the transliteration of the Russian word preserves the word play and sound similarity.

(stanza 50, lines 2–4) **thrown-in . . . blockhead** – a paraphrase of the name of the popular Russian card game 'podkidnoi durak.' The game is known in English as 'Shithead' or 'Idiot.'

(stanza 52, line 1) **clubscapades** – the author makes a word play of two Russian expressions – 'krestovye pokhody' (campaigns with crosses; crusades) and 'trefovye pokhody' (campaigns with clubs); to preserve the word play, a neologism 'clubscapades' is created to resonate with the word 'crusades.'

(stanza 52, line 3) **rags** – a slang word for low-valued cards.

(stanza 53, line 12) *va via* – be gone, be on your way (Italian).

(stanza 53, last line) *fuera* – out, outside (Spanish).

(stanza 53, last line) *a kysz* – shoo (Polish). In the Russian original, the author uses the English word 'shoo.'

(stanza 58, line 5) **a pair of bay** – a reference to and a paraphrase of a popular romance 'A Pair of Bays' ('Para gnedykh'), a free translation of

Donaurov's French poem 'Pauvres Cheveaux' by Apukhtin. The entire stanza is a play on the expectations of the Russian readers. The words 'para gnedykh' instead of being followed by 'zapriazhennykh s zareiu' (harnessed at dawn), like in the romance, is followed here by 'obretennykh zareiu' (procured at the dawn) and 'shtiblet iz ranguna' (shoes from Rangoon; in translation, the word 'brogans' makes the identification more difficult for English readers). Similar confusing 'horse' references follow in the word *troika* (traditionally, three horses or a sled drawn by three horses) used to describe a three-piece suit, and the word *arkhaluk* (a close-fitting Caucasian cotton or satin caftan) used after 'skewbald' and forcing readers to think about some exotic horse breed.

(stanza 58, line 8) **madapollam** – a soft, bleached or dyed cotton fabric manufactured from fine yarns and used in embroidery, the production of handkerchiefs, and as a base fabric in cloth printing; from Madapollam, a village near Narsapur, in India, where the British had a cloth factory.

(stanza 58, line 13) **che** – see Guevara, Ernesto 'Che.'

(stanza 59, last line) **steadfast tins of the guard** – a paraphrase of the title of Hans Christian Andersen's famous tale *The Steadfast Tin Soldier* (1838). In Russian, the plural *stoikikh gvardii oloviannykh* (steadfast tin of the guard) is an unusual expression because it is missing the subject, for instance, the word 'soldiers'; in English, a similar strange expression is created by using the plural of tin. Significantly, in the Slavic tradition the material from which the toy soldiers are made is *olovo* (lead).

(stanza 71, line 1) *sic* – thus, so, as such, in such a manner (Latin).

(stanza 75, line 6) *akmé* – pinnacle, acme. In the Russian original, the author uses the English word 'acme.' To make it more foreign for English readers, it is replaced here by a less familiar spelling in its original, Greek form.

(stanza 75, line 7) *kursaal* – literally, a 'cure room' (German), a public hall or room for entertaining visitors at watering places and health resorts.

(stanza 75, line 8) *rokambol'* – the Russian name of a rather complex card game for three players, with many variants, known around Europe under many names, for example, El Hombre, El Tresillo, Lomber, Rocambor, and Mediator. It was particularly popular in the seventeenth and eighteenth centuries, but later could not compete with *preferans* and whist and fell into oblivion.

(stanza 82, line 4) *kunstkammer* – see the note to 'Gazebo,' stanza 47, line 4.

(stanza 82, line 6) **special mould** – a reference to the title of Vasilii Ivanovich Kozlov's 1952 book *People of Special Mould* (*Liudi osobogo sklada*), about the partisans in Belorussia during the Second World War.

(stanza 87, last line) *arioso* – in Italian, *arioso* means 'airy' and is a term loosely used to describe a piece for solo voice that is neither quite an aria nor recitative. An arioso does not normally follow any strict rules, and it is sometimes used to identify a vocal or instrumental piece in lyrical style.

(stanza 88, line 3) **ragazza piccola mia** – my baby girl; my little girl (Italian).

(stanza 95, line 5) *cicerone* – guide (Italian).

(stanza 98, line 3) *trattoria* – an Italian eatery, less formal than a restaurant, often with no menus, casual service, and low prices; a tavern.

(stanza 98, line 4) **obolus** – also spelled *obol*; an ancient Greek coin or a small coin formerly used in Europe. In Greek and Roman mythology, an *obolus* was placed in the mouth or on the lips of the deceased to allow him to pay Charon for ferrying him across the Acheron and the Styx, the rivers separating the living from the dead.

(stanza 99, line 6) *ciao* – bye (Italian).

(stanza 99, last line) *arrivederci* – until we meet again; farewell (Italian).

Index of Names and Places

Acropolis – flat-topped rock in the centre of Athens; today, it features several famous partially preserved buildings (the Parthenon, the Erechtheion, the Temple of Athena Nike, and the Propylaea) constructed during the rule of Pericles. The area around the rock was, and still is, the most prestigious part of the Greek capital. 99

Adriatic – as part of the Mediterranean Sea, the Adriatic Sea separates Italy from the Balkans. 142

Aesculapius – Latin variant of the name Asklepios, god of medicine and healing in Ancient Greece. 41, 48

Afanas'ev, Valerii Pavlovich – (born 1947), also transliterated as Valery Afanasyev; Russian pianist, conductor, and writer, famous for his unorthodox, innovative interpretations of classical masterpieces. He studied at the Moscow Conservatory with Emil Gilels and won international Bach competitions in Leipzig (1968) and Brussels (1972). In 1974, he asked for political asylum in Belgium. He is the author of nine novels (seven written in English and two in French), two plays, short stories, poems, and essays on music and literature. 17, 33–4

Afula – provincial city in northern Israel, often nicknamed 'Capital of the [Jezreel] Valley.' xvi, 38, 76–9

Aksenov, Vasilii Pavlovich – (1932–2009), also transliterated as Vasily Aksyonov; Russian short story writer and novelist. In the Soviet Union, he published the novellas *Colleagues* (1960) and *Star Ticket* (1961). He is known in the West as the author of *The Burn* (1975), *Overstocked Packaging Barrels* (*Zatovarennaia bochkotara*, 1968), *In Search of Melancholy Baby* (1987), and the critically acclaimed *Generations of Winter* (1992). From 1980 until 2004, Aksenov lived in the United States and taught at George Mason University; he then moved to France. He won the 2004 Booker – Open Russia prize for his novel *Voltairiens and Voltairiennes*. 36, 147

Aleinikov, Vladimir Dmitrievich – (born 1946), Russian poet, prose writer, essayist, translator, and artist. One of the founding members of SMOG, for his participation in the group he was expelled from the Moscow State University in 1965, but reinstated in 1966. xiv, 154

Aleshkovskii, Iuz – (born 1929), also transliterated as Yuz Aleshkovsky (real name, Iosif Efimovich Aleshkovskii); Russian novelist and author of underground songs. While serving in the Pacific Fleet, he was sentenced to four years in labour camps for violations of military discipline. In the 1950s, he started writing songs, two of which, 'Comrade Stalin' ('Tovarishch Stalin') and 'The Soviet Easter Song' ('Sovetskaia paskhal'naia') became popular, and several were published in the almanac *Metropol'* (1979). He left the Soviet Union and settled in the United States, where he published the novels *The Kangaroo* (1986), *The Hand* (1990), and *A Ring in a Case* (1995). Aleshkovskii's humorous but often tragic tales are written in colloquial, colourful language full of expletives and obscenities. 20

Aleuts – native inhabitants of western Alaska and the Aleutian Islands, which stretch for about 1,100 miles (1,770 km) southwestward from the Alaskan mainland. The name Aleuts was given to this ethnic group by the Russians, even though they call themselves Unangan ('the people'). 25, 29

Allenby – famous street in Tel Aviv, Israel, known for its many bookstores, cafes, and restaurants. 76

Anubis – Greek name of a jackal- or dog-headed god associated in Egyptian mythology with mummification and the afterlife. 130, 175

Ardis – publishing house founded in 1971 by Carl and Ellendea Proffer as an outlet for those Russian authors whose works could not be published in the Soviet Union and for those important works of Russian literature from the past that, for some reason, were difficult to find or simply forgotten. ix, xii, 7, 9, 15

Avvakum Petrov, Archpriest – (1620 or 1621–82), Russian priest of Kazan Cathedral on Red Square in Moscow. He opposed Patriarch Nikon's reforms of the Russian Orthodox Church. His autobiography and letters are considered masterpieces of seventeenth-century Russian literature. Avvakum was repeatedly imprisoned and finally burned at the stake in Pustozersk, where he had been exiled by the government. 10

Baratynskii, Evgenii Abramovich – (1800–44), also transliterated as Evgeny Baratynsky; according to Aleksandr Pushkin, the finest Russian elegiac poet. 151

Index of Names and Places

Baryshnikov, Mikhail Nikolaevich – (born 1948), Russian-American dancer, choreographer, and actor; considered to be among the greatest ballet dancers of the twentieth century. After a promising start in the Kirov Ballet in Leningrad, he defected to Canada in 1974 and went on to become a principal dancer and artistic director with the American Ballet Theatre and the New York City Ballet. 36

Batiushkov, Konstantin Nikolaevich – (1787–1855), called the 'Russian Tibullus' and the 'Russian Parny'; poet whose work largely determined the evolution of Russian poetry in the Golden Age. His most influential poetic epistle 'My Penates' ('Moi Penaty,' 1811) inspired numerous poetic responses and imitations. 30

Bäckström, Lars David – (born 1925), Swedish poet and critic; editor of the Swedish-language journals *Word and Image* (1962–70) and *Journal* (1970–3) and publisher of the journal *The Power of the Word* (1974–9). 37

Beckett, Samuel – (1906–89), Irish prose writer, dramatist, and poet; one of the key playwrights of the Theatre of the Absurd, as evidenced by his *Waiting for Godot* (1952) and *The Endgame* (1957). Beckett's reputation also rests on three novels: *Molloy* (1951), *Malone Dies* (1951), and *The Unnamable* (1953). He was awarded the 1969 Nobel Prize for Literature. 34

Berberova, Nina Nikolaevna – (1901–93), Russian writer and educator. After living in Paris for twenty-five years, she emigrated to the United States and in 1959 became an American citizen. She started teaching Russian at Yale University in 1958, but in 1963 moved to Princeton University, where she taught until her retirement in 1971. Her autobiography, *Kursiv moi*, originally written in Russian, describes her early life and years in France; it was first published in English as *The Italics Are Mine* (1969). 36

Bergman, Ingmar – (1918–2007), Swedish film director; one of the most influential filmmakers of modern cinema. Bergman's films usually deal with questions of mortality, loneliness, and faith as well as with human sexuality, illness, betrayal, and insanity. He directed sixty-two films, most of which he wrote, and over 170 plays. Bergman achieved international fame with the two 1958 films, *The Seventh Seal* and *Wild Strawberries*; his other highly acclaimed films are *Through a Glass Darkly* (1961), *Winter Light* (1962), *The Silence* (1963), *Persona* (1966), and *Cries and Whispers* (1972). 35

Bergson, Henri-Louis – (1859–1941), French philosopher, influential in the first half of the twentieth century; famous for his concepts of duration, which can be only comprehended through intuition, and *élan vital*. Bergson elucidated his theories in *The Creative Evolution*, for which he received the 1927 Nobel Prize for Literature. 68

Beria, Lavrentii Pavlovich – (1899–1953), Soviet politician and chief of the Soviet security and secret police apparatus. Although most influential during and after the Second World War and immediately after Stalin's death (for which he might have been responsible), Beria was arrested in June 1953 and charged with various crimes; that December he was tried, sentenced, and executed. 8, 21

Blok, Aleksandr Aleksandrovich – (1880–1921), influential Russian poet and a leader of the Russian Symbolist movement. Blok's most important poetic works, characterized by their melodic quality and beauty of imagery combined with experimental stress patterns and rhyming, are 'Verses about the Beautiful Lady' ('Stikhi o prekrasnoi dame,' 1904), 'An Unknown Lady' ('Neznakomka,' 1906), and the longer poems *Scythians* (*Skify*, 1918) and *The Twelve* (*Dvenadtsat'*, 1918); his most famous plays are *The Puppet Show* (*Balaganchik*, 1906) and *The Rose and the Cross* (*Roza i krest*, 1913). 27, 150

Bodensee – Lake Constance; Central Europe's third-largest lake, after Lake Balaton and Lake Geneva. A natural bulge in the course of the Rhine River, the Bodensee is some 67 km (41.6 miles) long and 14 km (8.6 miles) at its widest. 90

Boguslawski, Alexander – professor of Russian Studies at Rollins College in Winter Park, Florida, translator, iconographer, and fantasy painter. A specialist in medieval Russian art and literature, Boguslawski has been a Sokolov scholar and translator for over twenty-five years. Besides authoring a number of articles in English devoted to Sokolov's works, he has translated into Polish the essays 'The Anxious Pupa' and 'A Portrait of an Artist in America: Waiting for the Nobel,' the novels *A School for Fools* (*Szkoła dla głupków*, 1984) and *Between Dog and Wolf* (*Między psem a wilkiem*, 2001), and an excerpt from *Palisandriia*. 16, 149

Bolkonskii, Prince Andrei Nikolaevich, also transliterated as Andrey Nikolayevich Bolkonsky; one of the major fictional characters in Tolstoi's *War and Peace*. 24

Borges, Jorge Louis – (1899–1986), Argentine writer, poet, critic, and translator; a master of technique, his experiments in fiction have influenced generations of Latin American and European writers. His most famous collections of 'fictions' are *The Garden of Forking Paths* (1941) and *The Aleph* (1949). 34, 37

Borneo – third-largest island in the world, located north of Australia; politically, Borneo comprises Brunei, Indonesia, and Malaysia. 136

Botkin, Sergei Petrovich – (1832–89), famous professor, internist, and the court physician to tsars Aleksandr II and III; generally considered to be the founder of modern Russian clinical medicine and health care. 45, 51, 153

Index of Names and Places

Brodskii, Iosif Aleksandrovich – (1940–96), also transliterated as Joseph Brodsky; Russian poet and essayist. Awarded the 1987 Nobel Prize for Literature, he was chosen 1991–92 Poet Laureate of the United States. He is buried at San Michele cemetery in Venice. xii, xvi, 77

Bug – pronounced 'Boog'; 772 km (479.7 miles) long, the Bug is the fourth longest Polish river. Flowing from central Ukraine to the west, forming part of the boundary between Ukraine and Poland, it passes along the Polish-Belarussian border and into Poland, emptying into the Narew River. 121

Bunin, Ivan Alekseevich – (1870–1953), first Russian writer to win the Nobel Prize for Literature (in 1933). Among his notable works are *The Gentleman from San Francisco* (*Gospodin iz San Frantsisko*, 1915), *Mitya's Love* (*Mitina liubov'*, 1925), and the semi-autobiographical novel *The Life of Arsen'ev* (*Zhizn' Arsen'eva*, 1933). His last book of fiction was a collection of short stories, *The Dark Avenues* (*Temnye allei*,1943), which is still widely read and appreciated in Russia. 28, 36, 151

Buttadeus, Johannes – also known as John Buttadeus, one of the names of the Wandering Jew; mentioned in the thirteenth-century work of Italian astrologer Guido Bonatti. 101

Caesar, Gaius Julius – (100–44 BC), Roman military and political leader who played a critical role in the transformation of the Roman Republic into the Roman Empire. 86, 166

Caldwell, Erskine Preston – (1903–87), American author; he wrote twelve books of non-fiction, twenty-five novels, and nearly 150 short stories. Following the ideas of his father, Caldwell depicted the life of the poor in the South. He is most famous for his novels *Tobacco Road* (1932) and *God's Little Acre* (1933). 25, 26

Calvino, Italo – (1923–85), Italian journalist and writer of short stories and novels. His best-known works include the collection of short stories *Cosmicomics* (1965) and the postmodern novels *Invisible Cities* (1972), *The Castle of Crossed Destinies* (1979), and *If on a Winter's Night a Traveler* (1979). 34

Carmel – name of the main market in Tel Aviv. 76

Catullus, Gaius Valerius – (ca. 84 – ca. 54 BC), Roman poet whose poems have been preserved in an anthology of 116 *carmina* (songs), including sixty short poems, eight longer poems, and forty-eight epigrams. xvi, 77, 78, 164

Celentano, Adriano – (born 1938), Italian singer, songwriter, actor, film director, and TV personality. He has released forty albums, and his songs are well known and popular around Europe. 144, 145

Cheju-do – also transliterated as Chejudo and Jeju-do; an island off the southern tip of the Korean Peninsula. The proper name of the island is Cheju; the *do* indicates the island's status as a province. 70

Chekhov, Anton Pavlovich – (1860–1904), Russian short story writer and playwright. His playwriting career produced four classics: *The Seagull* (1895), *Uncle Vania* (1896), *Three Sisters* (1901), and *The Cherry Orchard* (1904). Among his best short stories are 'The Steppe' (1888), 'The Grasshopper' (1892), 'The House with the Mezzanine' (1896), 'Ward No. 6' (1897), 'Gooseberries' (1898), 'Man in a Case' (1898), and 'The Lady with a Lap Dog' (1899). 9, 20, 60, 101, 168

Chaikovskii, Petr Il'ich – (1840–93), also transliterated as Chaikovsky or Tschaikowsky, in English commonly rendered as Peter Ilich Tchaikovsky; the most popular Russian composer of all time. His oeuvre includes seven symphonies, eleven operas, three ballets, five suites, three piano concertos, a violin concerto, eleven overtures, four cantatas, twenty choral works, three string quartets, a string sextet, and more than 100 songs and piano pieces. His most popular works, besides symphonies and songs, include *Sleeping Beauty* (1875–6), *Swan Lake* (1875–6), *Eugene Onegin* (1877–8), the *1812 Overture* (1880), *Romeo and Juliet* (1880), *The Nutcracker* (1891–2), and *Queen of Spades* (1890). 6, 65

Chud' – also rendered as Chud or Chude; term applied in the early Russian chronicles to Finno-Ugric peoples inhabiting the areas of modern Finland, Estonia, and northwestern Russia. 48

Chukcha – 'man with many deer'; an inhabitant of Chukotka, a territory stretching from the Arctic Ocean to the Pacific Ocean, covering 700,000 square km (435,959 square miles), separated from Alaska by Bering Strait. 25, 29

Cicero, Marcus Tullius – (106–43 BC), Roman statesman, lawyer, political theorist, and philosopher; one of Rome's greatest orators. His works include philosophical writings, speeches, orations, and letters. 51, 85, 166

Clairaut, Alexis Claude – (1713–65), French mathematician known for his work on celestial mechanics, including the shape of the earth and the motion of the moon, and for his computation of the date for the return of Halley's comet. 118

Coetzee, John Maxwell – (born 1940), novelist, literary critic, translator, and academic from South Africa (now an Australian citizen); winner of the 2003 Nobel Prize for Literature. 34

Coleridge, Samuel Taylor – (1772–1834), English poet, critic, and philosopher. Along with William Wordsworth, Coleridge was one of the founders of the Romantic movement in England and one of the Lake Poets; best known for his poems 'The Rime of the Ancient Mariner' (1797–8), 'Kubla Khan' (1797–8), and 'Christabel' (1797–1801), and for his prose work *Biographia Literaria* (1815). 59

Index of Names and Places

Cooper, James Fennimore – (1789–1851), prolific and popular American writer; best remembered for the series of novels known as the Leatherstocking Tales, featuring frontiersman Natty Bumppo: *The Pioneers* (1823), *The Last of the Mohicans* (1826), *The Prairie* (1827), *The Pathfinder* (1840), and *The Deerslayer* (1841). He was enormously popular in Europe, where he was admired not only by thousands of adventure-hungry readers but by such luminaries as Schubert, Hugo, and Balzac. 35

Copacabana – district of Rio de Janeiro that grew up around the famous Copacabana beach; well known for its night life and exuberant New Year's Eve celebrations. 40

Cyclops – or *kyklops;* in Greek mythology, a giant with a single eye in the middle of its forehead. 93

Dali, Salvador – (1904–89), famous Surrealist painter; born in Figueres, Catalonia, Spain. 41, 49

Damocles – hero of a classical story about King Dionysius II of Syracuse. After Damocles told the king how fortunate he was to wield such great power and authority, the wise king, in order to teach Damocles an important lesson, changed places with the courtier for a day. In the evening, at the end of a banquet, Damocles looked up and noticed a sharp sword hanging over his head fastened to a single horse hair. Terrified, he immediately lost his appetite and his wish to be as fortunate as the king. The expression 'sword of Damocles' is frequently used to indicate the imminent and ever-present peril faced by those in positions of power. More generally, it is used to denote the sense of danger caused by a precarious situation. 4

Dante Aligheri – (1265–1321), Italian poet whose major opus, the *Divine Comedy* (*Divina Commedia*), is considered to be the greatest literary work written in the Italian language and a masterpiece of world literature. The poem describes Dante's journey through Hell (*Inferno*), Purgatory (*Purgatorio*), and Paradise (*Paradiso*), guided first by the Roman poet Virgil and then by Beatrice, the subject of his love and of another of his works, *La Vita Nuova*. 35, 46, 49, 154

Darskii, Dmitrii Sergeevich – (1883–1957), Russian literary scholar and bibliographer, director of the library of the Theological Institute of the Moscow Patriarchate; author of studies of Fedor Tiutchev's poetry (1913), Aleksandr Pushkin's *Little Tragedies* (1915), and of Afanasii Fet's poetry (1916). 17

Da Vinci, Leonardo – (1452–1519), arguably the greatest mind of the Italian Renaissance and the author of the celebrated portrait of Mona Lisa (La Gioconda). 18, 149

Dickinson, Emily – (1830–86), American poet. Only a few of her almost 1,800 poems have been published, and those that were published during her lifetime were usually altered significantly by the publishers to make them more conventional and standardized. Her poems are unique for their short or irregular-length lines, they are usually untitled and often use slant rhyme as well as irregular capitalization and punctuation. 35, 161

Diurer, Evgeniia – (born 1981), photojournalist, wife of Viktor Erofeev. 80, 165

Dostoevskii, Fedor Mikhailovich – (1821–81), also transliterated as Fyodor Dostoevsky or Dostoyevsky; great Russian novelist, short story writer, journalist, and thinker. His most famous works include *Crime and Punishment* (1866), *The Idiot* (1869), *The Possessed* (1872), and *The Brothers Karamazov* (1880). 18, 24, 34, 39, 151

Drozhzhin, Spiridon Dmitrievich – (1848–1930), Russian poet who glorified the Russian village and nature in his works. He translated some of Rilke's poems, and his article 'The Contemporary German Poet Rainer Rilke' appeared in the journal *The Road* (*Put'*) in 1913. 6

Dürrenmatt, Friedrich – (1921–90), Swiss author and dramatist; known for his statement: 'a story is not finished until it has taken the worst turn.' He is famous for his plays, *Romulus the Great* (*Romulus der Grosse*, 1949), *The Visit* (*Der Besuch der alten Dame*, 1956), and *The Physicists* (*Die Physiker*, 1962), and for his short story 'The Tunnel' ('Der Tunnel,' 1952). 31

Dzaudzikau – Ossetian name of the capital of North Ossetia (founded in 1784); in Russian, Vladikavkaz. 136

Elbe – one of the major rivers of Central Europe; it originates in the Krkonose Mountains before traversing much of the Czech Republic and Germany and then flows past Hamburg into the North Sea, for a total length of 1,094 km (680 miles). 96

Ephron, Nora – (born 1941), American film director, producer, screenwriter, and novelist; best known for her romantic comedies. Ephron is a triple nominee for the Oscar for Original Screenplay for *Silkwood*, *When Harry Met Sally*, and *Sleepless in Seattle*. Her personal life inspired probably her best-known novel, *Heartburn* (1983), which in 1986 came out as a film starring Jack Nicholson and Meryl Streep. 29

Erenburg, Il'ia Grigor'evich – (1891–1967), also transliterated as Ilya Grigoryevich Ehrenburg; Russian writer and journalist. Among his satiric novels are *The Extraordinary Adventures of Julio Jurenito and His Disciples* (1921) and *The Stormy Life of Lasik Roitschwantz* (1928). The title of his postwar novel *The Thaw* (1954) became a term signifying the climate of optimism and the lessening of governmental controls in the USSR after Stalin's death. 31

Erofeev, Venedikt Vasil'evich – (1938–90), also transliterated as Venedict Vasilyevich Yerofeyev; Russian writer. His 1969 novel (poem in prose) *Moscow to* *the End of the Line* (*Moskva-Petushki*) became a sensation when it appeared in 1973 in Jerusalem; it was published in Russia only in 1989. 44, 153

Erofeev, Viktor Vladimirovich – (born 1947), popular Russian author of many books, including *Russian Beauty* (*Russkaia krasavitsa*, 1990), *Life with an Idiot* (*Zhizn' s idiotom*, 1991), and *Good Stalin* (*Khoroshii Stalin*, 2004). His works have been translated into twenty-seven languages, and *Life with an Idiot* was turned into an opera by Alfred Schnittke (1992) and into a film by Aleksandr Rogozhkin (1993). Since 1995, Erofeev has been the host of a popular cultural-literary TV program, *Apokrif*. 165

Ershov, Petr Pavlovich – (1815–69), also transliterated as Yershov; Russian poet, remembered today for his 1834 fairy tale in verse, *Little Hunchbacked Pony* (*Konek-gorbunok*). vii

Esenin, Sergei Aleksandrovich – (1895–1925), also transliterated as Sergey Yesenin; Russian lyrical poet. His unruly behaviour and a series of complex relationships (he was married five times) made him a celebrity, but his drinking and disagreements with official state policies led to his suicide by hanging in his hotel room. 30

Faulkner, William – (1897–1962), American novelist, short story writer, poet, and screenwriter; one of the most influential writers of the twentieth century and winner of the 1949 Nobel Prize for Literature. He is known for his complex, experimental style, the use of stream-of-consciousness, and for placing the action of most of his works in Mississippi. His most celebrated novels include *The Sound and the Fury* (1929), *As I Lay Dying* (1930), *Light in August* (1932), *Absalom, Absalom!* (1936), and *The Unvanquished* (1938). 35

Fedotov, Pavel Andreevich – (1815–52), Russian painter. Having mastered the technique of watercolour painting, in 1846 he started to work in oils. He produced small, intimate, mildly satirical paintings showing the foibles of Russian society. Fedotov is considered to be a precursor of Russian Realism. He died in a mental institution when he was thirty-seven. 16

Fellini, Federico – (1920–93), Italian director, one of the most widely recognized filmmakers of the twentieth century. Four of his works won the Oscar for Best Foreign Film: *La strada* (1954), *Le Notti di Cabiria* (1957), *8½* (1963), and *Amarcord* (1973); another famous Fellini film, *La dolce vita* (1960), won the Golden Palm at the Cannes Film Festival. 35

Flaubert, Gustave – (1821–80), French author, one of the great Western novelists; famous especially for his first published novel, *Madame Bovary* (1857), and for his unending search for *le mot juste* (the precise word). 20, 28, 35

Freud, Sigmund – (1856–1939), Austrian physician and founder of psychoanalysis. 32, 39

Galatas – small town at the eastern tip of the Peloponnese Peninsula, separated from the island of Poros by a narrow strait. 67

Galich, Aleksandr Arkad'evich – (1918–77), real name: Aleksandr Arkad'evich Ginzburg; Russian poet, screenwriter, playwright, and singer-songwriter. Galich was very critical of Soviet reality and was expelled from the Soviet Writers' Union and the Union of Cinematographers; in 1974 he was forced to emigrate, first to Norway and later, through Munich, to Paris. 20

García Lorca, Federico – (1898–1936), great twentieth-century Spanish poet and dramatist. As a poet, he is remembered for the *Gypsy Ballads* (*Romancero Gitano*, 1928), the *Poem of the Deep Song* (*Poema del Cante Jondo*, 1931), and *Lament for Ignacio Sánchez Mejias* (*Llanto por Ignacio Sánchez Mejias*, 1935). As a playwright, he is known for the three 'folk tragedies': *Blood Wedding* (*Bodas de sangre*, 1932), *Yerma* (1934), and *The House of Bernarda Alba* (*La casa de Bernarda Alba*, 1936). 83, 156

García Márquez, Gabriel – (born 1927), Colombian novelist, short story writer, screenwriter, and journalist. One of Latin America's most famous writers, he was awarded the 1982 Nobel Prize for Literature. His novels, such as *One Hundred Years of Solitude* (1967) and *Love in the Time of Cholera* (1985), popularized the style later called Magical Realism and widely used by Latin American writers. 34

Gertsen, Aleksandr Ivanovich – (1812–70), commonly rendered in English as Herzen; major Russian pro-Western writer and thinker. His memoir *My Past and Thoughts* (*Byloe i dumy*, 1868) is often considered the best example of autobiography in Russian literature. Gertsen left Russia in 1847 and founded in London the Free Russian Press which published, besides literary works, the periodicals *Polar Star* (*Poliarnaia Zvezda*), *The Bell* (*Kolokol*), and *Voices from Russia* (*Golosa iz Rossii*). 34

Goethe, Johann Wolfgang von – (1749–1832), German poet, novelist, and dramatist. Goethe's most important work is the two-part drama *Faust* (Part I, 1808; Part II, 1832). His other well-known works include the poems, *The Alder King* (1782) and *Roman Elegies* (1790); the Bildungsroman, *Wilhelm Meister's Apprenticeship* (1796); and the epistolary novel, *The Sorrows of Young Werther* (1774). 5, 153, 160

Gogol', Nikolai Vasil'evich – (1809–52), born in Ukraine but writing in Russian, he is often called the 'father of Russian Realism.' Gogol' was a great innovator and is a completely unique voice in Russian literature; his fondness for language combined with his stylistic brilliance make him a precursor of Russian Modernism. His most famous works are the novel *Dead Souls* (*Mertvye dushi*, 1842); the play *The Inspector-General* (*Revizor*, 1836); and the short story 'The Overcoat' ('Shinel',' 1842). 34, 163–5

Gol'dshtein, Aleksandr Leonidovich – (1957–2006), Russian writer, essayist, journalist, winner of the Antibooker and Andrei Belyi prizes; he was born in Tallinn and died in Tel Aviv. Sokolov's essay, 'About the Other Encounter' (published in *Zerkalo*, no. 27, in 2006, and devoted to the first meeting between Gol'dshtein and Sokolov in Tel Aviv) is a response to Gol'dshtein's 'About a Certain Encounter' ('Ob odnoi vstreche,' published in Gol'dshtein's longer work, *Aspects of Spiritual Marriage* (*Aspekty dukhovnogo braka*, 2001). xvi

Gor'kii, Maksim – (1868–1936), also rendered as Maxim Gorky, real name: Aleksei Maksimovich Peshkov; Russian writer, founder of Socialist Realism, and a political activist. A major street and a famous park in Moscow were dedicated to him (later Gor'kii Street was renamed Tverskaia, its original name). 24–6, 29, 158

Griboedov, Aleksandr Sergeevich – (1795–1829), Russian diplomat, playwright, and composer; murdered by a mob in Tehran. His fame rests on the verse comedy *Woe from Wit* (*Gore ot uma*,1823), still one of the most frequently staged plays in Russia. Many of the names in the comedy reveal characteristics of their bearers. He is also remembered as a composer of two waltzes, one in E minor and another in A flat major. vii, 50, 65, 157, 162, 164

Grimm Brothers – Jacob (1785–1863) and Wilhelm Karl (1786–1859), German scholars best known for their collections of folk and fairy tales. In 1812, they published eighty-six German fairy tales in a volume entitled *Children's and Household Tales* (*Kinder- und Hausmärchen*). This was followed by a second volume of seventy tales in 1814. The tales proved so popular (even though some were criticized as not suitable for children) that by 1857, in the seventh edition, their number had grown to 211. 67, 162

Guarneri – family name of famous luthiers from Cremona, Italy, and subsequently the name of instruments produced by them in the seventeenth and eighteenth centuries. The quality of the instruments is comparable to those crafted by the Amati and Stradivarius families. 117

Gubanov, Leonid Georgievich – (1946–83), Russian poet, one of the founders of SMOG. xiv, 155, 157

Guevara, Ernesto 'Che' – (1928–67), known as 'El Che' or 'Che'; Argentine Marxist revolutionary, intellectual, guerrilla leader, diplomat, and major figure of the Cuban Revolution. 136

Gulag – abbreviation of Glavnoe upravlenie lagerei (Main Directorate of the Labour Camps), now used to denote the system of Soviet labour camps. The term was popularized by Alexander Solzhenitsyn's novel *The Gulag Archipelago*. 35

Gumilev, Nikolai Stepanovich – (1886–1921), also transliterated as Gumilyov, Goumilev, and Gumileff; influential Russian poet, founder of the Acmeist movement. He and the poet Sergei Gorodetskii compared writing a good poem to building a cathedral. In 1921, he was accused of participating in a monarchist conspiracy and executed. Two collections of his poems were published: *The Pearls* (1910) and the *Alien Sky* (1912). His 1919 poem 'The Streetcar that Got Lost' ('Zabludivshiisia tramvai') is considered to be one of his best and most influential. 47, 156

Hegel, Georg Wilhelm Friedrich – (1770–1831), important modern philosopher; author of *Phenomenology of Spirit* (or *Phenomenology of Mind*, 1807), his account of the evolution of consciousness from sense-perception to absolute knowledge; *Science of Logic*, in three volumes (1811, 1812, and 1816; revised 1831); *Encyclopedia of the Philosophical Sciences* (1816; revised in 1827 and 1830), which is a summary of his entire philosophical system; and *Elements of the Philosophy of Right* (1822), explaining his political philosophy. Hegel has been an enormous influence on Western thinkers. 81

Heldt-Monter, Barbara – professor of Slavic Languages and Literatures at the University of British Columbia, in Vancouver, B.C.; critic, scholar, and translator. She has written on a wide variety of subjects and writers, including Karolina Pavlova, Tolstoi, Koz'ma Prutkov, Solzhenitsyn, and Nabokov. 17

Hellas – pronounced *Ellás*; Greece. 67

Hemingway, Ernest – (1899–1961), highly acclaimed American novelist, short story writer, and journalist; winner of the Pulitzer Prize in 1953 for *The Old Man and the Sea* and the 1954 Nobel Prize for Literature. His distinctive writing style, which significantly affected the development of twentieth-century literature, is characterized by economy and understatement, in contrast to the style of his literary rival William Faulkner. xiii, 26, 31

Hesiod – early Greek poet and rhapsode, presumed to have lived around 700 BC. His writings serve as a major source on Greek mythology, and also discuss farming techniques, astronomy, and time-keeping. 31

Hessen – in English, Hesse; one of the German states (Länder), with Wiesbaden as its capital. 67

Hiawatha – leader of the Onondaga and Mohawk nations of Native Americans who lived in either the 1100s, 1400s, or 1500s. Hiawatha was a follower of the Great Peacemaker, a prophet, and a spiritual leader as well as the originator of the idea of the Iroquois Confederacy. The myth of Hiawatha and his lover Minnehaha was created by Henry Wadsworth Longfellow in his 1855 epic *The Song of Hiawatha*. 19

Iar – also transliterated as Yar; Moscow restaurant famous for its Gypsy music and 'decadent' atmosphere. 74, 163

Iasnaia Poliana – also transliterated as Yasnaia or Yasnaya Polyana; Tolstoi's estate and the place where he is buried. 62, 74, 161

Iauza – also rendered in English as Yauza; left tributary of the Moscow River and the largest river within Moscow's city limits. 48

Ionesco, Eugene – (1909–94), Romanian and French playwright and dramatist; one of the major playwrights of the Theatre of the Absurd. His plays depict the banality, solitude, and insignificance of human existence. Among the best known are *The Bald Soprano* (1948) and *Rhinoceros* (1959). 35

Johnson, Don Barton – professor emeritus of Slavic Languages and Literatures, University of California at Santa Barbara, where he was a founder of the Sokolov Archive; one of the most dedicated and prolific scholars of Vladimir Nabokov and Sasha Sokolov, and author of many books and articles. x, xi, xiii, xiv, xv, 4, 16, 149

Joyce, James – (1882–1941), Irish writer, noted for his experimental use of language; one of the most influential writers of the twentieth century. He is best known for his landmark novel *Ulysses* (1922) and its highly controversial successor *Finnegans Wake* (1939), as well as the short story collection *Dubliners* (1914) and the semi-autobiographical novel *A Portrait of the Artist as a Young Man* (1916). vii, 28, 34

Jupiter – patron deity of the Roman state, who ruled over laws and social order. In Roman mythology, Jupiter is the equivalent of Zeus in Greek mythology. Jupiter is the father of Mars and the grandfather of Romulus and Remus, the mythical founders of Rome. 86, 158

Kafka, Franz – (1883–1924), major German-language fiction writer; born into a middle-class Jewish family in Prague. Most of his works, published after his death, greatly influenced Western literature. The celebrated novella *The Metamorphosis* (1915), and two novels, *The Trial* (1925) and *The Castle* (1926), deal with individuals entangled in a nightmarishly impersonal and oppressive bureaucratic world. 35

Kaganovich, Lazar' Moiseevich – (1893–1991), Soviet politician, administrator, and close associate of Stalin. For his ruthlessness in executing Stalin's orders, he was given the nickname 'Iron Lazar'.' 8

Kaganskaia, Maia Lazarevna – (born 1938), essayist and literary critic. She left the Soviet Union in 1976 for Israel and has published in many Russian-language literary journals in Israel and Europe. She wrote introductions to the novels of Mikhail Bulgakov and Vladimir Nabokov. Her essays, devoted to literary and political topics, are characterized by virtuosity of form and paradoxical thoughts. 32–3

Kandinskii, Vasilii – (1866–1944), also transliterated as Wassily Kandinsky; Russian painter, printmaker, and art theorist. He is credited with creating the first modern abstract works. These were a result of a long period of experiments and theoretical considerations, which he formulated into the idea of *inner necessity*. He was influenced by theosophy, according to which creation is a geometrical progression, beginning with a single point, and the creative aspect of forms is expressed by a descending series of circles, triangles, and squares. Kandinskii elucidated his theories in two books: *Concerning the Spiritual in Art* (1910) and *Point and Line to Plane* (1926). 28

Kant, Immanuel – (1724–1804), last great philosopher of modern Europe during the Enlightenment. His most prominent work was the *Critique of Pure Reason* (1781, revised 1787), an investigation of the limitations and structure of reason itself and also an attack on traditional metaphysics and epistemology. 128

Khachaturian, Aram – (1903–78), Soviet-Armenian composer whose oeuvre was often influenced by Armenian folk music. His compositions include concertos for violin, cello, and piano; concerto rhapsodies for the same instruments; three symphonies; and the ballets *Spartacus* (1950–4) and *Gaiane* (1939–41) – the latter features in its final act what is probably Khachaturian's most famous work, the 'Sabre Dance.' 18

Khlebnikov, Velimir – (1885–1922), real name: Viktor Vladimirovich Khlebnikov; member of the most significant Russian Futurist group, Hylaea. He is known for poems such as 'Incantation by Laughter,' 'Bobeobi Were Sung the Lips,' 'The Grasshopper' (all 1908–9), and 'Snake Train' (1910); the prologue to the Futurist opera *Victory Over the Sun* (1913); dramatic works such as *Death's Mistake* (1915); prose works such as *Ka* (1915); and the so-called super-tale *Zangezi* (1922). With the poet Kruchenykh, he invented *zaum*, translated as 'transreason,' 'transrationality,' or 'beyond sense,' an experimental poetic language characterized by onomatopoeias and neologisms, and often difficult to comprehend. 30, 163

Khoroshevo – originally a small village known from the time of Ivan the Terrible. Its neighbour, the village of Mnevniki, was populated by fishermen. Today, the old villages form the area known as Khoroshevo-Mnevniki, a district of Moscow, incorporated into the city in 1960. 50, 157

Khrushchev, Nikita Sergeevich – (1894–1971), following the death of Stalin, served as the general secretary of the Communist Party of the Soviet Union from 1953 to 1964 and as the chairman of the Council of Ministers from 1958 to 1964. Khrushchev was responsible for the de-Stalinization of the USSR, as well as several liberal reforms in areas ranging from agriculture to foreign policy, but after the Cuban missile crisis he was removed from power and replaced by Leonid Brezhnev. 8

Kozlovskii, Vladimir Danilovich – (born 1947), Russian journalist, translator, and linguist. He emigrated to the United States in 1974, where he graduated from Yale University. His published works include *The Uncensored Russian*

Chastushka (1978), *The New Uncensored Chastushka* (1982), a four-volume compilation of thieves' dictionaries (1983), and *The Jargon of Russian Homosexual Subculture* (1986). Since 1979, he has been a BBC correspondent in New York City and a frequent contributor to *Novoe Russkoe Slovo*. 17

Kremer, Gidon – (born 1947), one of the world's leading violinists and a conductor. Born in Latvia, he studied at the Riga School of Music and later with David Oistrakh at the Moscow Conservatory. In 1980, he left the Soviet Union and settled in Germany. 33

Kuprin, Aleksandr Ivanovich – (1870–1938), Russian writer, explorer, and adventurer whose best-known novellas include *Moloch* (1896), *Olesya* (1898), *The Duel* (1905), *Junior Captain Rybnikov* (1906), *Emerald* (1907), *The Garnet Bracelet* (1911), and *The Pit* (1915). He left Russia in 1919, but returned in 1937. 34

Kuz'minskii, Konstantin Konstantinovich – (born 1940), Russian performance poet who left the Soviet Union in 1978; lives in upstate New York. To avoid problems with censorship, he memorized thousands of poems by unofficial Russian poets, and published them in the West as *The Blue Lagoon Anthology of Modern Russian Poetry* (1980). Among his other publications is a collection of Russian poetry, *The Living Mirror* (1972). 5, 36

Lacaille, Nicholas Louis de – (1713–62), French astronomer. Lacaille was the first to measure a South African arc of the meridian; he also compiled an extensive catalogue of southern stars. 118

Lalande, Joseph Jérôme Le Français de – (1732–1807), French astronomer; from 1762 professor of astronomy at the College de France and from 1768 director of the Paris Observatory. 118

La Pérouse, Jean François de Galaup, Comte de – (1741–88), French navigator and explorer. 120

La Plata – region surrounding Rio de la Plata, the estuary at the confluence of the Uruguay River and the Paraña River, separating Argentina and Uruguay; this region is considered to be the cradle of the tango. 106, 159

Lel' – in Slavic mythology, supposedly the son of Lada, goddess of beauty, and thus the equivalent of the Greek Eros and Roman Amor. However, many scholars believe that both Lada and Lel' were not Slavic gods at all, but late anthropomorphic transformations of sounds and words in folk songs, misinterpreted by the medieval clergy as names of pagan deities. 45

Lethe – in Classical Greek, Lethe literally means 'forgetfulness' or 'concealment.' In Greek mythology, Lethe is one of the several rivers of Hades: those who drank from it experienced complete forgetfulness. Cf. Mnemosyne. 6, 18, 19

Limpopo – river in central southern Africa that flows into the Indian Ocean; immortalized by Rudyard Kipling in his *Just So Stories* (1902). 94

Linnaeus, Carl – (1707–78), Swedish botanist, physician, and zoologist; developed what became known as *Linnaean taxonomy*, the system of scientific classification now widely used in the biological sciences. 91

Li Qingzhao – (1084–ca. 1151), also transliterated as Li Ch'ing-chao; Chinese writer and poet of the Song Dynasty, regarded by many as the premier female poet in the Chinese language and a master of delicate restraint. Only about 100 of her poems survive; they mostly trace her varying fortunes in life. 48

Lobachevskii, Nikolai Ivanovich – (1792–1856), also transliterated as Lobachevsky; Russian mathematician whose main achievement is the development of a non-Euclidean, hyperbolic geometry. He also developed a method for the approximation of the roots of algebraic equations; now known as the Dandelin-Gräffe method because of the two other mathematicians who discovered it independently, in Russia it is called the Lobachevskii method. 102

Lomonosov, Mikhail Vasil'evich – (1711–65), self-made Russian 'Renaissance' man, professor, artist, and statesman. Lomonosov made a brilliant career, studying first in Kiev, and then Marburg. After returning from Germany, he was appointed a professor of chemistry at St Petersburg University, and in 1755 he founded Moscow University. He made important contributions to astronomy, chemistry, physics, mineralogy, history, art, philology, and optics. Lomonosov was also a poet, instrumental in the development of the modern Russian literary language and poetry. 66, 67

Lu Lun – (737?–99), Chinese poet of the Tang period. 132, 133, 176

Luther, Martin – (1483–1546), German monk, theologian, university professor, and church reformer whose ideas inspired the Protestant Reformation and changed the course of Western civilization. He translated the Bible into the vernacular, making it more accessible to ordinary people, standardizing the German language, and influencing German culture; the translation also helped in the preparation of the *King James Bible*. 67, 162

Luther King, Jr, Martin – (1929–68), prominent in the U.S. civil rights movement. He was the leader of the Montgomery Bus Boycott (1955–6), a co-founder of the Southern Christian Leadership Conference (1957), and is best known for his 'I Have a Dream' speech delivered during the 1963 march on Washington. King received the 1964 Nobel Peace Prize for his efforts to end segregation and racial discrimination through civil disobedience and other non-violent means; in 1967, he was shot dead in Memphis, Tennessee. 67

Index of Names and Places

Maiakovskii, Vladimir Vladimirovich – (1893–1930), also transliterated as Mayakovsky; Russian poet and playwright, one of the foremost representatives of early twentieth-century Russian Futurism. In his poetry, he employed the graphic division of lines into intonation 'steps,' extended metaphors, hyperboles, as well as original and inventive rhyme. He described his poetic craft in an essay, 'How to Make Verses' ('Kak delat' stikhi,' 1926). Among Maiakovskii's best-remembered works are the poems 'A Cloud in Trousers' ('Oblako v shtanakh,' 1914–15), 'The Left March' ('Levyi marsh,' 1919), and 'Well' ('Khorosho,' 1929), and two plays, *The Bedbug* (*Klop*, 1928) and *The Bathhouse* (*Bania*, 1929). Despite his initial support for the Soviet cause and his glorification of Lenin, Maiakovskii became disillusioned with the regime as well as with his personal life, which led to his suicide. xiii, 27, 30, 160

Mal'tsev, Iurii Vladimirovich – (born 1932), Russian journalist, correspondent of Radio Svoboda in Italy. After graduating in 1955 from Leningrad State University, he taught Italian at the Department of History at Moscow State University. He emigrated to Italy in 1974 and published *Free Russian Literature, 1955–1975* (1976); he is also the author of a detailed study of Ivan Bunin (1994). 17

Mandel'shtam, Osip Emil'evich – (1891–1938), also transliterated as Osip Emilevich Mandelstam; Russian poet and essayist. He was one of the foremost members of the Acmeist school of poetry and the author of the Acmeist manifesto, *The Morning of Acmeism* (*Utro akmeizma*, 1913); his first collection of poems, *The Stone* (*Kamen'*), came out the same year. His second book of poems, *Tristia*, was published in Berlin in 1922. In 1934, he was arrested for writing an epigram about Stalin, but rather than being sent to a labour camp, he was exiled to Voronezh; however, in 1938, arrested again and sentenced to hard labour, he died in one of the camps. 25, 149

Mann, Thomas – (1875–1955), German novelist and short story writer; winner of the 1929 Nobel Prize for Literature. Mann is known for his series of epic novels and stories providing insights into the psychology of artists and intellectuals. His most famous works are the novels *The Magic Mountain* (*Der Zauberberg*, 1924), *Joseph and His Brothers* (*Joseph und seine Brüder*, 1933–42), and *Doktor Faustus* (1947), as well as the novella *Death in Venice* (*Der Tod in Venedig*, 1912). 35

Mao Dun – (1896–1981), pen name of Shen Dehong (Shen Yanbing); Chinese writer, cultural critic, and journalist, considered to be one of the best modern Chinese novelists and short story writers. He was China's minister of culture from 1949 to 1965. He is best known for *Midnight* (1933), a grand novel depicting life in Shanghai, and *Spring Silkworms* (1956). 62

Marburg – a city in Hesse, Germany; particularly in the nineteenth century, its university enjoyed a great reputation and attracted many foreign students. 66–7

Matathias – one of the names of the Wandering Jew. 121

Matich, Olga – professor in the Department of Slavic Languages and Literatures at the University of California at Berkeley, she specializes in Russian Modernism and émigré literature and culture, as well as problems of gender, decadence, and the relationship between literature and the other arts. 16, 149

Melpomene – originally the Muse of Singing, she became the Muse of Tragedy, as she is most commonly known today; her name derives from the Greek verb *melpo* or *melpomai*, meaning 'to celebrate with dance and song.' 73, 75

Melville, Herman – (1819–91), American novelist, short story writer, essayist, and poet. His first two books, *Typee* (1846) and *Omoo* (1847), were well received, but by the time of his death, he was almost completely forgotten. Today, his longest novel, *Moby-Dick* (1851), is considered to be a masterpiece of American and world fiction. xiii, 35

Methuselah – oldest person in the Hebrew Bible; mentioned in Genesis as the son of Enoch, the father of Lamech, and the grandfather of Noah. He lived 969 years. Today, Methuselah is a synonym for any person living to a great age. 70

Metula – also spelled Metullah; city in northern Israel, founded in 1896. 78

Michener, James – (1907–97), American author of more than forty works, mostly novels about various countries and about generations of their inhabitants. His major books include *Tales of the South Pacific* (for which he won the 1948 Pulitzer Prize for Fiction), *Centennial* (1974, and a TV miniseries), *Caribbean* (1989), *Alaska* (1988), *Texas* (1985), and *Poland* (1983). 28, 29

Miller, Henry – (1891–1980), American writer and painter, known for creating a new sort of 'novel' in which he mixes fiction, autobiography, social criticism, philosophy, free associations, and theology. His most characteristic works are *Tropic of Cancer* (1934), *Black Spring* (1936), and *Tropic of Capricorn* (1939). He also wrote travel memoirs and literary criticism. 66–7

Miłosz, Czesław – (1911–2004), poet, prose writer, and translator; one of the most important Polish poets of the twentieth century and winner of the 1980 Nobel Prize for Literature. After defecting to France in 1951, he moved to the United States, where from 1961 to 1978 he was a professor of Slavic Languages and Literatures at the University of California at Berkeley. His collections of poetry include *A Poetical Treatise* (*Traktat poetycki*, 1957), *City without a Name* (*Miasto bez imienia*, 1969), and *Chronicles* (*Kroniki*, 1989). His best-known prose works are *The Captive Mind* (*Zniewolony umysł*, 1953) and *The Issa Valley* (*Dolina Issy*, 1955); he also wrote *The History of Polish Literature* (1969). 33

Miretskii, David – (born 1939), also spelled Meretskii; painter. He studied at the Kiev Art Institute from 1965 to 1969. The unorthodox subject matter of his work forced him to exhibit 'underground' in Kiev and Moscow, which led to his arrest and the confiscation of certain of his works. After his release, Miretskii left the Soviet Union, and arrived in the United States with his family in 1975, first settling in Cincinnati and later moving to New York City, where he continues to live and work. 36

Mnemosyne – the personification of memory in Greek mythology. Mnemosyne was the daughter of Gaia and Uranus. After sleeping with Zeus for nine nights, she gave birth to the nine Muses. Mnemosyne is also the name of a river in Hades, the counterpart of the river Lethe. 5, 53

Mobutu, Joseph Désiré – (1930–97), one of the longest-surviving African dictators. In 1967, he established a presidential form of government headed by himself, and four years later, in 1971, he changed the name of his country from Congo to Zaïre. In 1997, shortly before his death due to cancer, he was ousted and went into hiding in Morocco. His full name, Sese Seko Nkuku Ngbendu Wa Za Banga, can be loosely translated as 'The Great Unstoppable Warrior Who Goes from Victory to Victory, Leaving Fire in His Wake.' 137

Moderati, Majorette – heroine of Sokolov's novel *Palisandriia* (in English translation, *Astrophobia*). 20

Moira – in Greek mythology, the personification of destiny. The Moirae controlled the metaphorical thread of life of every mortal and immortal from birth to death. Even the gods feared the Moirae. Their names were Clotho (the one who spun the thread of life); Lachesis (the one who measured the thread of life); and Atropos (the one who cut the thread of life and chose the manner of a person's death). Cf. Parcae. 39, 53, 66

Mokhovaia – street in the centre of Moscow, extends from the Borovitskaia Tower of the Kremlin to Manezh Square. Mokhovaia Ulitsa (Moss Street) derives its name from the dry moss, used for insulating wooden houses, sold at the market on that street. Moscow State University's Department of Journalism is located at no. 9, and the Russian State Library (formerly, the Rumiantsev Museum and, from 1921, the Lenin Library) is at no. 26. 65

Molotov, Viacheslav Mikhailovich – (1890–1986), Soviet leader. In 1939, he was appointed commissar of foreign affairs (foreign minister), and as such negotiated the non-aggression pact with Germany that August. Molotov is famous for his radio announcement of the German invasion of the Soviet

Union. A bitter conflict between Molotov and Khrushchev (then the general secretary of the Central Committee) in June 1957 led to Molotov's dismissal from all his posts. 8

Monteverdi, Claudio Giovanni Antonio – (1567–1643), Italian composer, viola da gamba player, and singer; credited with making in his compositions a transition from the Renaissance to the Baroque (developing the basso continuo). He is the author of one of the first complete operas: *L'Orfeo* (1608). 130

Nabokov, Vladimir Vladimirovich – (1899–1977), one of the literary masters of the twentieth century. Nabokov is the author of short stories, poems, plays, translations of prose and poetry, chess problems, scientific papers on lepidoptera, and celebrated novels, including *Lolita* (1955), *Pnin* (1957), *Invitation to a Beheading* (1959), *Pale Fire* (1962), and *The Gift* (1963). viii, ix, 16, 33–4, 42, 159

Nebuchadnezzar – (ca. 630–562 BC), properly Nebuchadnezzar II; ruler of Babylon from about 605 BC to 562 BC. He is remembered for his monumental building program, construction of the Hanging Gardens, and his role in the biblical book of Daniel. 3

Nedbailo, Nikolai Mikhailovich – (born 1944), Russian painter, one of the members of SMOG. In 1966, he was exiled for 'parasitism,' but allowed to return to Moscow after a few months. xiv, 50, 154, 157

Neizvestnyi, Ernst Iosifovich – (born 1925), famous Russian sculptor. His last name translates to 'unknown' in English. In 1976, he emigrated to Switzerland, and in subsequent years was a guest lecturer at the University of Oregon and at the University of California at Berkeley. In the late 1980s, he created for Magna Gallery in San Francisco his *Man through the Wall* series to celebrate the end of Communism. In 1996, he completed his *Mask of Sorrow*, a fifteen-metre-high monument in Magadan (a port on the Sea of Okhotsk and a gateway to the Kolyma region, formerly one of the most infamous locations of the Soviet labour camps) dedicated to the victims of the Soviet purges; the same year, he was awarded the State Prize of the Russian Federation. He currently lives and works in New York City. 36

Nekrasov, Vladimir – (born 1938), Russian painter and architect. He studied art at the Leningrad Academy of Fine Arts. In the 1960s and 1970s, Nekrasov was well known as an important non-conformist artist. He left the Soviet Union in 1976 and, after a few years working two jobs, purchased some property in Brooklyn for his studio. His house, which has been a safe haven for Russian poets, painters, and intellectuals, is called *Nekrasovka*. In 1993, Nekrasov had exhibits in Moscow and St Petersburg. 36

New Economic Policy (NEP) – introduced by Lenin to prevent the Russian economy from collapsing. The NEP permitted private businesses to reopen while the state continued to control banks, foreign trade, and large industries. The NEP also loosened trade restrictions, which allowed Russia to re-establish alliances with foreign countries, and it improved the efficiency of food distribution. However, many city workers resented the profits made by private traders. In January 1929, Stalin abolished the NEP and replaced it with the first Five-Year Plan. 12

Nietzsche, Friedrich Wilhelm – (1844–1900), German writer, philosopher, and philologist who wrote critical texts on religion, morality, contemporary culture, philosophy, and science, using a distinctive literary style. His most influential and controversial work is *Thus Spoke Zarathustra* (*Also sprach Zarathustra*, 1883–5), in which he introduced the concept of the *Übermensch* (Overman). 53, 159

Nikitskie Gates – originally, gate (*vorota*) in the wall of Belyi Gorod in Moscow dividing Nikitskaia Street into Nikitskaia and Voznesenskaia. Today, the Nikitskie Vorota is a small square. 68

Novodevich'e Cemetery – also transliterated as Novodevichy Cemetery; the most famous cemetery in Moscow, situated next to the sixteenth-century Novodevichii Convent. Among the many notables buried at the cemetery are Anton Chekhov, Nikolai Gogol' (moved there from the Daniilov Monastery), Vladimir Maiakovskii, Mstislav Rostropovich, Boris El'tsin, Nikita Khrushchev, Mikhail Bulgakov, and Sergei Eisenstein. 21

Oblomov – central character in the best-known novel of the same name by Russian writer Ivan Goncharov, first published in 1859. The hero of the novel is often seen as the ultimate incarnation of the superfluous man, a stereotypical character in nineteenth-century Russian literature. 40

Oder – river in Central Europe, 854 km (530.6 miles) long, and the second-longest river in Poland. Known in Czech and Polish as Odra, it begins in the Czech Republic and flows through western Poland, later forming 187 km (116 miles) of the border between Poland and Germany, and ultimately emptying into the Baltic Sea. 120, 121

Ogarev, Nikolai Platonovich – (1813–77), Russian poet, journalist, and revolutionary. A close friend of Aleksandr Gertsen, he emigrated in 1856 to England and headed the Free Russian Press. He wrote several longer poems (the best known, 'Humor') and many romantic short verses, even though he was a defender of realism in literature. 34

Ogiński, Michał Kleofas – (1765–1833), Polish statesman and composer. For many years an exile, he composed the celebrated polonaise 'Farewell to the Fatherland' ('Pożegnanie ojczyzny'). 121

Index of Names and Places

Olivier, Laurence – (1907–89), famous British actor. His career spanned six decades and included hundreds of theatre, movie, and television performances. 40

Orpheus – in Greek mythology, a great poet and musician whose playing of the lyre could charm animals and even make trees, rocks, and rivers move. 66

Ostapovo – railroad station (properly, Astapovo) where in 1910 Tolstoi died, after developing pneumonia during his flight from home. 19

Ostozhenka – one of Moscow's oldest streets, its origins date from the sixteenth century when it was covered with flood meadows; after the mowing, haystacks called *ostozhiia* stood there, giving the street its name. 57

Oyashio – cold subarctic ocean current (known also as the Oya Siwo, or Kurile Current), flowing south and circulating counterclockwise in the western north Pacific Ocean, colliding with the Kuroshio Current off the eastern shore of Japan to form the North Pacific Current (or Drift). 104

Oz, Amos – (born 1939), birth name: Amos Klausner; Israeli writer, novelist, journalist, and professor of literature at Ben-Gurion University in Be'er Sheva. He has written eighteen books, in Hebrew, which have been translated into some thirty languages. Oz was awarded his country's most prestigious prize: the Israel Prize for Literature, in 1998, the fiftieth anniversary of Israel's independence. 38

Palamedes – in Greek mythology, the son of Nauplius and either Clymene, Philyra, or Hesione; considered a great inventor. Unjustly accused by Odysseus of being a traitor, he was stoned to death. 86

Parcae – in Roman mythology, the personifications of destiny (often called the Fates in English). Their Greek equivalents were the Moirae. They controlled the metaphorical thread of life of every mortal and immortal from birth to death. Even the gods feared them. Their names were Nona (the one who spun the thread of life); Decima (the one who measured the thread of life); and Morta (the one who cut the thread of life and chose the manner of a person's death). 38

Parmenides – (early 5th century BC), Greek philosopher born in Elea, founder of the Eleatic school of philosophy. His single known work is a poem that has survived only in fragmentary form. According to Parmenides, reality is one; change is impossible; and existence is timeless, uniform, and unchanging; while appearances are false and deceiving. 46

Pasternak, Boris Leonidovich – (1890–1960), Russian poet and writer. In Russia, Pasternak is most celebrated as a poet. *My Sister – Life* (*Sestra moia – zhizn'*), written in 1917, is arguably the most influential collection of poetry published in the Russian language in the twentieth century. When it came out in 1921, it made Pasternak the model for younger poets, and decisively influenced the poetry of Osip Mandel'shtam, Marina Tsvetaeva, and many others. In the West, Pasternak is best known for his novel *Doctor Zhivago*, which became an instant sensation, and was subsequently translated and published in many countries. He was awarded the 1958 Nobel Prize for Literature, but was forced to turn it down. *Doctor Zhivago* was eventually published in the USSR in 1988. xv, xvii, 9, 52, 154, 158–9, 160, 161, 162, 163

Paz, Octavio – (1914–98), Mexican poet, essayist, and art critic; winner of the 1990 Nobel Prize for Literature. 37

Pechora – major river in European Russia (Komi Republic and Nenets Autonomous District), 1,809 km (1,124 miles) long. 121

Penates – in Roman mythology, the *Di Penates* or, simply, *Penates*; originally patron gods of the storeroom, but later guardian gods of the entire household. The name Penates was used metaphorically for home or familiar place. In the late eighteenth and early nineteenth centuries, this metaphorical meaning became popular, as the poem by Konstantin Batiushkov, 'My Penates' ('Moi Penaty,' 1811), exemplifies. 50, 61

Pericles – (ca. 490–429 BC), Athenian statesman who brought great prosperity to Athens, encouraging arts, architecture, drama, music, industry, and commerce; often considered a father of Athenian democracy and addressed as a citizen. 99

Petipa, Marius Ivanovich – (1818–1910), Russian ballet dancer, teacher, and choreographer; arguably the most influential ballet master and choreographer that has ever lived. While holding the position of Premier Maître de Ballet of the St Petersburg Imperial Theatres (1871–1903), he created over fifty ballets. 130

Pierrot – stock character of pantomime and Commedia dell' Arte; French variant of the Italian Pedrolino. His character is that of the sad, naive clown, in love with Columbine who inevitably breaks his heart and leaves him for Harlequin. 53

Piraeus – Greek port; today part of Athens. 106

Platonov, Andrei – (1899–1951), pen name of Andrei Platonovich Klimentov; Russian writer. His literary reputation rests on two dystopian novels, *Chevengur* (1926–9) and *The Foundation Pit* (*Kotlovan*, 1929–30). 66

Poros – Greek island in the Saronic Gulf, separated from the Peloponnese Peninsula by a narrow strait, only 200 metres (218.7 yards) wide. 67

Pravda – Truth; Russian newspaper established in 1912. After the 1917 revolution, *Pravda* became an official voice of the Communist Party; it was closed in 1991 by Boris El'tsin. 11

Prévert, Jacques – (1900–77), French poet and screenwriter. His poems were published in his books *Words* (*Paroles*, 1946), *Spectacle* (1951), *Rain and Good Weather* (*La Pluie et le beau temps*, 1955), *Stories* (*Histoires*, 1963), *Fatras* (1971), and *Things and Others* (*Choses et autres*, 1973). Prévert's *To Paint a Portrait of a Bird* (*Pour faire le portrait d'un oiseau*, 1946) is an exploration of art, creativity, and artistic sensitivity. 13

Prishvin, Mikhail Mikhailovich – (1873–1954), Russian writer whose ability and gift to describe the beauty of the natural world made him, together with Konstantin Paustovskii, an acknowledged master of lyrical 'environmental' prose. His reputation grew steadily during the 1930s and 1940s, and by the 1950s, he had achieved widespread popularity and literary influence in his country, despite remaining outside mainstream Soviet politics. 6

Procrustes – in Greek mythology, a bandit from Attica who lived in the hills outside Eleusis. He had constructed an iron bed and invited every passerby to lie down in it. If the guest proved too tall, he would cut off the excess length; those who were too short were stretched until they were long enough. Nobody ever fit in the bed because Procrustes would stretch or shrink it upon sizing up his victims from afar. He was captured and killed by Theseus. 4

Proffer, Carl R. – (1938–84), scholar, translator, and professor at the University of Michigan who will be remembered for opening in 1971 the publishing house Ardis (see above entry for Ardis). Carl Proffer and his wife, Ellendea, launched Sokolov's literary career by publishing his *Shkola dlia durakov* (*A School for Fools*) in Russian and following it with Proffer's English translation. Later, they also published *Between Dog and Wolf* (*Mezhdu sobakoi i volkom*) and *Palisandriia*. vii, ix, xii, 15

Prometheus – in Greek mythology, a Titan who stole fire from Zeus and gave it to the mortals. 4, 152

Protagoras – (ca. 490–420 BC), pre-Socratic Greek philosopher; considered by Plato to be one of the sophists. In his dialogue *Protagoras*, Plato credits him with having invented the role of the professional sophist or teacher of virtue. His most famous saying is 'man is the measure of all things: of things that are, that they are, and of things that are not, that they are not.' 11

Proust, Marcel – (1871–1922), French novelist, essayist, and critic; best known for his *À la recherche du temps perdu* (in English, *In Search of Lost Time*; earlier translated as *Remembrance of Things Past*), published from 1913 to 1927. Begun in 1909, the work consists of seven volumes populated by more than 2,000 literary characters. The last three volumes were published posthumously and edited by his brother Robert. 35

Pugachev, Emel'ian Ivanovich – (1740 or 1742–75), also transliterated as Yemelyan Pugachov; Don Cossack, deserter from the Russian army and pretender to the Russian throne who led a great Cossack insurrection (1773–4) during the reign of Catherine II. Pushkin wrote a history of the rebellion and recounted some of the events in his novel *The Captain's Daughter* (1836). 47, 155

Pula – largest city and port in Istria, Croatia; best-known and most valuable ancient monument there is the coliseum dating from the second century, the eighth largest in the world. 78

Pushkin, Aleksandr Sergeevich – (1799–1837), Russian Romantic author. Pushkin is arguably the greatest Russian poet and the founder of modern Russian literature. His poems and lyrical verse, prose, and dramatic writing greatly influenced later Russian writers. In addition to numerous short poems familiar to practically every educated Russian, Pushkin is most famous for his novel in verse, *Eugene Onegin* (1825–32); a collection of stories, *The Tales of the Late Ivan Petrovich Belkin* (1831); the short story, 'The Queen of Spades' (1833); the drama, *Boris Godunov* (1825); and the longer poems, *Ruslan and Ludmila* (1820) and *The Bronze Horseman* (1833). 17, 23, 74, 75, 147, 148, 149, 150, 154, 155, 167, 174

Rabin, Oskar Iakovlevich – (born 1928), Russian painter. From 1942 to 1945 he studied painting in the studio of Evgenii Kropivnitskii. From 1958 to 1965 a group of young non-conformist artists, later called the Lianozovo Group, gathered around Rabin. Despite official opposition, Rabin became the first unofficial artist to have his work exhibited in the West (in London, 1964). He was one of the organizers of the infamous 'bulldozer exhibition' in 1974. In 1978, while in France on vacation, he was exiled from the USSR; in 1990, shortly before the collapse of the Soviet Union, his right to Russian citizenship was restored. 36, 66

Rakhmaninov, Sergei Vasil'evich – (1873–1943), also transliterated as Rachmaninoff; Russian composer, pianist, and conductor. One of the finest pianists of his day, as a composer, he is the last great representative of Russian late Romanticism in classical music. Early influences of Chaikovskii, Rimskii-Korsakov, and other Russian composers gave way to a thoroughly personal idiom characterized by a pronounced lyricism, expressive breadth, structural ingenuity, and a tonal palette of rich, distinctive orchestral colours. 36

Rangoon – Yangon; capital of Myanmar (formerly, Burma). 136, 177

Rasputin, Grigorii Efimovich – (1869–1916), also known as Grigorii Efimovich Novyi; Russian mystic who became close to Tsar Nicholas II and his family because of his ability to ease the hemophiliac sufferings of the heir, tsarevich Aleksei. Rasputin's dual personality (saint/sinner) and his meddling in state affairs led to a plot to assassinate him organized by Prince Feliks Iusupov. The conspirators fed Rasputin arsenic- and cyanide-laced cookies, and then shot him point-blank, but they were unable to end his life; the coroner who examined the body found later in a canal declared the cause of death to be drowning. 21

Ratushinskaia, Irina Borisovna – (born 1954), prominent Russian dissident, poet, and writer. In the early 1980s, she was charged with writing anti-Soviet poems, convicted, and sentenced to seven years in a labour camp, where, however, she spent only four years; she was released in October 1986, on the eve of the summit in Reykjavík between President Ronald Reagan and Mikhail Gorbachev. 37

Ravel, Maurice – (1875–1937), French composer of works that defy the established rules of harmony; a brilliant orchestrator of works by other composers. His popularity rests mainly on the *Boléro* (1928), intended as a miniature ballet. 18

Reid, Thomas Mayne – (1818–83), Irish-American novelist; author of many adventure novels with the action taking place in exotic settings. His tales of the American West captivated young readers everywhere. Among his books, many of which were popular in translation in Poland and Russia, are *The Rifle Rangers* (1850), *Scalp Hunters* (1851), *War Trail* (1851), *Boy Hunters* (1853), *Boy Tar* (1859), and *Headless Horseman* (1865–6). 35

Rhine – one of the longest (1,320 km or 820 miles) and most important rivers in Europe, it originates in Switzerland and, after separating France and Germany, empties into the North Sea in the Netherlands. 96

Rilke, Rainer Maria – (1875–1926), one of the greatest German-language poets. His two most famous verse sequences are the *Sonnets to Orpheus* (*Sonette an Orpheus*, 1922) and the *Duino Elegies* (*Duineser Elegien*, 1922); his two most famous prose works are *Letters to a Young Poet* (published posthumously in 1929) and the semi-autobiographical *The Notebooks of Malte Laurids Brigge* (*Die Aufzeichnungen des Malte Laurids Brigge*, 1910). 6, 62, 161

Rimbaud, Jean Nicholas Arthur – (1854–91), French poet who greatly influenced modern literature, music, and art. Described as 'an infant Shakespeare' and a poetic prodigy, Rimbaud stopped writing before he turned twenty-one; he died prematurely, shortly after his thirty-seventh birthday. 28

Rimini – city on the Adriatic Sea in the Emilia-Romagna region of Italy and capital city of the Province of Rimini. 106

Rodin, Auguste – (1840–1917), great French sculptor. Rodin was commissioned in 1891 to create a monument to Honoré Balzac. The 1898 sculpture displays Balzac with deeply cut features, cloaked in a cape, looking into the distance. Rodin's intent had been to show Balzac at the moment of artistic inspiration; despite the initial criticism and its late casting (1939), today the sculpture is considered to be one of Rodin's best. 41, 152

Rostropovich, Mstislav Leopol'dovich – (1927–2007), Russian cellist and conductor; widely considered to have been one of the greatest cellists of the twentieth century. He left the Soviet Union in 1974 with his wife and children and settled in the United States. Banned from several musical ensembles in his homeland, his Soviet citizenship was revoked in 1978 because of his public opposition to the Soviet Union's restriction of cultural freedom. 36

Rubicon – river in northern Italy, 29 km (18 miles) long, made famous by Caesar's crossing in 49 BC during his advance on Rome. 95, 121

Rue Peshkov – Gor'kii Street (Peshkov is the real name of Gor'kii), one of the major streets of Moscow. Originally named Tverskaia because it led from Moscow to the city of Tver', it was renamed Gor'kii Street in 1935 in connection with the major reconstruction of Moscow and the widening of the old street. After the collapse of the Soviet Union, the old name of the street was restored. 50, 158

Rumiantsev, Nikolai Petrovich – (1754–1826), Russian statesman and historian, collector of Slavic manuscripts, and founder of the Rumiantsev Museum. Opened in 1831, the museum was transferred to Moscow in 1861 and located in Pashkov's House on Mokhovaia Street. In 1924, the Rumiantsev Museum was closed and renamed the Lenin Library. 68, 162

Saint-Saens, Charles Camille – (1835–1921), French composer, organist, conductor, and pianist; known especially for his *Danse Macabre* (1874), *Samson et Dalila* (1877), *The Carnival of the Animals* (1886), and *Symphony No. 3* (Organ Symphony, 1886). 49

Sakhanevich, Oleg Viktorovich – (born 1935), also spelled Sokhanevich; one of the legendary runaways from the Soviet Union. He studied art in Kiev (1948–54) and at the Repin Academy of Fine Arts in Leningrad (1956–62). In 1967, he bought a ticket for a cruise on the steamer *Rossiia* and, after carefully calculating the distance, jumped out at night from his cabin's window with a small inflatable rubber boat and but meagre provisions. Having inflated the boat when already in the water, he set out in the direction of Turkey and was found by Turkish fishermen several days later. He asked for and was given political asylum in the United States. 36

Salinger, J.D. (Jerome David) – (1919–2010), American author; best known for his 1951 novel *The Catcher in the Rye*, as well as for his reclusive nature. He had not published a new work since 1965 and had not been interviewed since 1980. He followed *Catcher* with three collections of short stories: *Nine Stories* (1953), *Franny and Zooey* (1961), and *Raise High the Roof Beam, Carpenters and Seymour: An Introduction* (1963). viii, 36

San Michele – Isola di San Michele, island cemetery in Venice. 77, 144

Sarasate, Pablo de – (1844–1908), Spanish violinist and composer; his compositions require exemplary technique and today are performed by violin virtuosos. Perhaps the best known of his works is *Gypsy Airs* (*Zigeunerweisen*, 1878), a work for violin and orchestra. Another piece, the *Carmen Fantasy* (1883), also for violin and orchestra, is based on motifs from Bizet's opera *Carmen*. 83

Sartre, Jean-Paul – (1905–80), French philosopher, dramatist, and novelist. He developed his existentialist philosophical ideas in the novel *Nausea* (*La Nausée*, 1938) and the short stories collected in *The Wall* (*Le Mur*, 1939). His philosophy is explained in *Being and Nothingness* (*L'Être et le néant*, 1943) and *Existentialism Is Humanism* (*L'Existentialisme est un humanisme*, 1946). In 1964, Sartre was awarded, but refused to accept, the Nobel Prize for Literature. 16

Scaevola, Gaius Mucius – probably a fictional Roman hero, famous for his bravery. During the siege of Rome by the Etruscans, Gaius Mucius attempted to kill the Etruscan king. The attempt failed and the young man was captured. Sentenced to die in the fire, Gaius proved his bravery by sticking his right hand into the flames and showing no pain. For this heroic act, he was released by the Etruscans and later, in Rome, nicknamed Scaevola (left-handed) because of his burned right hand. 87, 166

Scandello, Antonio – (1517–80), Italian composer. Born in Bergamo, he spent almost half of his life in Germany, employed by the Electors of Saxony; he died in Dresden. xvii, 96, 166

Schiller, Johann Christoph Friedrich von – (1759–1805), German poet, philosopher, historian, and dramatist. Schiller is recognized for developing the concept of the *Schöne Seele* (beautiful soul), a human being whose emotions have been educated by reason, so that *Pflicht und Neigung* (duty and inclination) are no longer in conflict with one another; his philosophical work was also particularly concerned with the question of human freedom. Schiller is considered to be Germany's most important classical playwright, thanks to his influential and popular dramas *The Robbers* (1781), *Intrigue and Love* (1784), *Don Carlos* (1787), *The Maid of Orleans* (1801), *Mary Stuart* (1801), and *William Tell* (1804). 60

Schubert, Franz Peter – (1797–1828), Austrian composer; particularly noted for his original melodic and harmonic writing. Schubert wrote some 600 lieder, nine symphonies (including the famous 'Unfinished Symphony'), liturgical music, operas, and a large body of chamber and solo piano music. 68, 164

Scylla and Charybdis – in Greek mythology, two monsters guarding the passage between Sicily and the mainland (the Strait of Messina). Trying to avoid one monster would inevitably make the unfortunate navigator a victim of the other. Today, the expression 'to be between Scylla and Charybdis' means to have to choose between two equally bad alternatives. 36

Selene – in Greek mythology, Selene ('moon') was an archaic lunar deity and the daughter of the Titans Hyperion and Theia. In the traditional pre-Olympian divine genealogy, Helios (the sun) is Selene's brother. After Helios finishes his journey across the sky, Selene, freshly washed in the waters of Earth-Circling Ocean, begins her own journey as night falls upon the earth, illuminated by the radiance of her head and golden crown. 44

Seneca, Lucius Annaeus (also Seneca, Seneca the Younger) – (ca. 4 BC – AD 65), Roman Stoic philosopher, statesman, and dramatist of the Silver Age of Latin literature. He claimed that the universe is governed by a rational providence, happiness is achieved by a simple life, human suffering should be accepted and has a positive effect on the soul, study and learning are important, and one needs to come to terms with one's own mortality. 55

Shakespeare, William – (1564–1616), English poet and playwright; widely regarded as the greatest writer in the English language and the world's pre-eminent dramatist. Shakespeare is often called England's national poet and the 'Bard of Avon' (or simply 'the Bard'). His surviving works consist of thirty-eight plays, 154 sonnets, two long narrative poems, and three shorter poems. 60, 150, 160

Shaliapin, Fedor Ivanovich – (1873–1938), also transliterated as Fyodor Chaliapin; the most famous Russian opera singer of the twentieth century, credited with establishing the tradition of naturalistic acting in opera. Thanks to his powerful and flexible bass voice, employed in conjunction with a mesmerizing stage presence and superb acting ability, Shaliapin is considered to be one of the supreme performers in the history of opera. 36

Shostakovich, Dmitrii Dmitrievich – (1906–75), Russian composer. Initially influenced by Prokof'ev and Stravinskii (*Symphony No. 1*, 1924–5), Shostakovich began experimenting with modernist aesthetic (*Symphony No. 2*, 1927, and *The Nose*, 1927–8) before developing a hybrid style combining many traditions in one work (*Lady Macbeth*, 1930–2, and the *Fourth Symphony*, 1935–6). 28

Shpet, Gustav Gustavovich – (1879–1937), Russian philosopher, student and follower of Husserl. Shpet's best-known works include *Phenomenon and Meaning* (1914), *History as a Problem of Logic* (1916), and *Hermeneutics and Its*

Problems (1918). In the last years of his life, he translated English authors and Hegel's *Phenomenology of the Spirit*. Like many other Russian intellectuals of his time, Shpet became a victim of the purges; arrested in 1935, he was sent into exile and executed in Tomsk. 68

Sibelius, Johan Julius Christian – (1865–1957), Finnish composer of the later Romantic period. The music of Sibelius played an important role in the formation of the Finnish national identity, as in *Finlandia* (1899) and his musical renderings of themes from the Finnish-Karelian epic *Kalevala*, e.g., *Lemminkäinen Suite* (1893) and its popular third part, *The Swan of Tuonela*. 62

Sisyphus – in Greek mythology, a king of Ephyra (Corinth), who was punished in Tartarus by being forced to roll a huge boulder up a hill, only to watch it roll down again, and to repeat this throughout eternity. Today, 'Sisyphean' is used as an adjective to mean an activity that is unending and/or repetitive; it is also used to refer to tasks that are pointless and unrewarding. 4

Sitnikov, Vasilii Iakovlevich – (1915–87), Russian painter. After failing to gain admission to Vkhutemas (Higher Art Studios) in 1935, he worked as an animation artist and as a slide projectionist for the professors at the Surikov Institute. Arrested in 1941, he was declared insane and sent to a mental institution. During the Thaw, he returned to Moscow and became a part of the circle of 'non-conformist' artists. In 1975, he emigrated to Austria and later to the United States, where he worked until his death. Sitnikov's remains are interred in Moscow's Vagan'kovo Cemetery. 36

Skriabin, Aleksandr Nikolaevich – (1872–1915), also transliterated as Scriabin, Skryabin, and Skriabine; Russian composer and pianist, a representative of Symbolism in music. His works are original and contain very unusual harmonies and textures. Skriabin's ten piano sonatas show his progress from a late Romantic composer to a creator of experimental, atonal music. 63, 64, 65

SMOG – society formed in 1965 by a group of young Moscow writers and artists; acronym for Samoe molodoe obshchestvo geniev (The Youngest Society of Geniuses) or *smelost'-mysl'-obraz-glubina* (daring-thought-image-depth). To preserve the acronym, the letters SMOG can be rendered in English as 'Society of the Most Outstanding Geniuses' or 'Sense – Mind – Originality – Greatness.' The name also can be associated with the past tense of the Russian verb 'to be able.' The society was banned after a year and a half. Most members were persecuted and suffered in some way: the painter Nikolai Nedbailo and the poet Vladimir Batshev were exiled, the poet Leonid Gubanov spent time in a psychiatric hospital, and the poet Vladimir Aleinikov was expelled from Moscow State University. xi, xiv, 44, 47, 154, 155, 157

Index of Names and Places

Sokolov, Aleksandr Vsevolodovich – (born 1943), full name and patronymic of Sasha Sokolov. vii–xx, 73, 77, 148, 150, 153, 155, 156, 158, 160, 161, 163, 166, 168, 171, 173

Solzhenitsyn, Aleksandr Isaevich – (1918–2008), Russian novelist, dramatist, and historian. Through his writings, Solzhenitsyn made the world aware of the Gulag, the Soviet labour camp system. For these efforts, Solzhenitsyn was both awarded the 1970 Nobel Prize for Literature and exiled from the Soviet Union in 1974. He returned to Russia in 1994. He is remembered for his three early novels, *One Day in the Life of Ivan Denisovich* (1964), *The First Circle* (1968), and *The Cancer Ward* (1968), and for his expose of the Soviet labour camp system in *The Gulag Archipelago* (1973–78). 36

Sulla Felix, Lucius Cornelius – (ca. 138–78 BC), Roman politician and general. Thanks to his combination of cunning and bravery, Sulla was once described as being half fox and half lion. The ancient sources mention his piercing grey eyes that could intimidate all but the bravest. 78

Tabito, Otomo no – (662–731), minor Japanese poet; known primarily for being the father of Otomo no Yakamochi and for writing *Thirteen Poems in Praise of Wine*. 132

Tacitus, Publius or **Gaius Cornelius** – (c. 55–120), Roman historian. 51

Tanguy, Yves – (1900–55), French surrealist painter. At the outbreak of the Second World War, he emigrated to the United States and became an American citizen in 1948. His paintings have a unique, immediately recognizable style of non-representational surrealism; they show strange abstract landscapes, rendered mostly in a limited palette filled with angular or rounded shapes. 69

Taormina – small town in Sicily. 106

Terman, Douglas – (born 1933), minor American writer of apocalyptic thrillers dealing with nuclear war. Among his novels are *First Strike* (1978), in which a nuclear war is averted at the last moment; *Free Flight* (1980), about a Russian nuclear war victory and a lone rebel in New England; and *The 3 Megaton Gamble* (1978), which deals with the potential misuse of nuclear weapons. 28

Thessaly – large geographical region of Greece, with Larissa as its capital. 84, 165

Tibullus, Albius – (ca. 54–19 BC), Latin poet and writer of elegies; little is known about his life. Only his first and second books of poetry (describing his love for two women, Delia and Nemesis) are extant; many other texts attributed to him are questionable. 85

Tintoretto, Jacopo – (1518–94), real name: Jacopo Comin; one of the greatest painters of the Venetian school, who may be considered the last great painter of the Italian Renaissance. For his phenomenal energy in painting he was nicknamed *Il Furioso*, and his dramatic use of perspective and light effects make him a precursor of Baroque art. 62

Titicaca – located on the border of Bolivia and Peru, it is the highest commercially navigable lake in the world, notable for a population of people who live on its Uros, a group of artificial islands made of floating reeds, *totora*. 93, 94

Tiul'panov, Igor' – (born 1939), also known as Igor Tulipanov; Russian painter. He studied at the Leningrad Polytechnical Institute and worked as head stage designer at the Theatre of Comedy in Moscow, but gradually moved into painting. Influenced by Hieronymus Bosch and Van Eyck, Tiul'panov calls his painting style Symbolic Naturalism, rather than Surrealism, the term most often applied to his works by critics. In 1978, he emigrated to the United States. 36

Tobol'sk – founded 1587; historic capital of Siberia, located at the confluence of the rivers Tobol and Irtysh, approximately 1,861 km (1,156 miles) southeast of Moscow. 30

Tolstoi, Lev Nikolaevich – (1828–1910), also transliterated as Tolstoy; great Russian novelist, short story writer, playwright, social thinker, and philosopher. His most famous works are the novels *War and Peace* (1865–9), *Anna Karenina* (1875–7), and *Resurrection* (1899). 19, 24, 40, 150, 152, 159, 161

Trubetskoi – the last name of three Russian philosophers: Sergei Nikolaevich (1862–1905), his son Nikolai Sergeevich (1890–1938), and his brother Evgenii (1863–1920). Sergei was the first elected rector of Moscow University and a professor of the philosophy of religion, Nikolai was also an outstanding linguist, and Evgenii wrote the famous essay on Russian icon painting, 'Theology in Colours' ('Umozrenie v kraskakh,' 1915). 68

Tsinandali – village in Kakheti, Georgia, situated in the district of Telavi, 179 km (111.2 miles) east of Tbilisi; noted for the estate and its historic winery that once belonged to the nineteenth-century aristocratic poet Aleksandr Chavchavadze (1786–1846). The highly regarded dry white Tsinandali is still produced there. 49

Tsvetaeva, Marina Ivanovna – (1892–1941), Russian poet and writer. Her poetry, praised by such poets as Voloshin, Pasternak, and Mandel'shtam, was influenced by her own life, the places she visited, and the people she met. She emigrated in 1922, but in 1939 decided to return home. Unable to find work, she committed suicide after the attack by Germany on the Soviet Union. 30

Tsvetkov, Aleksei Petrovich – (born 1947), Russian poet, literary critic, and translator. He emigrated to the United States in 1975, where in 1983 he received his Ph. D. from the University of Michigan; since 1989 he has worked for Radio Svoboda. 32, 33, 149

Tula – city located 311 km (193 miles) south of Moscow, on the river Upa. In the eighteenth century, Tula became the greatest ironworking centre of Eastern Europe; subsequently, it achieved prominence as the centre of samovar production in Russia. 74

Tungus – Siberian ethnic group, closely related to the Manchus, divided into the Evenki, who inhabit the area between the Yenisei and Ob rivers and the Pacific Ocean and between the Amur River and the Arctic Ocean, and the Lamut, who inhabit the coast of the Okhotsk Sea. 48

Turgenev, Ivan Sergeevich – (1818–83), Russian novelist, short story writer, and playwright. His novel *Fathers and Sons* (*Ottsy i deti*, 1862) is considered to be one of the major works of nineteenth-century fiction. Turgenev became famous after publishing *A Sportsman's Sketches* (*Zapiski okhotnika*, 1852), also known as *Sketches from a Hunter's Album* or *Notes of a Hunter*. 18, 34, 147, 152, 173

Tver' – city 160 km (99.4 miles) north of Moscow, situated at the confluence of the Volga and Tvertsa rivers. Once the capital of a powerful medieval principality, Tver' was conquered by the army of Ivan III of Moscow in 1485. From 1931 to 1991, it was called Kalinin. ix, 6

Urals – large geographical area around the Ural Mountains; considered to be a natural boundary between Europe and Asia. 56

Vagan'kovo – one of Moscow's largest cemeteries; the resting place for many victims of the Stalinist terror and for many famous individuals, including Sergei Esenin and Vladimir Vysotskii. Vagan'kovo Cemetery is part of Moscow urban folklore and a topic of many graveyard jokes. 50

Väinämöinen – mighty and wise hero of the Finnish epic, *Kalevala*. 19

Vega, Lope de – (1562–1635), also known as Félix Lope de Vega y Carpio or Lope Félix de Vega Carpio; Spanish Baroque playwright and poet. His popularity in Spain is second only to that of Cervantes, while his literary output is enormous: he may have written between 1,500 and 2,500 plays of which 425 have survived. His most celebrated plays belong to the class called *capa y espada* or 'cloak and sword.' Part of de Vega's reputation rests on his stormy love affairs, reportedly almost as numerous as his plays. 21

Venclova, Tomas – (born 1937), Lithuanian scholar, poet, author, and translator of literature. He was educated at the University of Vilnius. As an active participant in the dissident movement, he was deprived of Soviet citizenship in 1977 and had to emigrate; he is one of the founders of the Lithuanian Helsinki Watch group. Since 1980, he has been a member of the department of Slavic Languages and Literatures at Yale University, where he received his Ph.D. in 1985. He has published collections of his poems, translations of poetry, essays, and articles. 33

Verdi, Giuseppe Fortunino Francesco – (1813–1901), Italian Romantic composer; one of the most influential composers of the nineteenth century. He wrote twenty-eight operas, the most famous of which are *Rigoletto* (1851), *La traviata* (1853), *Il trovatore* (1853), and *Aida* (1871). 130

Verkhniaia Maslovka – street in Moscow where, before the Second World War, workshops for artists were established. Nikolai Nedbailo was one of the artists who lived in the communal apartments on this street. 50

Vertinskii, Aleksandr Nikolaevich – (1889–1957), also transliterated as Vertinsky; Russian singer, composer, cabaret artist, and actor. He considerably influenced the Russian art-song tradition. In 1920, he left Russia and performed in many countries, including the United States. In 1943, the Soviet government allowed Vertinskii to return to the Soviet Union, where he gave about 2,000 concerts and appeared in films. The most famous Vertinskii's songs belong to his early period, the years before and shortly after the Revolution. They include such favourites as 'Never' ('Jamais'), 'The Little Creole' ('Malen'kii kreol'chik'), 'The Purple Negro' ('Lilovyi negr'), 'Your Fingers Smell of Incense' ('Vashi pal'tsy pakhnut ladanom'), and 'The Thing I Need to Say' ('To, chto ia dolzhen skazat''). 49

Vespucci, Amerigo – (1454–1512), explorer and cartographer. Vespucci was the first person to demonstrate that the New World discovered by Christopher Columbus in 1492 was not the eastern appendage of Asia, but rather a previously unknown 'fourth' continent. The continents of North and South America (and, by extension, the United States of America) derive their name from the Latin version of his first name. 41

Vitti, Anne or **Anna** – neither the name of this author nor the title of her work could be confirmed. 29

Vonnegut, Kurt – (1922–2007), also known as Kurt Vonnegut Jr; prolific American novelist famous for works blending satire, black comedy, and science fiction, such as *Slaughterhouse-Five* (1969), *Cat's Cradle* (1963), and *Breakfast of Champions* (1973). 29

Voroshilov, Kliment Efremovich – (1881–1969), Soviet military commander and politician. During the Civil War, Polish-Soviet War (1919–21), the Second World War, and the Winter War (1939–40), he exhibited personal bravery, but also incompetence. He was elected to the Central Committee in 1921 and remained a member until 1961; he is buried in the Kremlin Wall Necropolis. 8

Voznesenskii, Andrei Andreevich – (1933–2010), also transliterated as Andrey Voznesensky; Russian poet and writer. His first poems were published in 1958 and brought him recognition for their unique style, original rhymes, and originality of metaphors and imagery. xiii, 27

Vrubel'-Golubkina, Irina – (born 1943), Russian journalist and writer. She emigrated from the Soviet Union in 1971, and since 1993 has been the main editor of the journal *Zerkalo* (Mirror) in Tel Aviv. xvi, 77

Whitman, Walt – (1819–92), American poet, essayist, journalist, and humanist; one of the most influential American poets, famous for his use of free verse and for his poetry collection *Leaves of Grass* (1855). 42

Woolf, Virginia – (1882–1941), English novelist and essayist; regarded as one of the foremost literary figures of the twentieth century. Her best-known works include the novels *Mrs Dalloway* (1925), *To the Lighthouse* (1927), and *Orlando* (1928), and the book-length essay *A Room of One's Own* (1929). Woolf's literary experiments, among them the use of stream-of-consciousness, were instrumental in the development of literary modernism. 35

Zholkovskii, Aleksandr – (born 1937), also transliterated as Alexander Zholkovsky; professor of Slavic Languages and Literatures at the University of Southern California, Los Angeles, and author of numerous articles and books. His scholarly interests include linguistics and poetics. In the 1990s, he started researching *plokhopis'* (bad writing) and intertextuality. His *Text Counter Text: Rereadings in Russian Literary History* (1994) investigates the influences of classical Russian authors on the modern masters. 16, 149

Zurbagan – imaginary port in Aleksandr Grin's *Captain Duke* (*Kapitan Diuk*, 1915), *The Ships in Liss* (*Korabli v Lisse*, 1918), and *She Who Runs on the Waves* (*Begushchaia po volnam*, 1928). 66